Can't Wait Till Monday Morning

Can't Wait Till Monday Morning

Syndication in Broadcasting

by

Marvin A. Kempner

RIVERCROSS PUBLISHING, INC.
New York • Orlando

ISBN: 0-944057-73-0

Library of Congress Catalog Card Number: 97-36456

First Printing

Library of Congress Cataloging-in-Publication Data

Kempner, Marvin A.
    Can't wait till Monday morning : syndication in broadcasting / by
Marvin A. Kempner.
        p.   cm.
    ISBN 0-944957-73-0
    1. Radio broadcasting—United States—Finance—History.   2. Radio
programs—United States—History.   I. Title.
HE8698.K46   1998
384.54′0973—dc21   97-36456
                                                                          CIP

Contents

Preface

When broadcasting first got started in America, it was made up of small radio stations spread out all over the country. Each station reached only a local audience, and each station produced all of its own programming, or what passed for programming. This was expensive and it couldn't, and didn't, last. Income from advertising revenues was limited by the size of a station's audience, and that income could pay for only so many organists, tenors, comedians, writers and actors. Radio stations had to find another answer and that answer was networks.

Production organizations sprang up in a few large metropolitan areas and began to turn out programs the local stations couldn't afford to produce. These production organizations encouraged local stations to affiliate with them, and supplied those that did with the bulk of their programming. For more than twenty-five years, that was the way it worked. A local station did some modest production, pushed the network button and raked in the profits. Without a network affiliation a small station was hard pressed to make ends meet.

But in the early fifties it all changed. Licenses to operate radio stations, frozen during the war years, were suddenly readily available, and soon there were more stations in more markets than there were networks to service them. Once again, broadcasters had to shoulder the responsibility for providing their own programming.

Enter the syndicator.

The new process of magnetic tape recording made it possible for producers to turn out programs of every description, record them, and sell them nationally to individual stations. It was door to door sales.

From big town, to small town, to smaller town, salesmen of syndicated product blanketed the country. With a burst of creative marketing innovations, syndication became a major player in the broadcast industry.

Television provided the syndicator with even greater opportunities. First on film, and later on video tape, syndicated programs filled the air time of network affiliates which was not filled by the network. History had repeated itself. As with radio, television flourished so that soon there were more stations than the networks could service. Again, salesmen went door to door, out into the hinterlands to deal with the people who made broadcasting work—program directors and general managers, sales managers and engineers, newscasters and copywriters, and, often as important as any of them, the secretaries and receptionists who were the backbone of so many local broadcasting operations.

I became involved in developing some of the "nuts and bolts" for radio and television: the first jingle library; the first musical game show; the first nationally-syndicated woman sportscaster; the first usable "morgue" for television; the first, most successful interactive game show; and the first accurate, computerized telephone polling equipment.

This is my story, the story of American broadcasting from the bottom up, from the inside out. It is not about Ed Sullivan in New York, or Lucille Ball and Jack Webb in Los Angeles, but about a legion of people whose names nobody knows, who got up every morning and went to work in Terre Haute and Upper Sandusky, and who made it all possible for Ed and Lucy and Jack, and for all the others whose names everyone knows.

I am a syndicator, and the first to tell the syndicator's story. It's actually a hundred stories, or a thousand. It's more than an anthology of my comings and goings in the broadcast industry for half a century. It's the story of America as it has shaped, and been shaped, by an electronic industry that has come to be much more than the sum of all its parts.

My story is of those parts not easily seen unless you get out there and look very, very carefully. Person to person. Eye to eye. Door to door.

1.
The Beginning

The years 1936 through 1941 were my growth years—school and working part time doing emcee work in theaters, selling ladies shoes, and working as an inspector for the Curtis Wright Corporation which built P-40 fighters and C-46 transport planes. Then on into service.

I was discharged from the Army Air Force on March 6, 1946, having spent several months in hospitals from an injury sustained during the war. I received my discharge in San Antonio, Texas, and was offered a place on the manifest, a ride on an Air Force plane to New York. But having had a forty-two-day convalescent leave during the war when I took a plane from San Francisco to New York, flew east for nine hours and landed in Los Angeles (due to weather), I decided "No Way". So I took a train from San Antonio to Buffalo, New York. That way, I was assured of being home in a day and a half.

Several hours out of San Antonio, we ran into a cloudburst, and part of the track was washed out. I did arrive home eventually, but approximately two days late. While stewing on the train, I firmly resolved that I was going to stay home, find a job and begin my life anew. I had had enough of traveling, having been with the Air Force in the Air Transport Command (ATC), which we commonly referred to as the "Army of Terrified Civilians", the "Asshole Trucking Company", and "Allergic to Combat". Few people realize however that ATC boys flew into combat areas all the time, dropping supplies and bringing out litter cases of wounded GI's. I was much luckier than most, since I was with

9

a command training pilots to fly "The Hump" (the China, Burma, India route) in C-46 aircraft.

A few days after arriving home and getting into my first civilian clothing in a long, long time, I ran into an old friend, Alvin Goldberg, who was a market research analyst. He suggested I do some door-to-door survey work for him. He had a client, Colgate, and was trying to find out the identification of their jingle with the public. Bear in mind, those were the days when jingles were very few and far-between on radio. He took me to Robert P. Mendelsohn Productions, and introduced me to Bob Mendelsohn and Dick Ullman. Bob had been out of the service about ninety days and, with Dick, had formed a small recording company.

Dick was sales manager of Buffalo Broadcasting Corp. (WGR-WKBW Radio). He had written a limerick which became very successful, called "Wildroot Cream Oil Charlie". Wildroot, at the time was one of the largest hair cream companies in the country. He had also written one for the electric company ("I'm ready kilowatt, your electric servant at your beck and call") and several other jingles. Dick loved music and was quite a pianist, having written several local musical shows. He had also written a song that Bing Crosby recorded and sang on his radio show, but it never became popular.

Alvin was having the Colgate jingle re-recorded on soft acetates, and had small, portable record players to do the door-to-door survey. Having nothing else to do, I went out on the street and did several days of surveying for him. I remember some very humorous incidents, and one in particular comes to mind. A very attractive young woman in a robe answered the door one day, very pleasantly invited me in and then took her robe off. She was stark naked—and dammit—I ran.

Several days later, I went back with Alvin to Mendelsohn Studios where they started talking about having a man to represent them in New York City. After vowing never to leave Buffalo again, three weeks after my Army discharge, I suddenly found myself in the big city with a $35 per week expense account but no salary (commissions, maybe!). I had a sister, Shirley Grossman, living in Brooklyn, and had been told that I was welcome at any time to stay with her if I ever came down to New York. But I stayed with friends in New York, Queens, the Bronx, Long Island and New Jersey, making sure I never spent more than a few days in any one place for fear I would wear my welcome out. I also slept several nights on park benches, until my sister discovered this and demanded that I stay with her and her husband, Harold.

10

My office at 521 Fifth Avenue, between 40th and 41st Street, was a beautiful, large office building. Each Monday morning I would take the subway to the city, go to the bank, and get $10 worth of nickels. The truth is, my office was a telephone booth, in a long line of telephone booths!

When I finally reached, say Reggie Scheubel, who did all the buying for the Bulova Watch Company and their time signals, or anyone else in the major agencies in New York, they would ask me for my telephone number so they could call me back. That was impossible, so I had to say, "Don't call me—I'll be running—I'll call you!"

Six months in telephone booths attempting to make appointments was one of the greatest educational experiences I have ever had. It taught me how to get to the right people and find ways to get in to see them, and served me well in the years that followed.

I found telephone operators and secretaries to be the most valuable people to talk with. In many cases, top secretarial personnel have the authority to make an appointment for their bosses, particularly if what you tell them proves interesting. Be charming, have a sense of humor, and tell them just enough to whet their appetite. After a half dozen calls to a secretary, one gets to know her, and a friendly approach almost always works. She will even confide in you after a while, telling you the best time to call, or what day is best for you to try again. One trick I used was to ask a secretary what time her boss came in mornings. If he arrived at 8:00 in the morning, which many of them do, it gave me an opportunity to call and reach him directly, since most of the girls do not arrive until 9:00 or 9:30, depending on what time the office opens. Get friendly with the secretaries and when you do have an opportunity to make an appointment, be sure to thank them personally.

Another trick which works is to give her a little sampling of why you want to see her boss. If you make it interesting enough, it is amazing how quickly you can get through. I remember once attempting to get past a secretary who was very, very difficult. As a last resort, I said, "I really called because I heard he had died." Boy, did he get on the phone fast to find out about this rumor, and believe it or not, I made an appointment with him. Always remember: enthusiasm and simple tricks like calling him prior to the office being opened will often work.

At the time, I owned one sport jacket, two pairs of slacks and one navy blue suit. At 5 p.m., as my office was between 40th and 41st Street, I would walk over to 42nd Street and Times Square to catch the BMT out to Brooklyn. Those of you who have worked or lived in New

York know how mobbed the subway is during evening rush hour. I would find the spot where the train was to stop and, when the doors opened, I would let the mobs in front of me get on so as to be first in line for the next train. I was pleased with myself until one day the train stopped about three yards beyond where it should have. With a mob behind you, you go where they push you. I was not only forced onto the train sideways, but a woman behind me got hold of my jacket, and I heard a tremendous "rip." Have you ever had only the sleeves of your jacket left covering your arms, as you're handed the rest of your jacket by a stranger?

Those were tough days for me, but in time it proved very educational. I found in the years following that I had no problem reaching the right people in order to make an appointment.

In late October, I left New York City and returned to the Buffalo area much wiser. From then until the 90's, I never unpacked my suitcase. It was the beginning of a lifetime of meeting and working with the most unusual and exciting people in the world.

While I was still in New York, Dick Ullman and Bob Mendelsohn had signed a contract with a barbershop quartet known as the Lamplight Quartet. They thought it would be a great idea to produce a quarter hour of harmonies. They suggested I make a trip with the audition disc and attempt to sell the program. I was on three different lists to buy a car, but I still had several months to go before this would prove successful, so Dick Ullman suggested I take his car, a 1937 Ford two-door—another of the interesting experiences in my life.

I picked the car up behind the office and drove home, planning to leave the next day. I couldn't figure out why there were two pillows tied to the driver's seat with rope, but thought perhaps the upholstery was torn or badly worn. When I got to the first stoplight and stepped on the brake, I suddenly found myself in the back seat and the brakes weren't holding. I soon found that by pumping them I would eventually stop, and I was not deterred in my quest to make that first business trip. I put two large cardboard boxes behind the driver's seat. That worked fairly well, and I was able to reach the brake pedal and would start pumping at least 200 feet before I wanted to stop. I put 1400 miles on that automobile in the next two weeks. Youth and a sense of humor were all that kept me going.

My first stop was WENY in Elmira, New York, and I made my first sale to the general manager of the NBC and Mutual Broadcasting station. It was a 250-watt broadcasting facility, which in those days was plenty powerful enough for that market. I stayed in a delightful little hotel called the Mark Twain, and I was very pleased with myself. I continued on, with stops in Binghamton, Scranton, Wilkes-Barre, Allentown, Reading, Lancaster, and then on to the big city of Philadelphia.

During this trip, I discovered that the 1937 Ford also had a little problem with the clutch—it could not be put in reverse. I drove into a garage in Philadelphia, and the attendant grabbed the keys. I attempted to tell him that it would not go into reverse, but like all garage attendants, he paid no attention to what I said. From a distance, I got a kick out of seeing him trying to back up the car, then call another attendant to help him push it into a parking space.

Dick Ullman told me that the radio worked fine except when you hit a bump. There was a short somewhere, but all you had to do was stick your left hand out the window and hit the aerial. One Saturday afternoon, Army was playing Notre Dame and those two great players, Glenn Davis and Doc Blanchard, were on the Army team. I had quite a pounding afternoon listening to that football game, and my left hand was like raw hamburger that evening.

I ended my trip in Harrisburg, Pennsylvania. Although I had many potential sales, I had only been able to close Elmira.

I got up at four 4 o'clock in the morning to drive from Harrisburg back to Buffalo. It was mid-November. There was frost in the air, and there were some slick spots on the highway, but I was bound and determined to get that car home. When I dropped the car off I found out something that shook me up. The car did not have a spare tire, and worse, all four tires were showing fabric. I took my suitcase and went home—by bus. Dick never drove that car again. It was picked up and hauled off to the scrap heap, because he had purchased a new car while I was away. He got me involved in some wild things, but through the years, with all his eccentricities, I learned to love him.

Dick was always an idea man, and he had some great ones. He thought it would be wonderful if he could produce a five-minute radio show with Joe McCarthy, manager of the New York Yankees. "Marse" Joe was a delightful human being, when you got to know him, but had very little talent for talking in front of a mike. Even with scripts written for him, it took several hours to get a half dozen shows out of him. I was to make the sales trip.

I had had no real training in sales other than as a youngster selling ladies shoes, but, believe me, if you can sell ladies shoes, you can sell anything. I didn't know what was going to happen, but I went out

13

and attempted to sell *Joe McCarthy Speaks*. The program was three and a half minutes, with the additional minute and a half for the commercial. The half dozen shows I took with me on a soft acetate could be auditioned on the radio station's turntables. We did not have tape in those years, and quarter-inch tape recording materials were still in the future. I started out by heading for Rochester, New York, where I learned my first lesson in negotiations.

I met Gordon P. Brown, president, general manager and chief engineer of his own radio station, WSAY in Rochester. Gordon was a very wealthy man and an engineer who held several patents which were currently being used by RCA. If you got into a fight with him, he would throw his bank book at you. But regardless of what price you quoted, Gordon would always offer you half. He had a wonderful program director who became a close friend of mine years later, named David Olds. Dave ended up as program director of WNEW in New York, and was there for many years.

Gordon and I hit it off very well—I literally got thrown out. Years later I did get even with him when he bought my product after offering half my quote. He later discovered that I had doubled my price, and I was persona non grata until the next good program idea came down the pike.

I went on to Syracuse, then down to Wilkes-Barre, Pennsylvania, where my first call was to radio station WBRE. Louis G. Baltimore was the owner and general manager. I never met him, but I did meet his son, David M. Baltimore, who was assistant to his father. David was my age and believed he was born with a platinum spoon in his mouth. (I always felt "platinum foot" was more appropriate.) Through the years, David and I got along famously, like sandpaper on raw skin.

The sales manager was Abe Baltimore, brother of Lou. Abe had purchased my *Barbershop Harmonies,* after I finished that first trip, and had been quite delightful to me. On this second trip with *Joe McCarthy Speaks,* David Baltimore tried to throw me out of the office, and Abe, his uncle, gave him one of the great reamings I have ever heard. Abe looked at me and said, "I would like to take *Joe McCarthy Speaks* out to a major client." He picked up the phone, made an immediate appointment, and took me with him to see Stegmeier Brewery. The Brewery bought every market in Eastern Pennsylvania, and it was my first major sale in syndication.

To this day, David Baltimore and I do not get along. I have met him many times at NAB (National Association of Broadcasters) and

NATPE (National Association of TV Program Executives) conventions and been given a charming "hello, how are you," only to send a salesman into the market and be told he is not welcome.

Dave spent his life at WBRE radio, and later at WBRE-TV, fighting a losing battle. The Scranton/Wilkes-Barre/ Hazleton, area is mountainous, and, a television signal being "line of sight" does not carry too well there. It was one of the first major cable market areas to become successful, and Dave did nothing but fight against cable. If he had used his head, he'd have known that "if you can't beat 'em, you should join 'em." Dave Baltimore is still a horse's ass.

I returned to Buffalo a conquering hero because that one contract was large enough to pay for the entire production of *Joe McCarthy Speaks,* and show a profit. Bear in mind that, unlike today, programming was inexpensive, and production costs were a fraction of what they are now. I continued to sell *Joe McCarthy Speaks* and *Barbershop Harmonies* until March of 1947. In many instances I was just lucky, while other times I felt that I had done a very good sales job. My education in the field was growing.

In March of '47, Bob Mendelsohn and Dick Ullman were approached by Lou Cowan regarding taking over national sales of both properties, and I was part of the agreement.

Lou Cowan had spent twelve years attempting to sell an idea to the networks. Finally, they agreed to give him a thirteen week summer replacement on the CBS network. The program happened to be *Quiz Kids,* which became an immediate success and stayed on the network for many years.

Lou, having produced a half-hour series called *Murder at Midnight* wanted to go after the top syndication company in the United States. The number one syndicator in the country, and the father of syndication in broadcasting, was Frederick W. Ziv, who headquartered in Cincinnati. Fred had come up with a slogan, "The Freshest Thing in Town," which he had built into a complete promotional package. With two salesmen, he started selling this nationally, going to bakeries all over the United States, with great success.

What is syndication? Simply stated, it's a program distribution system for broadcasting. Syndication was developed primarily to give local advertisers the same "clout" that national advertisers had on the network. In the 40's and 50's, a national advertiser could buy a half hour for fifty-two weeks on one of the networks and spend approximately a half million dollars. A local advertiser, depending on the size of the

15

market, could spend from $2500 to $15,000 a year on advertising. Syndication offered the same quality programs that the networks offered, but instead of selling them to one or two advertisers nationally, the syndicator could sell them to 100 advertisers in 100 or more different markets. If one took a program to the networks and they bought it, one could normally make a small percentage of profits over costs. With syndication, the program was bought by dozens of advertisers which proved to be a much more lucrative way. There were only so many prime time commercial hours available on the networks, but the stations needed programming throughout their broadcast hours. Syndication also gave independent producers a wonderful entree into broadcasting, and thousands of programs were produced and sold through the years.

In the early years of syndication, the grand-daddy of them all, Fred Ziv, had the *Wayne King* show, featuring one-half hours of the waltz king; the *Barry Wood* show, quarter hours featuring Margaret Whiting; *Kenny Baker*; *Romantic Tenor; Pleasure Parade*, which included Vincent Lopez, Milton Cross, Jimmy Wallington, and The Modernaires with Paula Kelly; *Boston Blackie*, half-hour mysteries; *Philo Vance*, half-hour famous detective mysteries; *The Guy Lombardo Show*; *It's Show Time from Hollywood* with Freddy Martin; and *Favorite Stories* with Ronald Coleman as host and narrator.

The major radio network stations were always first in line to buy this product and at the time, Ziv had little, if any, competition. His training process was unique. He would bring in his entire sales staff and go through a complete presentation for them. They spent a day or so going through the material and then went up to their rooms and memorized the presentation with the use of flip cards. They could not leave for home until they had the presentation completely mastered.

All of Ziv's salesmen were trained to sell the client rather than the station. The reasoning was simple, and it worked tremendously well to the advantage of Ziv, becaise if a client became disenchanted, it was difficult for him to cancel. By the same token, if he sold the radio station and they, in turn, wanted to cancel before the end of the contract, it might cause ill feeling at the station, and no syndicator wanted to hurt their potential sales for future products. I know of few cancellations ever being allowed, either by Ziv or by other companies. Another good reason for selling the advertiser directly was that so many stations would not take you to their top clients, who were already under contract. Selling a client, which Ziv always tried to do, made a great deal of sense.

Once, in Roanoke, Virginia, when one of the Ziv's salesmen was making a presentation at the CBS station. John Harkrader, who at the time was general sales manager, sneaked me into the presentation. In the middle of the flip card presentation I asked a question and the salesman, Bill Christian, got so flustered he had to start all over again.

Years later, Fred Ziv, John Sinn and several of the other top executives of Ziv tried to get me to join them, but I couldn't see selling that way. Every person I ever called on was different, and you had to sell to them individually. How wrong I must have been! The Ziv sales were spectacular, and most of their salesmen became top broadcast executives.

Another form of syndication became extremely popular when years later tape became the standard in both radio and television. Off-network programs became gold mines in re-runs, forcing the fin-syn rules to be enacted by the FCC. This meant those with off-network programs could not place their shows in what became known as "prime access" time, normally 7 p.m. to 8 p.m. in the top fifty population centers. It helped the independent producers become factors in what became the most valuable available time, just before evening network took over.

Getting back to Lou Cowan: Lou had decided to form a syndication company with his major product, "Murder at Midnight", and picking up the Ullman-Mendelsohn's "Joe McCarthy Speaks" and "Barbershop Harmonies". Part of the deal was that they would hire me as a salesman, and I was to be given the New York, Pennsylvania, New Jersey, Delaware and District of Columbia territories. I was very excited, particularly when I discovered that I was to be paid $216 twice a month to cover my salary and traveling expenses. In 1947, hotel rooms cost from $1.50 to a maximum of $3.00 a night, with the exception of Statler Hotels, which charged $4.50 for a single room, and gasoline was 19-27 cents a gallon. When I got that bi-monthly check, I would go out to the finest restaurant I could find and have the biggest steak with all the trimmings, at a cost of no more than $2.00.

I now had only one problem—being able to buy a car. Although I had ordered one back during the war, I soon found out that the dealer had three lists. List #1, those who paid cash under the table; list #2, those who paid a little *less* cash under the table; and #3, those who thought car dealers were honest.

Heading for Main Street and "new car alley", I went from dealer to dealer pleading my case, only to be continually turned down. Finally,

I called on the Mercury-Lincoln dealer, and the sales manager took pity on me. He said, "Take the elevator to the second floor and pick out your car." What a thrill! I got off the elevator and discovered thirty cars, and I had my choice of any of them—thirty four-door, gun-metal-gray cars with radio, heater and stick shift. I finally had a car.

My boss in my new job was Bob Michels, vice president of sales out of Chicago. Joe Bailey and an Alfred Hollander in New York were also vice presidents but I initially reported to Bob. I now had three products to sell with the top territory, at the time, on the east coast, and I proceeded to work like hell. Seven weeks later, after doing any, and every, thing I could dream of to make a sale, I was called by Bob Michels and told that they felt I did not have enough experience so they were bringing in a very experienced syndication salesman by the name of Frank O' Driscoll to take over the New York-Pennsylvania territory. Frank *was* a very good salesman, and a very serious drunk and womanizer, but I always got a kick out of how he would try and close a sale by taking his hand and placing it vertically between the eyes of a potential buyer and say, "Either you buy it or buck it."

I was told they were giving me the Maryland, Delaware, New Jersey, District of Columbia, Virginia, West Virginia and Kentucky territory. I was distraught, but it turned out to be the true beginning for me.

2.

Louis G. Cowan Inc.

I arrived one morning in Staunton, Virginia, population 7,500, with an additional 2700 people in a state asylum. Since the census showed over 10,000 people, I had to quote a higher rate. I called on Charles Blackley, owner and general manager of WTON, a 250-watt station whose sales manager was Charles Seebeck. The station, in the heart of town, was a store front—plate glass window and all. Inside, it was sparsely furnished with what appeared to be second-hand furniture, giving it a somewhat shabby appearance.

I quickly learned that Charlie Seebeck ran that radio station, and proceeded to make a presentation to him for the sale of *Murder at Midnight.* I got half way through my pitch when he put his hand up and said, "Stop." He looked at his watch and said, "Marv, within ten minutes I have a client coming in and I am going to present NBC's *Haunting Hour*", another half-hour mystery that NBC's syndication division was selling. He continued, "Your price is $10 a half hour for this market. I can buy *Haunting Hour* for $7.50. If you will meet that rate, I will pitch your show instead, on one condition—you keep your mouth shut." Now anyone in sales who has gone through seven weeks without a nibble is not going to worry about whether the home office will accept a special deal or not. Get the contract. If the home office turns it down, at least you made the sale. So I immediately said "yes".

I kept my mouth shut, as told, and Charlie Seebeck, within about thirty minutes, signed a contract for twenty-six weeks. After the client left, Charlie invited me to have dinner with him at the best restaurant in town—a diner. Dinner was an education.

Charlie told me that evening, "Marv, you don't know how to sell in the South. All you need is a license to steal, but you have to know how. You may not know it, but I am Brooklyn-born and raised. You come on like gangbusters, with pressure. It won't work here. When you walk into a station, look around—it could be a shithouse, but tell them what a delightful facility they have. Talk about the weather; talk about sports; talk about politics, their interests, whatever, but never tell them why you're there. When they ask what they can do for you, tell them very simply. In the next eight weeks I wrote twenty-four contracts.

Charlie Seebeck was a most incredible man with a golden voice. He had been hired by Charles Blackley under an unusual contract. Charlie would receive 15 percent of the station's annual gross. He did all the selling, wrote all the commercials, opened the station early in the morning with the news, and did the eleven o'clock evening news. He still found time to do a weekly newspaper in four cities (Staunton, Harrisonburg, Charlottesville and Lexington) for which he wrote all of the columns and sold all of the space.

Charlie literally had every commercial business in the Staunton/Harrisonburg market on the radio station. We were all taught to get twenty-six, 52-week contracts from advertisers. Charlie would try to get an advertiser on a 52-week contract, and then keep them on what he called an "Until Forbid" basis. In other words, most contracts were signed for one year. After that, he'd service them by calling constantly, but he seldom asked for a renewal. Like buying a car on time, the client continued paying for years until he finally asked to cancel. WTON in the mid-40's shortly after the war, never did less than $100,000 a year, and a $15,000 income in Staunton, Virginia, in 1947 was a small fortune.

20

3.
Charlie Seebeck's "Radio Invented Me"

Charlie Seebeck wrote a story about himself titled "Radio Invented Me". He never published the twenty-five page memoir. Following are a few excerpts which date back to his start in 1934 at the age of eighteen.

He tells of his exuberance in returning home after making his radio debut, to be greeted by his mother who asked, "How much did they pay you?" "Nothing," he replied. "The son of a bitch cheated you!" she screamed. "When you go back next week, you ask him what the pay is." Chapter One continues:

"The week had passed, and screwing up my courage, I asked what the remuneration was for appearing on last week's show. The program director, from whom I was to learn much in the months to come, gave me a quizzical look, muttered an oath, and said, 'No money now—maybe after a while after you get enough experience.' I didn't know then that I should have quit while I was ahead for it would be some eighteen months before I would begin earning $15 a week. Few people realize what the early days in radio were like, how stations shared time with other stations.

"My start came at WLTH in Brooklyn, one of four stations sharing the 1400 KC band. To those of you who weren't in radio in the early thirties, let me explain: It was common for two, three or even four stations to share the samewave length, with each station having specified

21

hours, operating some thirty hours a week. This was the WLTH schedule

Sunday: 1:30 - 3 p.m., 10:30 - 12 midnight
Monday: 4 - 6 p.m., 9:00 - 10:00 p.m.
Tuesday: 11:30 - 1 p.m., 6:00 - 7:30 p.m.
Wednesday: 1:30 - 4 p.m., 10:30 - 12 midnight
Thursday: 8 - 11:30 a.m., 7:30 - 9:00 p.m.
Friday: 4 - 6 p.m., 9:00 - 10:00 p.m.
Saturday: 10 - 1:00 p.m., 6:00 - 7:30 p.m.

"Unlike today, radio was glamourous It was fun. Chain operators, projections and conglomerates were unheard of. There was more "show" than business. No matter how small a station might be, one would approach its reception room with awe.

"Out of a thirty-hour schedule, we had some eight hours of Yiddish, four hours of Italian, three hours of Polish, with early morning and late night being English. As with all "no-speaka-da-English" stations, the announcer would introduce the program, turn it over to the ethnic emcee and then return every fifteen minutes to give the call letters. I think one reason I never got too far in this business was due to my having a terrible cold one Friday night and, thinking he was doing me a favor, the Polish announcer signed the station off and gave my name as the announcer.

I think the most ambitious attempt ever made by a 100-watter, sharing time with three other stations, was a station with a studio in the Jewish section of Brooklyn, a crystal studio on the fifth floor of Namm's, a downtown Brooklyn department store, and for the "elite," (maybe for book reviews or travel talks) a studio in the Pierre Pont Hotel, in still another section of Brooklyn—three origination points for thirty hours of programming.

Getting back to the "Brooklyn Case", as it was known for some years to the Federal Radio Commission (and later in 1934, the Federal Communications Commission), in those days, licenses were not renewable every three years, as they are today, but every six months, so it was a constant battle with each station fighting for the others' facilities.

It was a strange mixture. One of the "infamous four" went to jail during World War II for selling USO-donated cigarettes. Another was broadcast by a Rabbi, who advertised not only bar mitzvahs over the air, but circumcisions as well! The third changed his call letters to

22

WVFW, I guess with the thought that the government wouldn't do anything to hurt "the boys." The fourth guy, I think was pretty decent. What I remember most about him was that his was the station that always came on banging the chimes. (When one station signed off, the next one came on a second later and over-modulated like hell to make the guy just signing off sound weaker, although they were all low wattage)"

Charlie also tells the story of a radio owner from Kansas City coming to New York and, when Charlie went after a job with him, left him with this lesson about job hunting: "Don't come to me to take money out of my cash register. Tell me what you can do to put money in!" It is a lesson that applies today even more than years ago.

Charlie proceeded to educate me in many other areas. He wrote me one time, "Why does the show always have to go on? Is it because of 'Love of the art'—the ego of a performer—is it theatrics? No! The show *must* go on—because nobody wants to give the money back!"

Charlie went through the service and had many, many stories of his experiences with getting enough advertising during days off so that in the evenings at camp he could print a weekly newspaper.

In 1946, fresh out of the Army, he met Charles Blackley in Staunton, Virginia. They proceeded to put WTON on the air after four months of construction slowed by shortages of materials. He sold eighty-three advertisers initially, most on an annual basis, and had to promise that no string music or cowboy yodeling would ever be heard on the station. They didn't want any more "live talent" country stations in the market such as the one found in Harrisonburg twenty miles down the road.

Some of Charlie's stories about personnel were most interesting. They paid their announcers well, in relation to other area stations, but were never able to find what he called a "eunuch. Once, two announcers journeyed together looking for jobs. Both were excellent. They stopped off in Roanoke first, naturally, for Staunton was just a comfort stop on the bus line, and the Roanoke station took the man without children. We got the other one. He had five kids and financial problems, and because he was always in hock, it was ten years before he was able to make it to the next town.

Then there was the time we hired a man with three children. He was so happy to join the station he screwed all night, and before he knew it, he had four on his hands. Another twelve-year financial problem."

23

Charlie used to say that over the years they loaned their air men lots of money to keep their heads above water but, strangely enough, never lost out because of it.

Then there was the time the wakeup man was reporting the amount of rainfall, which seemed to increase every day, until it dawned on him that it hadn't rained for ten days. It seems the night man had been pissing in the rain gauge, and for days that was the rainfall report!

He had one announcer who married the ugliest woman he could find because he didn't want any men in bed with her while he was working, but even that strategy failed. In 1953, Charlie began to check out the credentials of announcer applicants with their former employers to verify that they had no financial problems, weren't chasing women, didn't drink, paid their bills, and were dependable and honest. If they passed, he used to ask, "What's wrong with him?"

Charlie Seebeck became one of my closest friends. He was tall, overweight and looked a little like a man down on his luck. He had developed a southern drawl, but when he hit that microphone on the air he was absolutely brilliant in tone and enunciation. Dozens of station managers throughout the country became involved with Charlie because he always had fresh ideas for going after advertisers. I have never met a man who worked harder, and he was loyal to everyone around him. His worst setback was when Charles Blackley sold the station and he had to find employment elsewhere. But that wasn't a problem, and he worked until his death in 1989.

About a year after I first met Charlie, I received a phone call from Joe Bailey in the New York office. He said, "Marv, you've sold every program we have to Charlie Seebeck, and he's called asking to cancel the Tommy Dorsey show." I said, "Please don't do anything until you hear from me." I got up the next morning at 5 a.m. and drove the four hours to Staunton, Virginia. In those days, Virginia had ABC stores where you could buy alcohol. It was a brown bag state. Bars and restaurants couldn't sell booze. I bought two bottles of scotch and had them put in two separate brown paper bags, went over to the station and walked into the office. Charles Blackley and Charlie Seebeck shared the same office, with desks on opposite sides of a large room. As I appeared in the doorway with two paper bags over my head, Seebeck turned to Blackley and in a loud, clear voice yelled, "The son-of-a-bitch! Now we can't cancel!" Charlie and I went out that morning and resold the show, and the contract was honored.

I ran into him once at a Regional Virginia Association of Broadcasters convention in Richmond, Virginia. It was held at the beautiful John Marshall hotel, which had a long and fairly high stairway leading up to the lobby. This was before Charlie had purchased the Dorsey show, which was the only show I had not been able to sell him. Charlie's coming down the stairs, and he is drunk out of his mind. He grabs me, demands a blank contract for the Dorsey show and signs it, telling me to fill it out and mail it back to him. I found him the next morning after he had sobered up, and handed him the blank contract, stating there was no way I could accept it—he had been drunk. He looked at me and said, "I wasn't *that* drunk. Put it through."

I credit Charlie with my many, many years of success. He taught me to relax when selling, take my time, and leave high pressure out of my presentations and, most importantly, to have fun.

4.
The Tommy Dorsey Show

Aside from Washington, Baltimore, Charleston-Huntington, Richmond and Wilmington, my new territory was made up of many small radio markets.

West Virginia was an education in itself. I met a man in Morgantown who was younger than I, but who had been general manager of the radio station for almost two weeks. When I asked him what his past experience had been, he mentioned that he had been with AP. I immediately assumed he meant Associated Press, but I soon discovered he had been chief meat cutter at the Atlantic & Pacific Tea Co. supermarket, the A&P. "Mama" had bought him the radio station. Fortunately, I never saw him again and I don't know what happened to him.

In Logan, I discovered the mayor was in prison on a murder rap, but he was allowed out to run the city government from 9:00 to 5:00 Monday through Friday.

In Beckley, I met Joe Rahall, who owned the bus line as well as several radio stations. He had a violent temper. His screaming arguments with his brother, replete with vitriolic language, were something frightening to experiece. But Joe was a great businessman. He built quite a list of stations, not only in radio, but later in television as well. His brother Sam was also involved in broadcasting.

Lou Cowan continued to give us new products to sell. We had the *David Street Song Shop; Red Rider,* a Western, and *Smiths of Hollywood,* a 26-week comedy series of half hours. During this period, our big show was released, namely, *The Tommy Dorsey Show,* in which Tommy Dorsey became the disc jockey on a syndicated basis. It was made up of intros and talk, with lead-ins, but it allowed the stations to add his suggested records and their own commercials. It proved to be the first syndicated disc jockey show in the country, and was quickly followed by Harry Goodman's release, *The Duke Ellington Show,* later followed by Martin Block of New York City fame (the Martin Block *Make Believe Ballroom).*

My first big sale of the Dorsey show was to Tom Tinsley, owner of WITH in Baltimore, Maryland. He also owned WLEE in Richmond, Virginia.

WITH a 250 watter was on East Baltimore Street in downtown Baltimore. One climbed a long flight of stairs to get to the station, which proved to be anything but lavish in furniture or studios. (I later found out that the studio was rented for $300 a month, had a rate card of $9 for a one-minute commercial, and was doing well over $300,000 a year gross).

Tom Tinsley proved to be a strange character. He was of average height, thin and "Kojak"-bald, with a haughty attitude, his family having been given a land grant by the King of England in the seventeenth century. I always received a curt and reserved greeting from him. His family was wealthy and, in his early years, Tom had been quite a play-boy. His mother had placed him in several other broadcasting facilities, but with little success. She bought him radio station WITH but main-tained controlling stock interest. I give Tinsley credit in that he hired some brilliant people to run the operation, particularly Jake Embry. He later put WLEE and WXEX-TV on the air in Richmond, Virginia, and to my knowledge Mama didn't own any part of them.

My presentation to Tinsley started about 3:00 p.m. and wasn't completed until 7:00 that evening. His secretary, Mae Hughes, was a beautiful blonde about 5'2" tall, a carbon copy of June Allison with a body that wouldn't quit. I couldn't take my eyes off her.

Each time we wrote a contract, Tom would find something he didn't like and would change the wording, and Mae had to go back and re-type the entire agreement. She had a date that evening but couldn't get out of the office because of that contract, and the fire in her eyes could almost kill. When she finally left, Tom suggested I see his general manager, Irvin Abeloff, of WLEE in Richmond, Virginia, and mention to him that WITH had bought *The Tommy Dorsey show.*

That evening, being embarrassed because of what Mae had been put through, I sent a dozen roses to her in care of the station with a short note of apology. Then I headed my car to Richmond, where I immediately made another sale to WLEE.

The Dorsey show gave a radio station five hours of programming (one hour per day) Monday through Friday. In markets the size of Baltimore, it cost $125 per week for fifty-two weeks, while Richmond was $75 per week.

Cowan had an interesting schedule of commissions. As I mentioned, we were paid $216 twice a month, which had to cover all our travel and living expenses. Each quarter we were to receive a 10 percent commission after the first $10,000 of sales with a sliding scale up to a maximum of 25 percent. Those first two sales were worth more than $10,400 to me and I now was working on the next scale which would bring me even higher commissions.

I headed for Washington, D.C., my biggest market, and made an appointment to see Wayne Coy of WINX. At that time, the station was owned by the Washington Post and was a 250 watter. Wayne had recently taken the station over. It was in poor financial condition with low ratings, and he was looking to change its entire program format. He proceeded to buy every program I had. I was on a roll.

While at WINX, I met one of the local salesmen, Bill Ostrow, who invited me back to his apartment for dinner. There I met Art Wagman, who shared the apartment with Bill, and they suggested I share their apartment with them. Since it was in the center of the territory I was covering, I accepted. I was delighted to have a place that I could come back to when I was in or near the area, and save some dollars on hotels.

The apartment was at 5518 Connecticut Avenue, one block from Chevy Chase, Maryland. It had two bedrooms, and was on the second floor behind a photography studio, above a small family supermarket. My "share" was Bill Ostrow's bedroom. He had a queen-size bed, while I had a cot whose mattress was a Sears Roebuck wooden door covered with a sheet that had been sewn to it. But I was in my mid-twenties, and it was ample for my needs. I never had a problem sleeping in soft beds, hard beds or any type of bed. It was just part of life on the road.

Bill couldn't drink, which I soon discovered for myself at a house party with Art and our dates. Something in his body reacted to alcohol and, although it was hilarious to see, it could be serious. After one or two drinks, Bill passed out and went stiff as a board. February in Washington meant temperatures in the teens, and when we decided to take him home and put him to bed, he just wouldn't fit in the car. We got Art's convertible, put the top down, and drove him home literally standing up. Fortunately, he was fine in the morning, but he gave up alcohol—I never saw him take another drink.

Art owned a 1941 Lincoln Zephyr convertible, a most unusual and aggravating car. The doors, windows and top all worked by buttons, which would prove unreliable at times. One evening, we both had dates from Baltimore. I wanted to get some paper work finished, so Art offered to take the girls home in my car while I drove the Zephyr to the apartment and get a couple hour's work done. After bruising both hands, I waited two hours in that car for Art to come back and free me. All buttons were *stuck,* and it was the last used car of Art's I ever got involved with.

We had a guest for several months by the name of Marty Weissman. Marty was down on his luck and used the couch in the living room as a bed. He also had collected dozens of parking tickets and totally ignored them. One evening, there was a knock on the downstairs door and Bill went to answer it. A police officer was looking for Marty, who raced out the back door, down the stairs, and ran the one block into Maryland where they couldn't touch him.

A lamp with two bulbs was by the entrance to our apartment. One bulb was red, the other white. If the red bulb was on, you didn't open any door; if the white bulb was lit, it was all clear. I came up to the apartment one evening several months later with a date, and the red light was on. Not only were the two bedrooms in use, but the living room as well.

Art Wagman was studying for the bar and kept his head above water by selling used cars. Each Sunday he would put several ads in the Washington Post. One ad, I remember, said "exceptionally clean". He was quite truthful. He took me downtown in that car one day, and I discovered there was no floor board. Going through a puddle was a cleansing experience! Art would study in bed Monday through Friday until 6:00 p.m., then he would get up, shower, and go out on a date. That lasted several months until he took the bar and passed with flying colors.

Bill Ostrow had left WINX and was unemployed for several weeks. I soon discovered if I didn't get back to Washington on the weekend and replenish the food in the refrigerator, things might have gotten quite difficult for both Art and Bill. Marty had left us, having decided to get married after finding a job.

Several months later, Art's mother came for a visit. For days we had complained about the lack of clean sheets and pillowcases. Art's mom solved the mystery. It seems whenever a sheet or pillowcase was needed, Bill would simply put a clean one over the dirty one. Art's mom found ten sheets and sixteen pillowcases on Bill's bed, and then gave our apartment quite a cleaning.

I left West Virginia one evening about 6:00 p.m. and drove straight through until early morning to get back to Washington on Saturday. (In those days, we didn't have expressways. Travel was basically on two-lane highways.) I walked into the apartment about 3:00 a.m., not paying any attention to what the light in the hall might portend, took my clothes off and went to bed. About 7:00 in the morning, something awakened me, and I very slowly turned around and discovered Bill Ostrow in bed with his girlfriend, Rosalie, both up on their elbows looking somewhat quizzically. I just turned over and went back to sleep.

In late summer, I received a telegram from the home office which was one of the funniest I had ever read. The Cowan organization had decided to hold a contest. Anyone writing a minimum of $25,000 of business in the next six weeks would earn an extra 5 percent commission. With a rate card that started at $10 a half hour, and went up to approximately $150, with most of my major markets already sold, it was a real joke.

By early fall, 1947, I had approximately $5,000 in sales for the contest and I decided to go deep into my territory, namely Kentucky and West Virginia, hitting the small markets there.

I learned another lesson about selling: when you get hot, don't stop until you get the feeling that it's over. There comes a time in a salesman's life when, no matter what he does, he is at the right place at the right time. When that happens, you work every possible moment because it will not last forever. You will know when it's over because the manager will be out of town, or his wife's having a baby, or he has been in an automobile accident, or for one reason or another, he is unavailable.

I went through West Virginia and Kentucky and made a sale a day for the next three weeks. They were small sales and, surprisingly, most of them were for *The Tommy Dorsey show.* I had a minimum rate (which all these markets called for) of $50 a week, or $2600 for the year. I not only made it into the contest, I wrote $37,500, which meant a bonus check of $1875. It also put me over the top of the sliding scale commission, which meant I had reached the plateau, or 25 percent of every contract I wrote for the rest of the year, ending in April, 1948.

I bought my mother a fur coat and purchased one of the first 100 television sets sold in the Buffalo, New York, area for Mom and Dad. The television set proved to be quite unusual. The box was about the size of today's thirty-five-inch TV set, with a nine-inch black and white tube. WBEN, owned by the Buffalo Evening News, was a 5,000-watt CBS network radio station and had the first construction permit in the market granted by the FCC. Their offices were on the top floor of the Statler Hotel in downtown Buffalo and every day for 15 minutes at twelve noon they would take a camera and pan from the studio the sights around the downtown area. When I was in Buffalo visiting my parents, I would run back to the house at noon and we would turn our set on for that 15-minute programming. One day, the camera panned into one of the hotel rooms, and the few of us who owned television sets witnessed two people "honeymooning away". The camera man, realizing what was going out on the air, froze, but only for 30 seconds or so. That may have been the first x-rated show on TV!

Early in December, I received a call from Chicago asking me to come in for a general sales meeting. I arrived at the office about nine o'clock on the given date and spent almost three hours being patted on the back and told what a wonderful, incredible job I had done. At the same time, they rewarded me with the state of Tennessee. Later on, when I got into this new territory, I discovered I had been preceded by a bad check artist—not a fun situation.

I learned another lesson at this meeting on how to treat people. I was told to go out and have a leisurely lunch, *by myself*, which seemed strange. Here I am invited to a general sales meeting, where I'm the only salesman present, and then I am told to have lunch by myself and return at 2:00 p.m.

The second shoe fell in the afternoon when I was told I was making too much money. I had from December through April remaining, and anything I sold would be at 25 percent commission. It was too much. I was also told that I was making more money than they were. In all my years in marketing, to me the greatest compliment was when my account executives or sales personnel were making more than I was. If you own the company and have large stock interests, they were really making it for you in the long run.

They cut my commission down to a straight 17 percent, and I later discovered they called each salesman in one at a time, to try and make the best deals they could. I still believe to this day that was the end of the Louis G. Cowan Company's chances of becoming the big name in the syndication field in broadcasting. I vowed to keep my eyes and ears open, and not make any long term plans of staying with the company.

31

In December of 1947, (Albert) Wayne Coy became chairman of the Federal Communications Commission. The Washington Post people brought in John S. Hayes, former station manager of WQXR in New York, to replace him at WINX. WQXR was a good music station, and John decided to totally change the programming at WINX. Unbeknownst to me, John called Al Hollander, vice president of Cowan, and claimed that Ziv and the other syndication companies had let the station out of all their contracts because Wayne Coy was now the FCC Commissioner, and John was changing the programming. Without calling anyone to verify, Al Hollander authorized the cancellations and I was out several thousand dollars in commissions. He called me to tell me, and I lost my cool. We got into a screaming session, and he told me to shut up or he would fire me. I told him to go ahead and do so, but it never happened.

Al Hollander was a 5'2" dynamo, or so he thought. I have always believed he had a terrible inferiority complex, and tried to compensate by throwing his weight around. Not too long after, he went back to Grey Advertising as a vice president. I have not talked to him since, but I have always felt double-crossed.

John Hayes had also called Fred Ziv with the same story, and Ziv's retort was, "If the salesman will let you out of the contracts, we will be very happy to oblige." Naturally, nothing happened. The contracts went on until expiration.

When you travel, you meet some very unusual people and you make some lifelong friends. This happened to me in Roanoke, Virginia, when I first met John Harkrader, who was sales manager of WDBJ a CBS affiliate.

I spent many weekends in Roanoke in a beautiful, seven-story, old English inn known as the Hotel Roanoke. It was furnished southern-style, like the pre-Civil War era. It was purchased by the Norfolk and Western Railroad, whose home offices were across the street. The dining room was staffed by waiters and waitresses whose jobs had been handed down from generation to generation. It was a showplace in the South, and their breads, cornsticks and other foods (even peanut soup) were sensational.

In the late summer and early fall, John and I would hit every county fair within a sixty or seventy-mile radius of Roanoke. John was engaged to a delightful young lady, Marg, from Kansas City, but at the time he was living in a boarding house. I recall one Sunday afternoon arriving at the boarding house and finding John sitting in a rocking chair on the porch waiting for me. He had taken two large glasses, put a glass straw in each filled them with crushed ice up to the top, with mint leaves interspersed. He had then poured bourbon to the top and put the glasses in the freezer. We spent the afternoon sipping mint juleps of solid bourbon and, as the ice melted, getting higher and higher.

John had a 1946 Nash automobile. Once, while driving with him on a two-lane highway, we got behind a farmer in a little Model A Ford coupe who was riding the center line so no one could get past him and doing about twenty miles an hour. John quietly sneaked up on him, hit his bumper, and stepped on the gas. That poor farmer desperately tried trying to steer at forty and fifty miles an hour until John finally let him go.

I had sold John *The Smiths of Hollywood,* a comedy Harry Von Zell as the father, Brenda Marshall as the mother, and several starlets as the children. We had sold it to Heironimus Department Store, and my rate was $50 per week. I had only twenty-six shows, so I could only sell for a six-month period. Ray Jordan was the general manager of WDBJ, and John, Ray and I went out for lunch one day. Ray looked at me and said, "Marv, do you think it was fair selling *The Smiths of Hollywood* for $50 a week when the half-hour time cost is only $25?" That should give you an idea of the rate structure of radio in its early days. At the time, Roanoke was the 103rd market in the United States.

When Ray Jordan retired, John became general manager of WDBJ, and continued as general manager of WDBJ-TV, the CBS affiliate in the market. He was so well-loved in Roanoke that, upon his retirement, they named a park after him.

When traveling, I quite often would get up at five o'clock in the morning, drive 150 to 200 miles to my destination, work until 5:00 or 6:00 in the evening, and then find a hotel or motel in the area. I would do that five days a week and, wherever I ended up on a Friday night, I would normally sleep until noon on Saturday, have a big brunch, do a little sight-seeing, relax, and plan my trip for the following week.

Now that I had the state of Tennessee, it was time to go into those markets. They were wide open, and most cities had not been properly sold. The salesman who preceded me wrote bad checks at every station he went to, so there were a few trying moments in several of the markets, but I never really had too much of a problem.

On Friday night, leaving Virginia, I decided to get started and drove to the little city of Johnson City, Tennessee. At the time, I did not realize this was known as the tri-cities area, with Bristol, Virginia-Tennessee and Kingsport, Tennessee, within twenty miles. I found a little hotel, the John Sevier (named after one of the great pioneers in Tennessee history). It was Saturday, my time to sleep in and catch up on some rest. The hotel was charming, true early-south architecture. It's now a retirement home. In those days, the railroad track was in front of the hotel, and business had to stop to allow trains to go through.

At 5:00 a.m. Saturday morning, my eyes opened, and although I fought and tried to sleep, it was impossible, so I got up, showered and shaved and went to see if there was a radio station in the market. There were several in the tri-city area, but the only one in Johnson City with management in at the time, was WETB, a 1,000-watt day timer. I walked in about 9:00 and asked for the general manager, who was not in, but his commercial manager, a guy by the name of Charlie Powers, saw me. I presented *The Tommy Dorsey Show* to him, and he looked at me and said, "Will you help me sell it?"

We then called on a small milk company, called Pet Milk Products co. It was a southern company not affiliated with the national company, and it was the first in the South with fresh milk products. I was introduced to Major Ballew, and with my small record player presented *The Tommy Dorsey Show* to him. After five minutes he said to me, in a marvelous southern drawl, "Mr. Kempner, that is a very fine program, but we are looking for a family-type show." What an opportunity! I immediately switched to *The Smiths of Hollywood.* I was making the presentation to Major Ballew (his first name was Major—he was not a former officer) and his sales manager, when, just a few minutes into the presentation, he asked me to stop. He then brought in his entire staff, from the people who milked the cows on up, and there must have been thirty to thirty-five of us in the room. I started over with the program, and the laughter in the room made me certain I had made a sale.

After most of the personnel had left, Major Ballew looked at me, and in that wonderful soft southern voice said, "Mr. Kempner, can you clear that program from Washington D.C. to Miami for me?" At that time, that meant twenty-six markets, most of which were out of my territory. We set a meeting for 9:00 Monday morning, at which time I would have to have cleared the markets which he indicated.

I went back to the hotel and called my boss, Bob Michels, in Chicago. Naturally, he was not in the office on Saturday so I did what any red-blooded American salesman would do—I called him at home. I said. "Mr. Michels, this is Marv Kempner—",and that is as far as I got. I have had my ass reamed before and since, but never the way Bob Michels gave it to me that day. How dare I call him at home! Office

34

hours were 9:00 in the morning to 5:00 at night, Monday through Friday! The office number was such and such! While he was berating me, I kept saying but one word, "but—but—but." I finally screamed into the telephone, "But I've got to clear twenty-six markets by 9:00 Monday morning for *The Smiths of Hollywood.*" There was dead silence, followed by, "Call me at the office in thirty minutes." When I called back, he apologized for a good five minutes. I got all the markets cleared except Roanoke, Washington and Richmond, which I had already sold. Michels asked me to make sure I got a photographer to take pictures of the signing of the contract, and my picture with story appeared in *Broadcasting Magazine* two weeks later.

On Monday morning, I sold Major Bailey a fifteen-minute block of *The Tommy Dorsey Show* in Roanoke on WROV, in Washington on WWDC, and in Richmond on WLEE. The sale ended up with twenty-nine or thirty markets, and was the largest individual syndication sale made to one company to that time. Joe Bailey from the New York office called me and said, "Marv, I know what Al Hollander did to you, but I am seeing to it that you get full commission on this entire sale."

My territory had expanded through the Carolinas by the spring of 1948 and, although we were not getting much new product, I had enough to continue selling consistently. Lou Cowan had gone the network route with *Stop the Music* and that, coupled with the *Quiz Kids* and *Elmo Roper,* was doing exceptionally well. He was a very fine gentleman and always treated me well. Lou was married to a delightful lady who was a Spiegel, of Spiegel Catalog fame. It is interesting that the Spiegel family never authorized the use of any broadcast. They stayed with their catalog only, and Lou Cowan, being so successful in broadcasting, never tried to change their minds.

One day I received a call from New York asking me to meet Tommy Dorsey and spend several weeks with him on his one-night-stand tour of the southeast. I had heard many stories about Tommy, all of which I found to be untrue. He worked very hard, his men were loyal to him, and he had a little darling who was the "mother" of the band, Connie Haines. There was an unwritten law among the members of the band regarding Connie: "You may look, but do not touch." She was a sweetie, still looking for the man of her dreams, whom, I discovered years later, she found when she was in her late twenties, had three or four children in the next six or seven years, and remains happily married. Connie really didn't know me, but I watched her many, many evenings on the bandstand. I also met Charlie Shavers and Ziggy Elman, two of the great trumpeters of that era. The band was very solid. My primary job was as a "front man"—to arrange personal appearances at the stations that had his program.

I was having dinner with him one evening, when he called the waitress over and asked her to bring a box of Saltines and a bottle of Heinz ketchup. That seemed a strange request, and he proceeded to eat the Saltines after pouring ketchup on them. I tried several, and they weren't that bad. Tommy told me how when he and Jimmy were growing up, their mother baked fresh bread every day. When they came home from school, they would finish off a loaf of bread and a bottle of ketchup as an afternoon snack.

Tommy would be on the bandstand from 8:00 at night until 2:00 in the morning, and we would carry him off the stage soaking wet, take him to the hotel and put him to bed. By 6:00 or 7:00 the next morning, he was raring to go. He never required more than three or four hours of sleep. I also remember how every night of the week he would call his mother in southern California. He was married at the time, but not working at it, and I never recall him calling his wife.

One time, I met him at the airport in Lynchburg, Virginia, a town about fifty miles from Roanoke. He arrived in a single engine plane, and I drove him to the hotel where he asked me to call two people who he hadn't seen in twenty years. I looked at him incredulously and said, "Tommy, nobody has had any sleep for days. Why bother?" He turned to me and said, "Marv, when you are going up the ladder of success, make all the friends you can because some day you may be coming down and you might need them." The two people came with their families, and probably talked about it for the next twenty years.

The orchestra was playing that night at the gymnasium at Virginia Military Institute. They had a small stage at one end, only about twenty feet wide, so the band set up in a pyramid with the brass section on top. Unbeknownst to any of us, Ziggy Elman was so drunk he was staggering. Everything went along famously until Ziggy's solo of "And the Angels Sing", made famous while he was with Benny Goodman. There was Ziggy, seemingly thirty feet above the floor, with his horn raised to the sky, when he suddenly lost his balance and went over backwards. He was so drunk he fell to the floor unhurt. The whole brass section started blowing air, and Tommy stopped the band. Ziggy, red as a beet, came out from behind the stage and climbed all the way to the top, Tommy started over, and we went through "And the Angels Sing" a second time.

36

*　*　*　*　*

In many markets, particularly the larger cities, radio stations could usually be found in downtown hotels. Most were in the basement, others were anywhere from the second floor mezzanine on up to the top floor. A 250-watt radio facility in Chattanooga, Tennessee, had their studios at the Patten Hotel. The manager, Vann Campbell, and I became quite friendly and we set up a meeting for lunch. I walked into the station a few minutes early and discovered two well-dressed gentlemen sitting in the lobby. All stations had speakers in their waiting rooms so you could listen to their programming while waiting for an appointment. It was noon, and a big fanfare came on, "And now, *Queen for a Day* with Jack Bailey, brought to you by Alka Seltzer and Miller Brothers Department Store." Never did have lunch with Vann that day because he had to explain to the two gentlemen in the lobby, who were vice presidents of Mutual, how he had cut in and used a local store in the program opening.

Earlier, the first edition of the afternoon newspaper had come out, and in the center of the first section was a two-page double-truck ad for Miller's Department Store. As anyone discharged after World War II knows, looking for a white shirt at that time was like looking for a needle in a haystack. Here, in bold print headline, was "5,000 WHITE SHITS". In the second edition later that afternoon, it was corrected.

The Patten Hotel brings back many memories because so many things happened to me. My car was hit in the parking lot, I had a flat tire, but the most memorable moment came one Sunday afternoon. I had driven to Chattanooga that morning, checked into the hotel, bought a newspaper and was lounging quietly on the bed. I had my left leg stretched out and my right leg was almost touching the floor. I decided to call my mother and dad in Buffalo. I always managed to contact them at least once a week to make sure they were all right. My mother got on the phone, and we were having a delightful conversation when I felt something on my ankle. I didn't pay any attention until it felt like it was crawling up towards my knee. I kicked my right foot only to see a mouse thrown across the room and scurry under the radiator. My poor mother didn't know what was going on so I calmed her down by saying, "Oh, it's nothing very serious," and continued with the conversation. When I finished the call, I phoned downstairs, a bit angry. They were very apologetic and told me to come down immediately and they would change my room. When I appeared, the room clerk again apologized and said, "We very seldom have problems with mice, Mr. Kempner—only bedbugs." I quickly checked out and went a couple blocks down the street to another hotel.

37

When we brought Tommy to Chattanooga, he was interviewed live on the station, and he made the delightful remark (which we were able to delete before it went on the air), "This is Tommy Dorsey broadcasting from the Patten Hotel in Chattanooga, Tennessee, Chattanooga's leading flea trap."

By that time, I was following Tommy through many areas of the U.S. and, basically, it was the end of my having a true territory. I continued to work in the southeast until I left the Cowan organization, then the United States became my territory. When a band is on the road, they are usually either practicing, playing, or sleeping on the bus or in a hotel. Tommy used to have a once-a-month shindig where he would rent an entire floor of a hotel and have no appearances set for that weekend. It was known as "Tommy's Orgy", and I tell this story only to illustrate the type of man he was with his players.

Tommy had a youngster in his early twenties playing in the brass section. He played a mean trumpet. He had told Tommy he was engaged, had bought a ring for his young lady, and was very, very happy and excited. Tommy knew something, but never opened his mouth. That weekend was "Orgy" weekend, which meant the men could let their hair down, get as drunk as they wanted, and just have a ball. At the party, every call girl in the area was there, and one of them was this boy's girlfriend. For four days afterward, no one saw this youngster, but Tommy kept his seat empty and the band played without him. The young man finally showed up with a four-day growth of beard, bloodshot eyes, looking terrible. Tommy put his arms around him and said, "Go upstairs and get a few hours sleep—we start playing at 8:00." Not another word was ever said.

We were in Chicago once playing a gig and the band went to a place called Jazz Unlimited for a jam session at 2:00 in the morning. It proved to be quite exciting because on the bandstand was Satchmo Armstrong and several other name musicians. They just kept coming up and taking turns, and they played for several hours. When Tommy walked in, he saw Jack Teagarden, probably the greatest trombonist ever, on the bandstand. With a smile on his face he said, "Nobody plays trombone when Teagarden's around,"—and borrowed a trumpet.

I left Tommy in August and a few days later received a call from his manager. Lou Cowan was not picking up a second year of *The Tommy Dorsey show,* even though we had been successful in selling ninety-three markets. Tommy suggested that I take over the selling of the show for the second year, and he would pay all my travel expenses, plus a very nice salary and commission. I jumped at the chance, and headed back to the apartment in Washington.

Bill Ostrow had left, having recently been married, and Art Wagman had found an idiot, Lester Pearl, as a replacement. Lester was a very strange human being. He would take inventory every day to see what cans of food were missing, how many slices of bread you had eaten, how much was left in the peanut butter jar, how much milk you had drunk, and worst of all, believe it or not, he would count the sheets of toilet paper.

I went into the apartment, called the long distance operator and said I would be making dozens of long distance calls. Would it be possible to have an operator available so that I didn't have to start from scratch, since I had the names and numbers of all the people I had to call? They gave me an operator to whom I gave forty or fifty calls at a time—I was planning to spend two or three days making appointments all the way down through Texas. Poor Lester! He walked in and that phone kept ringing and ringing as the operator kept getting the calls, and he looked at me and said, "Who's going to pay for this?" I said, with a straight face, "Well, you, Art and I are going to split the bill. We split everything else, don't we?"

I started on a trip that took me from D.C. to El Paso, Texas. Have you ever driven from Dallas to El Paso? It's just desert, more desert, and the only change is when the railroad track goes from the left side of the road to the right side. Then, suddenly, one sees a mirage! Skyscrapers in the distance! Finally, after 650 miles, there's Midland-Odessa.

I was gone until the Tuesday before Thanksgiving. I had some success, but nowhere near the success necessary for Tommy to spend the money or time to produce the show nationally, and I received a call from his business manager about 10:00 that evening in Asheville, North Carolina We agreed that it was time to quit. I left at 5:00 a.m. on Wednesday morning, and drove non-stop to Buffalo, arriving at 8:00 a.m. on Thanksgiving Day. Looking back, it is hard to believe the driving we did without expressways or turnpikes. Cars didn't have air conditioning, and most didn't have automatic transmissions. My 1947 Mercury had only a radio and heater. But in retrospect, it was a wonderful time in my life.

5.
The Ullman Years

On the Friday after Thanksgiving, I drove down to see Bob Mendelsohn and Dick Ullman to find out what they had been up to during the many months I had been away.

*   *   *   *   *

Dick Ullman had gone to Yale, something he never let any of us forget. He was an accomplished pianist, and I believe in his heart it was his true love. While at Yale, he spent many of his weekends in New York City with the Gershwin family. He knew Paul Whiteman and most of the other big names in music in the twenties. His parents were wealthy, but were wiped out in the stock market crash of 1929. He had a brother, Fred, who in the forties produced motion pictures for RKO, the last one being *The Window*. Fred had a heart attack and, to prove he was all right, decided to chop down a tree shortly after coming home from the hospital, and dropped dead.

Shortly after Pearl Harbor, the FCC had declared a moratorium on the granting of construction permits for radio or television. At the end of the war, in 1945, there were 933 AM licensed radio stations, and less than ten television stations (six on the air and three or four with construction permits.) By January 1, 1947, there were fifty-five television stations on the air, and in 1948, the FCC, with spectrum problems on the VHF-television band, declared a freeze on all TV construction permits until a way could be found to handle the twelve VHF channels.

By 1947, there were 1,062 AM radio stations on the air, and 458 were under construction. With the government selling used transmitters at bargain basement prices, one could be on the air for as little as $25,000. By the end of 1947, a new form of broadcast station was in its early stages. There were 84 licensed FM stations, with another 703 under construction.

The difference between AM (amplitude modulation) and FM (frequency modulation) bands is interesting. AM requires a ground system of radials (wires), rather than a tall tower, and the signal follows the curvature of the earth. FM is "line of sight", and tall towers on high ground are required. All television signals use the FM band.

I've always felt that David Sarnoff, one of the great pioneers in broadcasting and equipment, slowed the success of FM, particularly radio, because of RCA's dominance in network, patents and manufacturing.

In 1948, the FCC put into effect their "duopoly law", which meant that one could not own more than one radio station in a market. This was relaxed somewhat, and one could own one AM, one FM, and one TV station. Newspapers, which the government wanted out of the broadcasting business, were in many ways grandfathered in. One of many problems broadcasters had with newspapers was refusal to print their station's programming. If a paper owned a station, only that schedule was printed. The FCC, after many complaints, finally forced all schedules to be printed. Many changes have since been made, and the duopoly law in the 90's is almost nonexistent. But because of that law, Buffalo Broadcasting Corporation was forced to sell one of their two radio stations, either WGR or WKBW.

At the time, Dick was general sales manager of WKBW, a 50,000-watt AM radio station. The station was sold to Doc Churchill, one of the early radio Evangelists. Dick would not work for Churchill, so his contract was bought out and he was paid a year's salary. With his wife, Phyllis, he went to Nassau and spent months there until he had gone through all of his money.

*   *   *   *   *

I walked into the office that Friday morning after Thanksgiving, and the first thing I did was lend Dick Ullman $200 to buy groceries. He had just come back, decided he had to go back to work, and had the germ of an idea. He said, "Let's do three or four jingles for major

41

businesses—one for dry cleaners, one for clothing stores, jewelers, etc."
I looked at him and said, "Dick, if you're going to do it for three or four advertisers, why not do it for all of them?" And that was the beginning of Jingl-Library and Richard H. Ullman, Inc.

Ed Kavinoky, an attorney with his own law firm, set up the new company. He, Bob Mendelsohn and I put up most of the money with two or three others putting in smaller amounts. We raised a total of $25,000. At age twenty-seven, I was a vice president.

We decided to produce forty-eight jingles covering every conceivable business. Each jingle would have six twenty-second variations, six ten-second variations, and two tags. They would be open end and done in such a way that each station could sell to their own advertisers and incorporate them in the jingle. One of the more corny ones I remember was for fuel oil: "Everything's going to be oil-right. Fuel oil is a winter delight", followed by the musical bridge with the local announcer reading the copy over the music, then singing the tag.

We hired Bobby Nicholson as our musical director. He, Dick and a few others were to write and arrange the jingles. We hired dozens of musicians and produced each of the forty-eight jingles in a variety of ways.

Bob Mendelsohn and I were to be the engineers, using the old Mendelsohn Company equipment, including a Presto recorder. We recorded on soft vinyl and, upon completion, sent it to a lab where they made a mother and stamper, and could then stamp out vinyl recordings.

There were two types of records made on vinyl. The standard had horizontal grooves—the wider the groove, the higher the sound or tone. The original phonograph records used a "vertical" cut which was Thomas Edison's invention. With the exception of one company, everyone used horizontal or lateral equipment in those days.

With the Presto recorder, the needle cuts the groove through soft vinyl, and a powerful vacuum cleaner pulls away the vinyl as it is cut. This could cause tremendous problems if the vacuum cleaner didn't do its job and a groove wasn't cleaned out properly.

Within a few weeks, our recording sessions started. They went from 9:00 to 5:00 each day. Bob and I would re-record from the vinyl disc onto our master, a 13¼ inch disc which, when finished at the lab, would turn out a twelve-inch record. With luck, we would finish a day's recording at 2:00 or 3:00 a.m. Some nights were heart-breaking because we would get to the last cut on the master and something would go wrong, and we would have to start all over. It was six, very trying

42

weeks, but finally all masters had been shipped out for pressing. Soon the day would arrive when we found out whether the idea would sell.

On February 2, 1949, Dick Ullman decided we should have a party celebrating the completion of our first product, Jingl-Library. We invited the entire staff and their wives, and all the stockholders. With Dick's favorite bartender from the Buffalo Club making martinis in double martini glasses, using a perfume spray for the vermouth, it wasn't long before everyone let his hair down.

Bobby Nicholson told a story of when he was still music director at WKBW. In those days, major radio stations all had standby orchestras, and would have at least an hour-long musical program, normally in the morning. At WKBW, Foster Brooks, who later became famous with his drunk act in Las Vegas, was the announcer. He had a full set of false teeth, and one morning they bet him he could not do the commercial break without his teeth. The rubber face of Foster broke the band up, and for ten minutes they couldn't play a note.

It was a fun evening. At one point, Ike Lounsberry, president and general manager of WGR radio, and one of our stockholders, asked me in front of everyone how many sales I could make in a two-month period. Without thinking, I said fifty, and Ike thought that was the funniest thing he had ever heard. Looking back, it was a stupid thing to say on my part, but I was stuck with it. I never liked being made a fool of.

The following morning, Dick Ullman left for Toronto, Bob Mendelsohn headed for Ohio, and I took off for D.C. Dick made his only sale I recall in the more than thirty years we worked together, to All Canada, which was the largest station representative firm in Canada. They represented dozens of stations and had their own sales staff placing U.S. programming.

Bob came back two weeks later with lots of promises, but I don't recall any sales. Bob was a great local radio and agency salesman, but he never knew quite how to close a deal in this type of business. Through the years, I found this true of many good men, but I never understood why.

I arrived in Washington the night of February 3, and made my first call to Ben Strouse, general manager of WWDC. I had called his sales manager to tell him I was coming in to give them the first presentation of Jingl-Library. I sold the station, but only after a good three-hour workover by Ben Strouse. Ben and I became very close personal friends in the subsequent years, and his station became one of my first calls when breaking a new product.

43

I had made a promise of fifty sales in two months to Ike Lounsberry. Since there were only five working days in a week, that meant I had only forty selling days and had to make more than six sales a week.

In those days, one seldom made advance appointments to see the general manager, except in the top ten markets. Normally, you could just walk into a station, ask for the manager; and get an audience. I devised a very simple plan that worked wonders for me. We only gave a thirty-five-mile protection against sales to competitive stations, and one could normally find another station within a fifty to one-hundred-mile radius. After getting the signature on the contract, I would look at the general manager, telling him of my next stop, and nonchalantly ask, "Who would you suggest I see there first?" When I got to the station in the next market, I would say to the general manager, " 'John Doe' asked me to see you first." The first question usually was, "Did he buy it?", and when the answer was "yes", the hard work was done. Program or product sales were always a "follow the leader" game with broadcasters.

When breaking new products in any business, one looks for the leaders in the industry. At the time in the broadcasting fraternity, there were anywhere from six to ten leaders. They were the people you would try to see first, because their names were known to the rest of the industry. More importantly, you could get a decision from them. Make three or four sales to the leaders, and the next ten sales are much easier.

I have heard so often the saying, "New York is where it's at," but the leaders of the major market stations are not necessarily in New York. For ABC, it may be San Francisco or Chicago; for NBC, Los Angeles or Washington; and for CBS, it used to be Chicago and Los Angeles. Get to the top manager in one of the leader markets and they will set up a meeting with owned and operated stations. I never found New York City to be the leader in broadcasting.

On the thirty-eighth day of my two-month trip, I was in Raleigh, North Carolina, and had made forty-five sales. Although that was a great accomplishment, I was down in the mouth because I wanted those fifty markets in the exact eight-week period. (40 working days.)

I called on Fred Fletcher, general manager and commercial manager of a Mutual broadcasting system, Tobacco Network Station WRAL. It was a 250-watt station in downtown Raleigh, which in the late 40's was a sleepy, but beautiful city, reminding one of what the Old South must have been like. The offices were on the second floor of a somewhat

44

sleazy-looking building, but the people were southern-hospitality nice. Fred was one of the true "good old boys", with his Carolina drawl, delightful personality, and easy smile.

I presented Jingl-Library to him. He excused himself, saying he would be back in a few minutes. I learned later that he had gone across the street to his father, A. J. Fletcher, president and owner of the station, to get an okay. A.J. was in his eighties, but he was still the big boss man, known in Raleigh as "Daddy".

Fred came back about fifteen minutes later and said, "Marv, we're buying your Jingl-Library for WRAL here in Raleigh, but we also want to buy it for the entire Tobacco Network." I made the deal on a market-by-market basis from the rate card, adding $5 per week to each market, and then giving him a 10 percent discount. (I had learned that trick well.)

The markets after Raleigh included Durham, Fayetteville, Rocky Mount, Greenville, Newburn, Jacksonville and Wilmington—all in North Carolina. On the thirty-ninth morning of my trip, I headed home with fifty-three firm sales for Jingl-Library but I never got a chance to shove that down Ike Lounsberry's throat. He had gone to Detroit where he was involved with another station.

Several weeks later while working in the Alabama-Mississippi area, I would still get up at 5:00 in the morning, find a general manager at a station at 8:00, rather than 9:00, and drive to the next market only to discover it wasn't on daylight saving time, but standard time. My day would continue like that, ending up in Central time, rather than Eastern Standard Time. With the time changes, I was able to see and sell eight different stations in one day. The only problem was, at 7:00 that evening, I found myself 200 miles from the motel I had left my clothes in, figuring I would still be in the area that evening.

With the huge success of Jingl-Library, it was now essential to have salesmen traveling throughout the United States. Dick Ullman was the president, and he felt he knew how to pick and choose.

His first sales disaster was Jim McCormick out of Los Angeles, a bachelor and great bridge player, but the wrong type of man for our company. I had set the pricing of Jingl-Library based on population and area. I had also suggested that we set up a commission for any salesman of 17 percent against their draw, which was accepted by everyone else until Dick went to California. He was so enamored with Jim McCormick that he offered him 25 percent. Of the first four salesmen our president hired, all of whom I trained, none ever made it, so for the next year we had a revolving door. But sales were coming in, and the company was doing very well regardless.

* * * * *

I made many friends through the years—people from all backgrounds. In Baltimore, the lovely Mae Hughes, whom I had sent flowers to, was so thrilled with the gesture that the two of us became an item for several months.

In Memphis, I met the co-owners of WDIA, a 250-watt day-timer independent, which was the first all-black programmed station in the country. Their commercial manager became a very dear friend. He went on to a station in Orlando, where I found him a few years later.

I met a delightful and beautiful gal while in Richmond, Jo McKinnon, who was from Memphis and a former Powers model. She and another wonderful gal by the name of Helen Powers were both at WLEE in Richmond.

Helen Powers was from Baltimore, and was one of the brightest program people in broadcasting. Her husband, Ralph, had been the morning man at WFBR, which was the highest-rated morning show for years. He developed multiple sclerosis, which eventually affected his speech and forced him into retirement. Helen had worked for WITH in Baltimore for years, and then was sent to the sister station, WLEE in Richmond, when it first went on the air. She not only did programming but knew how to hire and work with a new staff.

Bill Spigler, another great friend, was the sales manager of WLEE. I recall one sales meeting at 8:00 a.m. when they lost their network feed, which was Mutual, and Bill was called out of the meeting to go into the studio and play the piano until the network came back on.

The general manager had just hired a new sports announcer, and I was invited to go to the Richmond baseball field with him and Bill to watch a night game. We lugged a thirty-pound battery-operated radio with us, (we did not have transistors in those days) to listen to the new director of sports announcing his first game.

The first batter, hit the ball and the new announcer screamed into the mike, "It's a long, long, long, long fly ball out to center field." There was a short pause and then, "and the short stop comes in and takes it." The search began for a new play-by-play announcer the following day.

Harold Krelstein was vice president and general manager of WMPS, a 10,000-watt powerhouse in Memphis owned by Plough

46

Broadcasting. Prior to joining Plough, Harold had worked for Harry Goodman in New York, a syndicator who was very well known for his singing time signals. I not only spent time with Harry while in New York, but also with his sons, Danny and Everett, both of whom continued for years in the industry.

Abe Plough, who owned the station, was also president of Plough Pharmaceuticals, now merged into Schering Plough. Harold invited me to have lunch with him and Abe, a day I remember vividly only because we went around the block at least twenty times because Abe would not pay fifty cents to park, if he could find a parking meter and pay a nickel. The rich get richer!

Harold called me at my hotel one day to tell me he would pick me up in his new Lincoln Continental. He asked if I would mind if he took the car to an automatic car wash before going to his private club for lunch.

We ended up stuck there about an hour because Ford had been promoting their automatic door locks which locked at twelve miles an hour. Now, when you put a car in an automatic car wash, it spins the tires to clean the whitewalls. The doors locked with the engine running, and we had to wait until Harold's wife came with an extra set of keys. Harold became a very close friend. Later, he was one of the major domos in the beginning of rock and roll.

*   *   *   *   *

In 1953, we sold the "Jingl-Library" to NBC for their Thesaurus Library. They did very well with it, and it was one of the big reasons that their library continued successfully for several years.

"Musical Tune-O"

Driving back to the Buffalo office, I kept hearing a strange program in many of the southern markets. I happened to stop at a market in North Carolina and asked the general manager if he had heard of it. He said he was running it three hours every afternoon and had paid $100 for the rights. He gave me a card and showed me how they ran the three-hour game show.

I was heading back to the office and had planned to go to New York the following Monday, having been given the opportunity to pick up the MGM product, which included half-hour radio shows of the Hardy Family, and many other MGM features produced for radio syndication.

47

Still being young and very naive, I mentioned to Bob Mendelsohn and Dick Ullman that I had run into this program which seemed quite interesting, and I produced the card. They looked at each other, then at me, and said, "Can you find this guy?" On the card, at the bottom, was written, "Robert D. Buchanan, Lake Charles, Louisiana" and the date of copyright.

At Dick and Bob's insistence, I called Lake Charles and found Bob Buchanan working for a local radio station. I told him I was interested in handling his product, and we agreed to meet in Atlanta, Georgia early the following week. Dick suggested I do everything in my power to get the rights for national syndication of his program, but never bothered to tell me what type of deal I should make. Remember,I wasn't yet twenty-eight years old, and my business acumen left much to be desired.

I met Bob Buchanan and offered him a deal, which he accepted. I felt I had taken advantage of him, so at the last minute I changed the agreement and headed back to the office. Sometimes, naivete—even stupidity—pays off in the long run. I had originally offered Buchanan 10 percent of gross sales of his product, then changed it to 10 percent of the first $100,000 and 15 percent thereafter.

When I got to the office, I looked at Dick and Bob and said, "I think I may have made a mistake. We are going to have to pay too much." When I outlined the deal, they were absolutely stunned! How was I to know the standard syndication deal at the time was either a 50:50 split or a 65:35 split, with sales normally getting the smaller amount.

That was the beginning of *Musical Tune-O,* the only program I have ever had that I could honestly say I could sell in any and every market in the country. Broadcasters today could use this program. The copyright is still in effect, but there is no way today that you can afford an on-air staff; and there is little talent left in broadcasting. Music at most stations in the 90's is garnered from a satellite. Someone else has done the programming and left openings for commercials, weather and news.

Musical Tune-O was a bingo card with 250 instrumental musical selections, numbered from 1 to 250. If you at home with your *Tune-O* card could identify the song being played, you looked it up alphabetically, found a number next to it, and checked your card. If you had five in a row horizontally, vertically, diagonally, or had all four corners on the card, you were a winner. You called the station, claimed your prize, and the station went on to the next game.

The station was instructed never to play more than three tunes in any sequence making up a row, or more than two of the four corners. When they wanted a winner, they were to segue ten seconds or less of each song, one right after the other. The game was so popular that, as you started the second song, they could pick up the phone before it rang and have a winner. It brought tremendous store traffic to the advertisers.

We had to clear the game against laws in broadcasting regarding lotteries. One had to have what was called "CCP,"—consideration, chance or prize. The ruling at the time said we had prize and we had chance, but no considerations, since no one had to buy anything, and after a few months we were allowed to pursue sales.

We had to find a prize broker. At the time, the best-known was George Kamen from New York. After several meetings with him, we devised a plan that would offer $100 worth of prizes for $15, and stations would give a plug to the manufacturer. Depending on their market, stations could order what they needed. There were a few snags, like watches with no mechanisms inside and some other poor quality items, but generally, it worked well for us.

I met George one day for breakfast at the Shoreham Hotel in Washington several months after we released the show. He received an emergency phone call, and when he returned to the table he was ashen. His brother was on a transatlantic plane from Europe, the same flight as Marcel Cerdan, the middle-weight boxing champion, and the plane was missing.

I took him over to WWDC where we spent several hours looking at the United Press and Associated Press bulletins, but to no avail. It was a terrible tragedy. His brother was a very personable fellow who had European rights to all Disney merchandising. (What would that be worth today!) I stayed with George all day, then put him on a train to New York that evening.

One problem with *Tune-O* was the cost of cards. If each station printed its own, they would cost at least $10 per thousand. We solved it by ordering the cards in million lots, whereby we were able to get them at approximately $2 and charge the stations $3, the extra dollar paying for warehousing and shipping.

We printed the cards on one side only. That allowed the stations to reprint their advertiser's message on the other, and charge an additional fee. We then printed up on heavy cardboard a master of all cards so the D.J.'s or program directors could plan their games. By using colored pins, they could program their music and have winners whenever they pleased.

With twenty-five different cards, and with only three or four released each week, we only had to change the combinations every thirteen weeks. By printing and releasing fewer of certain cards, we had some control, but all cards were released at the same time. In each thirteen-week cycle, we changed the card colors, so one had to go out to the advertisers each week to pick up a different card. Many people collected every card, and lots of Tune-O Clubs were formed.

The best way to break in a product that most of the United States has never heard of is to go to a small, medium market (or markets,) make the presentation, discover what the pluses and minuses are, and attempt to make strengths out of weaknesses before going to the major cities. I used to train salesmen, and I tried to teach them that 90 percent of selling was selling themselves, with enthusiasm, and 10 percent was selling their product. The perfect presentation, which is almost impossible, is one in which you answer all the questions before they are asked. Most importantly, you must make your presentation to those who can make the decisions.

I started out with several small medium markets, places like Jamestown (NY), Rochester, Syracuse, and a few more, and all were immediate sales.

I then headed for Washington, D.C., and went to see Ben Strouse at WWDC. Ben, at one time, had been a buyer at the Gutman Department Store in Baltimore, Maryland. He married Ruth Katz, daughter of Joe Katz of the Katz Advertising Agency in Baltimore. (It was said that the reason Joe Katz never lost his accounts like Arrow Beer and Ex-Lax was because he had control of their stock.) After Ben and Ruth were married, Ben went to work for Joe as a salesman at the original WWDC. In those days, it was a 250-watt station. Later they bought Cowles 5,000-watt frequency, switched call letters, and WWDC moved to the 5,000-watt station. WOL went to the 250-watt station, and was sold. It didn't take long for Ben to become the station and general manager. He was tireless and very capable. He was also very good to me through the years, and I became very friendly with him and his wife.

I presented *Musical Tune-O* to Ben Strouse and his national sales manager, Herman Paris, the local sales manager, Maxie Sherman, and the entire sales force. Ben said, "Marv, will you help us sell it?" When I agreed, he set up a plan. The following morning, I was to go on sales calls with Herman Paris. Maxie Sherman, Ben, and each of

50

the salesmen were to team up also. We would meet up in Ben's office at 5:00 p.m. that evening.

Herman and I sold out the show before noon, so we went for a leisurely lunch, and then went shopping before going back to the station. When we got in, we discovered that we had sold *Musical Tune-O* three times over. We had sold a large food chain, a chain of drugstores, music stores, a department store, a gas station chain, plus numerous several smaller advertisers.

At 7:00 that night, Herman called Ruth Strouse to apologize for Ben being late, and Ben called Herman's wife. Ben took a bottle from his desk drawer, we all had a drink, selected the advertisers and signed a contract between *Musical Tune-O* and WWDC. I then proceeded on to Baltimore, where Jake Embry picked it up immediately for WITH, and since I was only seventy miles away, I decided to go on to Wilmington, Delaware.

WDEL in Wilmington was a 5,000-watt powerhouse owned by the Steinman Group out of Lancaster, Pennsylvania. They owned stations in Lancaster, Reading, Wilmington, Harrisburg, York and Lebanon. The Steinman stations were an interesting operation. They were newspaper-owned, paid their people very poorly, and, until the FCC stopped it, never printed any radio station's programming schedule but their own. They were top dog in most of their markets with 250-watt stations, and 5,000-watt stations in Wilmington, Delaware and Lancaster. Wilmington was the powerhouse and, for years, maintained their number one status, primarily because their rate card was so low other stations in the market had problems making a profit.

Steinman never made multiple buys; each station manager had authority to program his own station. In Wilmington, I used to work with the sales manager, Bernie Millenson, and then have to get on my hands and knees with Gorm Walsh, the general manager, and beg him to put my program on. I felt Gorm was heartless because he would look at me and say, "I would have to replace a public service show, and I am not willing to do so."

When I arrived in Wilmington with *Musical Tune-O,* Gorm Walsh was out of town. Bernie Millenson took one look at it and said, "I have to have that!" I said, "Fine, Bernie, sign my contract"—which he couldn't do, and I would not save it for him. I took it to WILM and, an hour later, left the market with a contract, feeling I finally got even with Gorm Walsh. Bernie threatened me with not being welcome again at the station, but I told him I would just have to take my chances. His

51

wife, Esther, had just had a baby girl. Before leaving the city, I sent a gift to her, and I was welcome the next time I went into Wilmington.

Jake Embry of WITH bought it immediately, so I knew all I had to do was go down to WLEE in Richmond, their sister station, and they would purchase it also. While drawing up the contract in Richmond with Irvin Abeloff, I suggested to Irvin they order 50,000 Tune-O cards. He said, "I want 10,000," and when I said it was not enough, he told me "where to go". Ten days after the show hit the air, Irvin was on the phone, livid with rage because I had not sold him 50,000 cards. He had run out in less than a week, and his advertisers were screaming, as were his listeners.

About this time, we hired Bob Buchanan, who had been an advisor, and brought him into the Buffalo office. He had designed *Musical Tune-O,* and had great expertise in station problems, so it was a very good move. Bob was a great idea man, worked well with the staff, and took over day-to-day management of the show. His experience in radio station operations was a big plus. I was especially pleased because Dick Ullman needed someone who could make decisions quickly. Dick was a great procrastinator and had problems making decisions. He would ask everyone's opinion, including the gardener and the trash collector—anyone who would listen—and still couldn't make up his mind.

Next door to our office, a woman and her two daughters worked at the oldest profession in the world, and Dick, in his naivete, used to say what a lovely family they were. We finally told him the truth. Dick asked them if they were prostitutes, and was shocked beyond belief at their reply.

In late February, 1950, I was in the office one morning when the phones started ringing off the hook. At the time, we had three secretaries plus Norma Seal, Dick's personal secretary. I couldn't understand what was going on until one of the station managers calling mentioned an article in *Time* magazine. We got hold of the February 20, 1950, issue, and under the radio & TV column, was the headline "Very Curious", containing the following article.

> "Very curious," said the Englishman. "First the man calls out a number, and you put a bean on it. Then he calls another number and you put another bean on it . . . until at last a lady screams, 'Bingo!' and everybody else cries, 'Aw, hell!' Very curious place, America."

Last week the baffled Englishman would have found America even more curious. The latest radio craze was *Tune-O,* an air version of bingo with a touch of *Stop the Music* thrown in. Players must first guess the name of the tune being played from a numbered list supplied by the sponsors, then match the tune's number with an accompanying bingo-type card. The first to plot five numbers in a row calls the radio station, screams 'Tune-O!' and waits for the prizes to roll in: $1,000 in cash, jewelry, a new automobile.

Started in Manhattan only three months ago, 'Tune-O' has stormed its way into six other large cities (Atlanta, Detroit, Louisville, Miami, Norfolk, San Diego), and last fortnight made a dizzying debut to a wildly enthusiastic audience in Washington, D.C. By last week more than 30,000 Tune-O cards had been given out and station WWDC had to install three special lines to handle the crowd.

Although the article stated that *Musical Tune-O* had stormed its way into "six other large cities," we actually were in most major markets. The sales had been made but start dates had been held up awaiting authorization by the FCC. By 5 o'clock all 3 of our girls were crying hysterically with phone calls driving everyone crazy. I recall one incident where 3 stations in one market wanted to buy it and we accepted the one who offered cash up front.

One of the fun stories is what happened in New York City with "Musical Tune-O". The Weintraub Advertising Agency purchased the program for Seaman Brothers. Among their products were Air Wick and White Rose Tea. *Tune-O* was purchased specifically for White Rose to promote a new product, White Rose Coffee. What happened is one of the true success stories in broadcasting and advertising. The program had to be cancelled after a six-month period, making all the newspapers and trade magazines because it was too successful.

Seaman Brothers had approximately 200 trucks distributing in over 5,000 locations. They promoted *Musical Tune-O* on the Bond building sign at Times Square, and the public went wild.

Since the cards had to be changed every week, and one had to go into the stores to get each week's card, it soon became evident that getting the cards to all the stores would be a major problem. In that six-month period, Seaman Brothers and White Rose handed out more than 18 million cards.

Near the end of the six-month run, the station had over one hundred telephone operators. I believe it is the only time a program

53

failed because it was too successful. Many more than two hundred trucks couldn't deliver the cards to what was estimated to be from 25,000 to 30,000 locations in the greater New York area. That, plus the fact that White Rose couldn't supply their stores with coffee and tea in the quantities that sales demanded. During the early days of Tune-O the general manager of WMCA was so angry when the rating services did not show a substantial increase in the station's audience, he took the controls off one afternoon and played TUNE-O with regular cards. The response was so overwhelming that the telephone system was knocked out in two borroughs of New York City.

In Philadelphia, I called on Roger Clipp, vice president and general manager of one of the top stations, WFIL. I made my presentation to Roger, who said, "If you can sell it, we will buy it." I spent the next few days working with one of his salesmen, Irv Teetsell. I had known Irv in Atlantic City, where he was general manager and commercial manager of WFPG. We sold the program to the largest drugstore operator in the greater Philadelphia area, Sun Ray. I went back to Roger with the contract for the Sun Ray stores, and I will never forget his response. He read the agreement, tore it in half, threw it in the wastepaper basket, and with a sneering smile said, "Sorry—we can make more money selling spots." In all my years in broadcasting, it has been seldom that people like Roger don't get their just desserts.

The station was owned by Triangle, which also owned a newspaper and several other major-market stations. Roger had made Triangle the powerhouse in the market, in both radio and television, but as my attorney in New York once said to me, "Marv, remember this—the man doesn't make the station, the frequency or channel makes it." Years later, Roger retired, and with his incredible background and genius, bought a radio station in the Sarasota, Florida, market. If my memory is correct, he went broke within a year.

I started over, going back to the client, getting an okay to change stations, and took the program to WPEN. It was an outstanding success (and one that I hope Roger found a bit distressing). I never called on Roger again.

During my absence on one trip, Dick Ullman had hired a new salesman, Laurence Chalker, to handle the southeast territory. Dick signed a company note to help him buy a car, and asked me to spend a week training him. Lawrence appeared to be very talented, but something didn't seem right. He liked the bottle too much, I like an occasional drink too, but not every day. Although he could make a good pitch, after a few months I found he didn't have that natural ability to close, so I had to let him go. I then discovered we still had to pay for the car, and Dick finally learned a lesson.

A few weeks later, servicing a station in Knoxville, Tennessee, I read that Oak Ridge, the east coast atomic bomb city, would be opened to the public. That sounded exciting. It had its own radio station and it was close to Knoxville, so why not investigate?

I made an appointment to see Marshall Pengra, general manager of the station, went through the gate at Oak Ridge and proceeded to the station. The city reminded me of an army camp, with most buildings like barracks and very few real houses. One felt an eeriness about the place; in 1951, the atomic age was still very young.

Marshall Pengra was a delightful man in his early forties, wiry, with a wonderful sense of humor. I pitched *Musical Tune-O,* and early in the presentation he stopped me, saying he had just purchased a similar show called *Chalk-O.* Laurence Chalker had stolen *Tune-O.* I suggested to Marshall that he sign my contract since the plagiarism was evident. He finally agreed and fortunately for everyone, it was the end of Laurence Chalker.

Musical Tune-O was an unusual program concept and, with 17 percent of the public being bingo-crazy, it could have been very successful for AM broadcasters in the '90's. Unfortunately there is no way to set up programming in the individual markets to play two to three hours each afternoon with live talent. The advertisers would be the easiest part because one can guarantee tremendous store traffic which advertisers love.

Financing proved very simple in those early years. We worked with the Buffalo branch of the Marine Trust Co., now known as Marine Midland, and rather than go in and borrow funds with one's signature, we would go in with contracts. We could borrow up to 75 percent of the contract valuation. When the stations paid, the money went towards decreasing the loan. If a contract became sixty to ninety days delinquent, we would just replace the original contract with a new contract. Unlike most businesses, broadcasting, because it is government-licensed, was seldom a problem as far as collections were concerned. I don't believe, through the years, our percentage of loss was over a half of a percent.

Dick Ullman decided it was time for us to go "big time." He contracted with the infamous gay nineties singer, Beatrice Kaye, to do fifty-two-half hours of a musical show. I was not very excited because I never cared for that type of programming, but contracts were signed, and Beatrice with her entourage came into the Buffalo area to produce the show.

Beatrice, an old vaudevillian, was a total pain in the ass. I soon tired of her rantings and demands. I had been to many parties with stars, and I quickly realized how boring most of them are, talking only about themselves

Beatrice Kaye was a perfect example. God forbid if there was any noise while she was taking a nap! Her husband and manager, Sylvan Green, was a pathetic Milquetoast, always kowtowing to her idiotic demands. Tea better be the right color and flavor, bath at the exact temperature, and in the morning tip toe around—"You know how lightly I sleep!" When Sylvan was away from her, he was a different person—charming, with a good sense of humor, and a great storyteller. But when Beatrice called (or rather, screamed), he reverted back to Milquetoast. We listened daily to Beatrice's stories of working with Milton Berle, Ed Sullivan and the old-timers in vaudeville. It was the twilight of her career, and I might have been sympathetic, but her two personalities—one for the public, the other off-stage—bothered me. Nevertheless, the recording dates went as scheduled, with Bobby Nicholson directing and writing most of the arrangements.

It was a difficult time for me. I had met Aileen Juvelier, fallen in love, and married. I was distracted because I had finally found something that was more important than my work.

I hated the Beatrice Kaye show, and I learned that if I didn't like what I was selling, it was twice as difficult. I did, however, get very lucky on a trip to Pittsburgh. I made a presentation to the Duquesne Brewery and they bought several markets, enough to break even on a show that I never felt belonged in our stable.

Early in 1951, Bobby Nicholson left us to form a company called Soundac, to produce commercial jingles and other programming. His partner, Jack Schleu, was a commercial artist who had dabbled in animation. The company was formed over cocktails at Frank & Teresa's, (known as the Anchor Bar), where Buffalo chicken wings, now famous, originated.

After several months, Bobby left Soundac and headed for New York, having been hired by Buffalo Bob Smith, a close personal friend, to take over the duties of Clarabelle. Buffalo Bob had begun his career in broadcasting in upstate New York, where he developed and programmed Howdy Doody. He took it on to New York and NBC where it became the first big success story in children's television programming. Bobby helped write *The Howdy Doody Show* and did all the music and arrangements. He continued working with Bob Smith for several years, finally forming a company with Roger Muir the executive producer of Howdy. For years they were successful producing shows and pilots for NBC.

6.
Television

When Bobby Nicholson left Soundac, Jack Schleu asked Bob Buchanan to join him. When Bob did, he discovered no one had ever paid the musicians recording for Soundac. Subsequently, Bob paid the musicians and ended up with Nicholson's stock. A few months later, the company moved down to Hallandale, Florida, where Soundac flourished for many years.

Early in 1952, the FCC removed the freeze on television after setting up channels 2 through 13 on VHF (very high frequency), and UHF (ultra high frequency) for channels 14 and up. We nicknamed UHF television, "ultra high foolishness". With the FCC having only twelve VHF channels to allocate nationally, many major and mid-size markets received UHF channels in addition to the twelve sought after VHF Channels. Many, many, radio broadcasters filed for construction permits, and many, many broadcasters went broke with their UHF grants. There was very little cable, and with the aerials needed for UHF among the many engineering problems, very few markets with both VHF and UHF were successful. In cities with all UHF channels, however, most stations did survive.

Our first television program was developed in 1952 by Jack Schleu and Bob Buchanan of Soundac, and was called *Dollar Derby*, the original TV auction. It helped make 7-11 stores famous in Texas, and was very successful with supermarkets. The format was a simple one: when you purchased anything from the store, you were awarded paper money, and each week on the program we auctioned off products to the highest bidder using that paper money.

I made a presentation to the Pepsi Cola Company in Buffalo, New York, and their account executive, with the client present, was dead set against it. But one learns in selling, that there are many ways of getting a contract. There is the soft sell, telling your story very quietly; the "up tempo" presentation, with a great deal of enthusiasm throwing out facts and figures, etc.; and there's the hard sell, used only as a last resort when you're sure you're heading for an emphatic "no". The hard sell is what we call the "insult pitch". It is used sparingly, and it makes or breaks your presentation.

I used the insult pitch with the account executive, in front of his client, called him every name in the book and telling him how stupid he was not to understand what the program could do. I told him that, because of his thick-headedness, I was going to present it to his competitors.

I got the sale, and it was very successful for Pepsi Cola, but the account executive called Dick Ullman to tell him I was not welcome again and had too high-pressure to ever be successful in selling in the Buffalo market. That insult sale came back to haunt me many years later when I managed a radio station in the Buffalo market and couldn't even get an audience with the account executive for Pepsi Cola.

With so few stations then on the air, one had to travel throughout the United States. In Omaha, Nebraska, a station was interested in purchasing *Dollar Derby*. It was my first visit, and I spent a weekend there in a hotel. In those years, Pennsylvania still had blue laws, but they were mild compared to what I encountered in Omaha. It was as if they rolled up the streets on Friday night. I didn't know anyone, and when Sunday arrived, there were no movies, *nothing*. Alcoholic beverages were out of the question, and I even wondered if you could buy a Pepsi Cola because it had fizz.

In the spring of 1952, I was at a NAB Convention in Chicago, staying at the Hilton Hotel on Michigan Avenue. Lew Avery, of Avery-Knodel, one of the top station representatives in New York, invited me to his suite at the Blackstone Hotel to have a drink with him. We got to talking about broadcasting and its future. I was still young and naive, and Lew made a remark that I have never forgotten. He said, "Marv, the broadcast industry as we know it now is a 300 million dollar business. Believe me when I tell you it will someday be a multibillion dollar industry." As I walked across the street back to the Hilton an hour later, I thought Lew didn't know what he was talking about. In the early '90's, radio alone grossed something like 11 billion dollars.

By 1953, I was becoming tired of traveling and Bob Mendelsohn, who was still with the company, suggested we buy a radio station. At the time, the price for radio broadcasting facilities was at its all-time low because of the overwhelming popularity of television. We found a wonderful opportunity and an incredible buy in Providence, Rhode Island. The *Providence Journal* owned WPJB, a 5,000-watt directional station at 1420 on the dial. General Tire, which owned several facilities as well as the Yankee Network, had station WEAN in Providence that the *Journal* wanted to buy. The newspaper planned to then sell WPJB. We had the opportunity to buy WPJB, all of its facilities, and take over the Yankee Network, at a total cost of $150,000.

Bob and I flew to Providence, where we were met by Bill Koster, general manager of the *Journal's* station. He took us out to a beautiful old mill, circa 1780, which had been converted into a charming restaurant called The Grist Mill. Over dinner, we discussed details of the potential purchase and I fell in love with New England.

In a meeting with Tom O'Neil, our contact at General Tire, we shook hands on the deal and were to get back to him on terms. We raised a portion of the $50,000 down payment from Jake Embry of WITH in Baltimore, Ben Strouse of WWDC in Washington, and even Fred Ziv, the top syndicator in broadcasting. Together with our own investments, we had the $50,000, and we and were waiting for final papers from General Tire to file with the FCC.

For weeks we got phone calls from General Tire's attorney, Jack Poor, telling us the papers would be forthcoming in the next day or two. After almost three months, we discovered that the *Journal* was paying General Tire an additional $50,000 and allowing WPJB to go dark so there would be one fewer competitor in the market. Since the *Journal's* station was directional, and one that our attorneys felt would never be granted by the Commission, we had wasted almost six months.

Bob Mendelsohn left the company shortly thereafter to become sales manager of one of the trade publications in New York. Two years later, he bought a radio station in Wilmington, North Carolina. His dream had come true but in retrospect, I don't think I would have been happy as a station owner, even in Providence.

While planning to head for New York and look for a job (something I wasn't too worried about), I stopped in to see Dick Ullman. As we were talking, the phone rang and, overhearing the conversation, I became intrigued with what was going on.

I asked Dick if he had any new product, and he mentioned they had made a deal with Soundac and Bob Buchanan to handle a new property called Ad-imation. He smiled at me and said that was one of the salesmen on the phone who had just made a sale of Ad-imation for $500. The salesman was his son, Dick, Jr., who had come to work for the company several months earlier.

Dick told me that he was making a sale a day, so I asked to see the product. Soundac had produced an animated intro package for television, somewhat similar to our Jingl-Library. The animated intros could be sold to local advertisers, they would fit any type of business. I asked Dick why he was selling it outright, and why for as little as $500. If the product was as good as I suspected, he should be leasing the materials and not selling anything on an outright basis.

I then made my most foolish remark ever, stating, "I can get five times that on a two-year, or more contract." I was still the second largest stockholder in the company, but Dick made me a sporting proposition: I would be paid a 25 percent commission if I went out on a two or three-week trip. He would pay my traveling expenses as well. I picked up the audition materials, made my airline reservations, and took off on the three week trip.

Having worked out the rate card, I was gone for almost the entire month. I came back with two year contracts, with a certain number of immediate releases and, thereafter, monthly releases for two years. Dick and I worked out an agreement wherein I was to become executive vice president to handle all marketing promotions and sales. We still had some radio products, as well as Dollar Derby and Ad-imation, and we made a substantial profit for the next two years.

The Animation Years

Soundac, headed by Bob Buchanan and Jack Schleu, in addition to building products for the Ullman Company, was heavily involved in animated ideas for movie promos, sports promos, film services for shopping centers, syndicated commercials for beer sponsors, TV news, map services and many other innovative ideas.

We referred to Bob Buchanan as "the inventor", while Jack Schleu was the creative genius with the art. They became the most creative and productive group in the industry, producing over 4,000 local and regional commercials, all the video for the Seattle World's Fair, and the advertising and marketing for Mountain Dew until that company was purchased by Pepsi Cola. There are currently books on the history and development of animation which give ample credit to Soundac and Jack Schleu for making creative use of limited animation through sophisticated design elements and pioneering production techniques which since have become standards in the animation industry.

While in Hallandale, Florida, I visited Jack and Bob at Soundac and saw some of the story boards Jack was working on, covering a new program which they had titled *Watch the Birdie*. When Bob gave me the format of the show, I immediately authorized a go-ahead on a pilot presentation, called Dick Ullman and told him I was picking up another product on a percentage basis for the company.

Watch the Birdie was a call-out television show. Contestants were asked to register by filling out blanks at the sponsor's store or dropping a postcard to the station, whichever they desired. Names of contestants were selected on camera, and then called on the show and asked a multiple choice question. If the contestant could not answer the question, a second and third contestant were called. If none of the three could answer the question, the answer was given on the air, a second question was asked, and additional contestants were called. The questions were clever, but fair, and the TV audience had little trouble answering them correctly. When a contestant answered an animated question correctly, he became qualified for a try at the "Watch the Birdie Jackpot". Twelve different film clips were supplied, each with the clock spinning around the dial twice and then stopping on a number. When the clock stopped in animation, the hour was repeated over and over again, and the birdie came flying out of a clock and the clock fell apart.

The object for the contestant was to select a number from one to twelve at which the clock would stop. If he guessed the correct number, he won the jackpot; if not, a token prize. The jackpot film clips were placed in a projector in advance so no one would know the number that would be picked.

Two or three animated questions normally would be used in each 15-minute program segment, depending on the operating format which was set up by the individual station. The number of times the jackpot would run would depend on the number of correct answers to the animated questions.

We had great success selling *Watch the Birdie*. It was placed in most major markets and smaller cities.

Several weeks after its introduction, I received a call from an Arthur Lund, a vice president of Campbell Mithun Advertising Agency in Minneapolis. I made an appointment to meet him in Chicago the following week. Art Lund was a tall, fairly heavy-set man with a wonderful sense of humor. We sat at a bar in one of the local hotels and set up a spot buy for one of the agency's clients, Malto-Meal.

In the mid-50's, if you had a sale, or even a partial sale, for a television station, you were very popular indeed. Art sent me a list of the markets they wanted and the number of minutes they would purchase. It quickly became apparent that I was going into markets that were not on his list. I called him and asked if he had any budget for me in Madison, Wisconsin, and sure enough, he found some more money for me.

While in Madison, I met Morton J. Wagner, manager of WMTV, the Bartell-owned television station. It isn't possible to like everyone in an industry but Mort especially turned me the wrong way. I had a strange premonition that our paths would cross again in the future.

The Malto-Meal journey took me all the way to the west coast, and I enjoyed every bit of it: Milwaukee, the first big city to clean up its waterfront and make it absolutely beautiful; Minneapolis, the city of lakes and, at the time, Charlie's Cafe Exceptional, Harry's Bar, and McCarthy's; Chicago, with Michigan Avenue still more beautiful in the summer than walking up 5th Avenue, Park Avenue or Rodeo Drive; St Louis, a city that to this day I still can't understand how it exists, although the arch along the river and the original KMOX bring back nostalgic memories; Denver, still one of the most beautiful cities, where one can take one's children to pan for gold, see a mining town, the Brown Palace Hotel with the bullet holes in the original bar, the nostalgia of "Mollie Brown"; Kansas City, a great town with wonderful mid-westerners; and Salt Lake City, where Roger Smith found a home, with the old Hotel Utah, run by the Mormon Church, where people quietly go up and down the lobby saying, "If you have to drink, please do it in the room." Salt Lake City has no bars except in the back rooms of many little restaurants and the soup bar of the hotel, where for lunch you could order two different kinds of soup or chili, the largest roll you have ever seen, all homemade. For this old-fashioned European fare, one stood in line to get a seat at the counter.

I arrived in Salt Lake City and quickly sold KSL-TV, owned by the Mormon Church. I had three phone calls awaiting me when I returned to the hotel. One was from KTLA in Los Angeles, another from KTTV, and a third from the CBS network office. I called KTLA first and made an appointment, then called KTTV. Prior to my calling CBS, my phone rang and, lo and behold, it was CBS asking what time my flight arrived so they could pick me up in a limousine! As it turned out, however, I did not get picked up by CBS because I had a verbal commitment from KTLA, which was the station Malto-Meal wanted.

Few people understand what television was like in the 50's. We did not have tape at the time, so you couldn't tape the programming and re-broadcast it to the west coast. That meant that prime time network went on the air at eight o'clock in New York, and five o'clock on the west coast. By eight o'clock on the west coast, all network programming was over, and the network's affiliates had to program locally. Because of this, the independent television stations, many of which had purchased top feature films or sports, had all the ratings. One could use kinescope, but it was a very poor quality copy of the program from the east coast. Those days before tape and satellite were golden for independent television stations in the major markets of the mountain and west coast time zones.

I completed my trip after also hitting Seattle, Portland, Sacramento and San Diego. Most of my trip was flown on United Airlines, and I was told by one of the men at the United counter that, with such an itinerary, I should join their Red Carpet Club, which required 100,000 miles of flying. I thought it was a great idea, so he gave me an application which I filled out and mailed to United. A couple of weeks later, I received a very pleasant letter from them thanking me for wanting to become a member of their 100,000-mile Red Carpet Club, but their records showed that I had not flown 100,000 miles. I answered by stating that they had recently taken over Capitol Airlines, which was headquartered in the east, and if they would check Capitol Airlines's records, they would find I had over 100,000 miles. Two weeks later, I received my credentials from United Airlines with a plaque showing I had over 500,000 miles! I would be happy for just a dollar for every mile I have flown since.

"Colonel Bleep"

In 1956, Bob Buchanan called Dick Ullman, asking if he would be interested in a new cartoon series. The original concept was for fifty-two animated cartoons running from seven to eight minutes in length. They would be the first color cartoons produced for television, using new techniques that Jack Schleu had developed with Soundac's Oxberry animation stand. At the time, Jack had an artist by the name of Hal Lockwood who had worked with Disney, and who, to this day will tell

63

anyone who will listen that Jack Schleu and Soundac were probably the most creative and productive group in the industry at the time. Several other artists, wide-action cameramen, animation stand operators, and editors were also involved. Bob sent a one-page, full-color story board to the office depicting a little, round-faced animated character who lived in outer space and saved the world from all types of space villains.

Col. Bleep lived on Zero-Zero island and was an officer in the Futura Interplanetary Space Command. His companions, Squeak and Scratch, made sounds similar to their names. Squeak was a happy-go-lucky boy of the present, looking somewhat like a hinged wooden puppet who could not talk. Scratch was a powerful caveman who should have been extinct but, like Rip Van Winkle, fell asleep thousands of years ago and didn't wake up until an atomic bomb went off.

All three characters could fly, as well as the chief villain of the series, Dr. Destructo, who looked like a menacing black mountain with evil eyes. Jack Schleu developed the basic plots for the series by reading an encyclopedia of ideas. Other shows were based on current events. For example, soon after the Russians sent the first animals into space, Col. Bleep was busy rescuing them when they became stranded in orbit. Because of budget restrictions, Jack simplified his characters in the "modern" look of the time.

A story board is like the comic page of your newspaper, with approximately eight pictures drawn by hand telling the story of an episode. The characters are portrayed, but very basically. No one would use a story board to sell a series. Instead, two or three cartoons would be made in their entirety. During that period, very few cartoon packages had yet been released by the majors, and those that were available had been sold on the average seven-year unlimited-run basis. One interesting story of the time was how the Popeyes, owned by King Features, a division of the Hearst Corporation, refused to work on a percentage, and demanded 3 million dollars for a seven-year license. In the years that followed, first Gold Key, a syndicator, and then Len Firestone, wrote over 100 million dollars from that 3 million dollar buy. No one really knew in the early years of television what a product was worth, or would become worth.

Getting a new program off the ground is not only challenging but, in some instances, downright lucky. Somehow, some of us either have a sixth sense or been fortunate enough to be in the right place at the right time. When I looked at the story board, I just had a hunch to call Miller Robertson, in Minneapolis. I made an appointment to see him and flew out to one of my favorite cities in the midwest. I've spent many days in Minneapolis, and knew the Leamington, Curtis, Nicolet and Radisson hotels. Some are still there, but the original Radisson has been torn down. I always looked forward to staying there. Violins playing at dinner, the lobby and the shops made it one of my favorite hotels.

And can anyone who has ever been there forget Charlie's Cafe? You might wait hours without a reservation but it was always worth it. The lazy susan placed on the table with every conceivable delicacy was always a treat. Then there was Harry's Bar, the "Minneapolis' Toots Shor's" for the advertising and broadcasting fraternity. Minneapolis's wide streets, that marvelous landmark, the Foshay Tower in downtown, and those wonderful midwesterners always made me feel so welcome.

I presented a simple story board of *Colonel Bleep* to Miller Robertson, and after nine hours of work sold 100 cartoons for $39,000 from a simple colored piece of paper. (Bob Buchanan and Jack Schleu never forgave me since they had originally planned on making only fifty-two episodes.)

It wasn't until several months later that we finally received three shows. We made up a presentation reel on 16 millimeter film so the animation did not lose that much quality. With half-hour programming or film, the 35 millimeter was the norm. In order to get good motion in cartoons, you needed twenty-six pictures per second. That was a great deal of art work, but Jack Schleu found many shortcuts to save time, and although the 100 episodes were not all finished by start date, enough cartoons were available to start shipping to the stations.

After the audition (or presentation) tape with the three shows was received, I headed for New York where I met Milford Fenster at WOR-TV. Mil did all the buying for the General Tire-RKO Group, including stations in New York, Boston, Los Angeles, Detroit and Memphis. At the time, they had a working agreement with KPIX, the Westinghouse station in San Francisco as well. WNAC in Boston was the CBS affiliate, as was KPIX, while WHBQ in Memphis was ABC. WOR-New York, KHJ-Los Angeles and CKLW-Windsor-Detroit were independents.

After viewing the presentation, Mil told me that he would set up a meeting with Norman Knight, the president and general manager of WNAC-TV in Boston. If I would hit the other stations, and they wanted it, he would make a group buy. He also offered to meet me in Boston the following Monday morning and let the other station managers know I was coming, but he made it very clear that I was on my own; he would only authorize New York City unless the other stations wanted the product.

I caught a flight from Buffalo to Boston at 7:00 a.m. on Monday morning, planning to meet Mil at WNAC's offices for a 10:00 meeting with Norm Knight. Mil was waiting for me, and we sat from 10:00 a.m. until 12:30 p.m., when Norm Knight's secretary finally came out and suggested we have lunch since Norman was running late. We came back from lunch and were ushered into Mr. Knight's office a little after 2:00 p.m. Norman is a man of medium height, and an incredible bundle of energy. He had taken the station in Boston, made it number one in the ratings, and was very well thought of in the industry. He had a 16 millimeter projector in his office, and I quickly described the product while threading the machine. I pushed the start button, and thirty seconds later Norm jumped up, turned the projector off, looked at me and Mil and said, "I'm not interested."

I don't lose my temper often, but this time I really blew up. I called him every name in the book, and chewed him out for making me wait over four hours for a firm appointment. Mil Fenster was trying to calm me down, but I wouldn't stop.The next thing I knew Norman was looking at me and saying, "Marv, you're right." He walked over to the projector, pushed the start button, and proceeded to watch another two to three minutes. Again he turned it off and looked at me and Mil. Then he said, "Fine! We'll buy it." Before we left, by way of apology, he gave me a gold Cross pen and pencil set, a beautiful pocket secretary and perfume for my wife. From that moment on, Norm Knight and I were fast friends, and I never had a problem in seeing him and being given an opportunity to make my presentations. Norm amassed seven radio stations in the New England area and left RKO a year or two later, but we never lost touch.

When we left the station, Mil looked at me and said that he didn't know how I had done it. Several weeks later, I learned that he talked with Dick Ullman and mentioned to him that I was one of the finest salesmen he had ever encountered. I flew back to New York with Mil, visited my sister on Long Island, and then caught the "Royal Coachman" of American Airlines to Los Angeles at 11:30 that night. The flight left from New York's Idlewild Airport, which basically was an aircraft hangar. We flew in a DC-6, a four-engined pressurized aircraft, that took somewhere between nine and ten hours nonstop to L.A. I arrived about 6:00 a.m., caught a cab to Hollywood and had coffee and

66

read the paper in the dining room of the Hollywood Roosevelt Hotel, waiting for my 10:00 a.m. appointment at KHJ.

I got an okay at KHJ, caught the noon flight to San Francisco, got my authorization there, had dinner, bought a shirt, tie, underwear and socks, changed in the men's room at the St. Francis Hotel, went back out to the airport and caught the "redeye" to Detroit.

CKLW-TV's studios were in Windsor, Ontario, across the river from Detroit. RKO owned twenty-nine percent, the maximum percentage allowed for an American company in Canada, and operated it from Detroit. I met the general manager in the Detroit offices and quickly made my sale.

I called Mil Fenster from CKLW's office and asked him if I still had to go to Memphis since I hadn't been to bed since Sunday night. He laughed and said, "Go home, Marv. You've got Memphis as well." I'll never forget that trip and my reception by the stations.

A few months later, Mil, a Harvard Law School graduate, left RKO and joined the law firm of Hall, Casey, Dickler & Howley. He worked full time until his late seventies, and became the expert in broadcasting law. One of his accounts was Capital Cities, now known as Cap City's-ABC.

Broadcasting stations, in many instances, are "follow the leaders." With the sale of the RKO Group, most other major markets were sold quickly, and by mid-1957, *Colonel Bleep* had become very successful. Some promotions followed, including on-air hosts in space costumes, live audiences, daily quizzes, giveaways, local store promotions, and *Colonel Bleep* space cadet cards. It was a very exciting time for all of us at RHU (Richard H. Ullman, Inc.).

7.
John Kluge

I first met John Kluge at his food brokerage in Baltimore, Maryland, where I learned that he owned WGAY, a daytimer in Silver Springs, Maryland. A few years later, on a flight from New York to Washington, John was sitting next to me. I re-introduced myself, and we proceeded to talk about broadcasting. He asked me where I was from, and when he heard that I was working and living in Buffalo, he said, "I have always wanted to own a radio station in Buffalo." I told him I thought I knew of one that could be purchased, and he immediately came back with, "Find me a radio station, and I'll give you a $75,000 finder's fee." That was 1957, the Thursday before Memorial Day. John gave me his home telephone number and told me to call him with any information pertaining to a station being available.

I flew home on Friday afternoon, and early Saturday morning contacted Thaddeus (Ted) Podbielniak, who owned WXRA, a 1,000-watt daytimer at 1080 on the dial. I had heard that Ted was interested in selling his station, and asked whether that was true. When I received an affirmative reply, I said, "I believe I have someone who would be interested in buying it. I'll get back to you." I called John in Washington and told him of the station's availability. I also mentioned to him that they wanted a quarter million dollars. John then said, "Set up a meeting for me at 10:00 on Monday morning, and I'll call you back with the time of my flight's arrival." I called Ted, who set up a 10:00 a.m. meeting with his attorneys. I confirmed this with John, who called me later to tell me he would be on a 9:00 a.m. flight.

I picked John Kluge up at the airport and took him to the station, where Ted and his attorneys were waiting. I have never been involved in another meeting like that in my entire life. John said to them that he wanted to buy the station, and he would pay them $225,000. He would show them how to save on taxes, making his offer more valuable than the quarter million dollars they were asking. He was a genius with figures. I sat with my mouth open listening to a brilliant negotiator. Ted's attorneys were stunned. At 11:30, John said "Let's make our deal. I'll get the paperwork to you. I would like to catch a 12:30 flight back to Washington." And the deal was made, right on the spot.

On the trip back to the airport, John thanked me profusely, and as he got out of the car he said, "Marv, you now own fifteen percent of radio station WXRA, and you will be my managing director." I looked at him aghast and said, "But John, I don't want to run a radio station." His parting remark was, "I bought it for you. I'll talk to you next week."

I walked around in a daze for a few days trying to figure out what I should do. I had two beautiful children, ages five and three, and it would be nice to spend more time with them and their mother. Also, it seemed such a great challenge. I sat down with Dick Ullman and Ed Kavinoky, our attorney, and told them I was going to try it. I had been on the road for more than ten years, and felt I needed a change. It was decided I would take a leave of absence from the company and take on WXRA. I flew to Washington to see John ten days later, and spent an evening with him at his home, a beautiful house across from the Shoreham Hotel in Washington. Some of his art work and treasured possessions were, to say the least, unusual. He had a sailfish in his office, no larger than six or seven inches in length, that had been caught in a net and was so beautiful he had it framed.

John told me he had called several people regarding my background, and from the short period he had known me felt that I was probably what he had been looking for and fit into the great plans he had for his company. He also mentioned that we would not get FCC authorization before the end of September or the first of October, which gave me the summer months to clear up my affairs at the Ullman Company, and also plan the type of format I would use and what staff requirements I would need. Having never managed a broadcasting facility, I was excited and couldn't wait to get started. It was during that period that I met Ernie Tannen, vice president and general manager of a daytime station, WEEP in Pittsburgh. Ernie had worked for John at WGAY in Silver Springs, and when John bought the Pittsburgh station, gave

69

him a percentage and had him run the operation. Ernie had done an outstanding job at WEEP, and he helped me immensely. He told me a very interesting story about John Kluge.

John was a street urchin in New York who was taken into a school teacher's home and brought up, going on to college at NYU, where he befriended the son of the president of China. Subsequently, John spent his summers in China as secretary to the president.

After World War II, John's first success was in the food brokerage business. He would go out to the wholesalers with an attache case in which he had two cups, a jar of Nescafe instant coffee, and a jar of George Washington coffee. He would ask for cold water to pour in the cups and would add a spoonful of Nescafe in one, and a spoonful of George Washington in the other. The Nescafe would float on the top of the cold water because it needed hot water to dissolve. The George Washington coffee instantly dissolved, since it was the first coffee made using the crystallization method developed during World War II for producing blood plasma.

His next venture was a potato chip company, which was not successful. He sold the company, but had several days before closing and getting paid. His creditors were at his throat, so he devised a simple way to handle them. He sent every one of them a check, knowing that he would be able to cover in a matter of days when the sale of the potato chip company went through. The checks went out unsigned. Several days later, he sent apologetic letters with signed checks that would now clear the bank.

John taught me something else that, unfortunately, I didn't follow in later years. He said, "Never go into a business that has an inventory." Think about it. A radio or television station license is granted by the federal government through the Federal Communications Commission. It is a license for a channel or frequency which is a monopoly for the market area covered. No one else can have that channel or frequency. One builds the station and then sells air, or time. If you looked at John's businesses—radio stations, television stations, cellular telephones—he knew what he was doing.

I also knew several of John's managers. One in particular, Harvey Glascock, had been working as a salesman at WMAL in Washington. I saw Harvey just before he took over WKDA in Nashville, which John had recently purchased (along with stations in Fort Worth, Texas, Tulsa, Oklahoma, Silver Springs, Maryland, and the one in Pittsburgh). Both Harvey and Ernie were very helpful in my early days at the station.

Station WINE

During the summer of 1957, I had the opportunity to think about what I wanted to do with WXRA. I contacted Helen Powers, who was back in Baltimore, having finished doing the programming and setting up the operations at WLEE in Richmond, and I asked her if she would be interested in coming to Buffalo to be my operations and station manager. Ralph Powers, her husband, had died several months earlier and she jumped at the chance. I then decided WXRA as a call letter sounded too experimental, so upon authorization of the station's sale by the FCC, we immediately requested a change and picked the letters WINE. I flew to Memphis to see Harold Krelstein and ask whether or not he would let me have his "Plough format," only to discover that Harvey Glascock had stolen it in Nashville and had the top-rated station in the market.

I decided to change disc jockeys, and kept only the program director and an afternoon man who had a two-hour block of talk with his wife, putting him into the sales department. The job was going to be fun, and I never had a moments doubt. The day finally came. A wire was received from the FCC authorizing our taking over, Helen Powers arrived, and our staff was complete. John Kluge flew to Buffalo and spent an evening with me. His parting words were, "Do what you have to do. I'm behind you 100 percent." I filed for a call letter change, and it was immediately granted. We were now WINE. I then called Andy Williams's agent in New York to see if we could get Andy to come to Buffalo for a big promotion day for our call letter change. Andy had a top ten tune on the charts, "Lips of Wine," and we thought that would be a great start for our change in format and sound.

Understand, I had no place really to go but up. I had a C. E. Hooper rating of .03 in a 1:00 to 3:00 p.m. afternoon show. I don't think I had a trace in the Pulse ratings. The total gross of the station when we took over was somewhere between $3000 and $3500 a month, of which ninty-five percent was religion, and the Yankee Network fed us baseball for $17.00 a game. Try making money with 2 to 3 hour games, plus double headers!

Our promotion day arrived, and we proceeded to the airport to pick up Andy Williams. Andy, at the time, was in his early thirties and had just left the Williams Brothers Group to go out on his own. He arrived in a torn pair of blue jeans and a dirty T-shirt, and the most scuffed-up loafers I have ever seen. How do you take him to potential advertisers looking like a bum? So we headed to Kleinhans, a large men's store, and bought him a suit, shirt, tie, shoes and socks. Andy gave us that delightful grin of his and said, "I always arrive like that—how do you think I've built up my wardrobe?"

At sign-on in the morning, we started playing Andy Williams's "Lips of Wine," and we played it 477 times—nothing else all day long. We broke only for a five minute newscast every hour, and we drove everybody crazy. One of my disc jockeys got so upset that he found a record of Lawrence Welk, set it up to where Welk talked, and when the vocal went into the instrumental, the following words were heard, "Vunderful, vunderful." Then back to "Lips of Wine". We took Andy all over the city and made the front page of the Buffalo *Evening News*. I suppose if we did that in the nineties, we would probably lose our license, but one thing for sure, everyone in the Buffalo area knew that WINE was a radio station.

The second major promotion was to take eight transistor radios and glue the dial to 1080. We took them to barbershops throughout the city and gave them as gifts. We also bought eight transistor radios, scotch-taped the dial to 1080, put them on full volume, wrapped them in small boxes and mailed them to ourselves, dropping them in mailboxes all over the city. They went through the post office playing, and returned to us the next day. We sure as hell were being talked about! And our new sales staff started to pay dividends with sales coming in to our rock and roll format.

One month after takeover, our first rating showed us in third place in Buffalo, New York—a daytimer against 50,000-watt and 5,000-watt stations. Our biggest competitor was a full time 250 watt station, WBNY, and when their program director, Dick Lawrence, heard what our call letters were, he started changing his promos to "Listen to WBNY, the champagne of music." We countered with, "What is champagne? Wine with a sparkle!"

I decided to take on a station rep, Peggy Stone in New York, since she handled the Plough broadcasting stations and several others. Peg was a redhead in her early sixties, and still a beautiful gal. Although Harvey Glascock in Nashville had given me most of the Plough format, Peggy gave me the complete format. (Harold Krelstein actually got the format from David Segal of station KOSI in Denver, Colorado, and it was very successful because of its simplicity. Harold was having a rough time at WMPS in Memphis, and Abe Plough was getting impatient after several years of trying to build an audience. Dave suggested the changes, and Harold added his own ideas.)

The format required that every half hour you start with a fast, up-tempo musical selection followed by a slow, then a medium-slow, then a medium-fast and then back to fast and so on. Give the time, give the temperature, and don't talk—just play music. Disc jockeys had to make out music sheets in advance showing their breakdown, not only in tempo, but with a top forty list. The top ten on the list had to be played much more often during the broadcast day, at least once every two hours.

Les Paul invented the electric guitar, which was the driving force in the development of rock and roll. He had the idea, then went to Freddy Fender to develop and build it. Fender guitars are still the music industry's best and most expensive guitars. That invention led to electrifying many other instruments, making many new sounds and effects available for musical arrangements. Adding African rhythms, soul, country, rockabilly and pop gave us the "raunchy" (a word a rock tune in the late 50's added to our vocabulary) sounds so familiar and popular today.

Two pioneers in rock music were Todd Storz of Omaha and Gordon McLendon of Dallas. Todd's father owned the Storz Brewing Company in Omaha, and Todd for months begged his father to buy him a radio station. KOWH, a 500-watt daytimer, was Todd's first station and, in no time, it had cornered more than fifty percent of the afternoon audience. Upon the purchase of WTIX radio in New Orleans (1958), Todd literally re-wrote the book on independent radio and became revered by broadcasters who followed him.

Gordon McLendon, with his father, Barton, started the Liberty Network, an independent network which originally broadcast baseball games. Gordon himself did the play-by-play and quickly built a large following. He and his dad then purchased radio station KLIF in Dallas. Gordon was an innovator who through the years purchased stations in Houston (KILT), San Antonio (KTSH), Shreveport, Louisiana (KEEL), Louisville, Kentucky (WAKY), and southern California (XTRA), which was the first all news station. Later, he bought San Francisco's KABL and Chicago's WYNR.

With the advent of television, radio stations had slipped in popularity. Television became the media of choice, causing network radio stations huge problems. For several years, they tried telling their advertisers that rock and roll was for "teeny boppers" only, but they had no answer to the Hooper and Pulse ratings which gave the rockers more

73

than fifty percent of the audience. In one year alone, WKBW radio, a 50,000-watt station in Buffalo, went from $200,000 in national sales to just $20,000. The prime-time nighttime audience was now going almost exclusively to television, and when that happened, radio, no longer the entertainment media it had been, very quickly became a companion. It was in the kitchen, the bedroom, sometimes in the bathroom, and, most importantly, in the automobile. What became known as "drive time" were the most valuable radio time periods, normally from 6:00 a.m. until 10:00 a.m., and from 4:00 p.m. until 6:00 p.m.

All kinds of crazy things were happening. Harvey Glascock of WKDA flew to Memphis and quietly sat in a hotel room for a week monitoring WMPS, the Plough station, trying to figure out the format, something he finally was able to do. He took it back to Nashville at WKDA, implemented what he discovered, and WKDA very quickly became number one in the Nashville market against such powerhouses as WSM. By 1957, although the "teeny bopper" tag was still bandied about, most major markets had found a niche for themselves with the rock and roll phenomenon.

At WINE, although our promotions were proving very successful, selling was like pulling teeth. Early on, I went in to see Lou Bunis, president of the Sample Shop, a large department store in Buffalo. He was cordial, but he told me there was no way he would buy airtime on WINE because we had no audience. If I could prove I had an audience, would he give me a schedule? I asked. When he nodded affirmatively, I picked up the phone, called my program director and told him to put a special spot on the air immediately, stating the first twelve people to call the station would receive a free pair of nylon silk hosiery from the Sample Shop. I had a portable radio with me, and we sat in Lou's office until the spot went on the air. Five minutes later, my program director called and said the twelve pairs of hosiery had been given out. Thirty minutes later, the telephone company called the station and said if we ever did that again, they would pull our telephones. More than six hundred people had called in a matter of two or three minutes. I went back to see Mr. Bunis the following day, and he gave me a small ad schedule.

In November, 1957, we concocted a new promotion which proved to be fabulous. We had spent a lot of money in our first month, and we were asked to curtail costs until we could pick up our sales. I went to the president of the Pigeon Fanciers Association in the Buffalo area and asked him if we might be able to get fifty homing pigeons. Unbeknown to me, the pigeon fanciers are always looking for ways to

74

use or race their birds and although we had to go to ten or twelve different fanciers to get fifty birds, it was quickly arranged. I then sent the salesman out to shoe stores to collect fifty shoe boxes. We punched air holes in them, and took red and white crepe paper and wrapped the covers and boxes separately.

We selected the top fifty advertisers and agencies in the greater Buffalo market. We took the boxes to the pigeon fanciers' homes, where they put the birds in the boxes, tied the boxes with a big red ribbon, and placed a letter on the outside of each box. Our salesmen delivered the boxes to each of the fifty agencies and advertisers. The letter attached to each box was written by the pigeon, and signed with a claw mark. It stated that we were inaugurating the first special delivery service from WINE radio station, and asked them to take a moment to fill out the attached form, put it in the container on the pigeon's leg, and release the bird. We added a P.S., stating, "Please release me within an hour since it is getting awfully cramped in here." The promotion proved to be not only sensational, but in many instances, frustrating, because we could not get the messages back until the evening hours when the pigeon fanciers returned home from work.

We received many calls from the advertisers, who got a tremendous kick out of the promotion. I even got a call from BBD&O Advertising Agency saying that if this was the way we were going to be promoting, they would like to place schedules for their advertisers.

One Chrysler dealer was so enamored by the bird, he kept it all day long. When he finally threw it out the window, the bird kept coming back. After three attempts, he called me, and I asked him whether he had placed a schedule. His response was, "Hell no!" I laughed and said that the bird had orders not to leave unless given an order. Actually, the birds would not fly after dusk. There were two or three instances where we had to pick up the birds ourselves.

The next morning, the Buffalo *Courier Express* had the headline, "NO, THOSE WEREN'T SPUTNIKS FLYING AROUND." The story proceeded to describe in detail what we had done. The total cost of the promotion was two bottles of New York State champagne for the Pigeon Fanciers Club. Two weeks later, we followed it up by sending each of the advertisers a completely cooked squab with the message, "We sent you the bird—thought you'd like it cooked."

We came up with a wonderful promotion for Coca Cola, something that I think could have been used nationally. We sold them a large schedule of "time signals" that ran three to four seconds on the half hour, or within the first nine minutes after. The commercial, simplicity itself, went, "Coca Cola time—two thirsty", "Coca Cola time—two thirsty-five", etc. By December, people in Buffalo, when asked the time, would answer, "Two thirsty-nine," and subliminally they would think "coke".

From my travels, I borrowed many ideas that other stations had used. We had billboards going in both directions from the airport with nothing but bright red ruby lips on a white background, and at the base, the words, "Your wife loves us. She spends more time with us than she does with you." We followed with another billboard several months later showing a wife and two children smiling with hands outstretched, saying, "So glad you're home. We took care of your family while you were away." Naturally, our call letters were prominently displayed.

I wanted to use a promotion contest giving a month's payment on a car, as a first prize but decided against it when I discovered that a winner in another market was on his final payment—a balloon clause contract that cost a couple grand.

The Russian Sputnik had just gone into orbit so we dressed one of our disc jockeys in a space costume and had him run into a cemetery from a busy morning traffic highway, while we announced that a space alien was reported in the area. We Canceled that promotion quickly when we discovered we could get into a lot of trouble, however, and we announced that it was just a prank by one of our jocks.

Our sales picked up beautifully through the first three weeks of December, but I hadn't counted on the fact that the month of December is a poor one because from Christmas until New Year's, no one advertises. It's a three-week month. So you try to sell seasons greetings from the advertisers that last week. I spent many hours with our young sales staff, who were paid $65 per week as a draw against commissions, trying to teach them some of the things I had learned.

Bernie Millenson, whom I knew when he was a salesman at WDEL in Wilmington, Delaware, sales manager at WMAS in the same market, and general manager for Plough at WCAO in Baltimore, used to come in an hour before anyone else at the station, have his coffee and go through the newspaper picking out ads and finding potential advertisers. He would also go through the telephone book and, as I recall, he had more than 300 accounts on the air.

I would tell the salesmen a story about Tom Tinsley, owner of WITH in Baltimore, who invited me to a sales meeting at 8:00 a.m. one morning. He had called in a Western Union messenger boy and, in front of the sales staff, wrote out a simple sentence. Folding the piece of paper without the salesmen seeing it, and giving it to the messenger, he asked him to go up and down North Charles Street, the main street in Baltimore, ask for the owner or general manager of each store, ask the question on the piece of paper, and mark down the response. He handed the youngster enough money for lunch and told him to be back at the station at 4:00 that afternoon.

When the messenger returned, Tom had the salesmen reconvene. He asked the messenger boy to read out what he had written on the piece of paper, to wit, "You don't want to buy any radio time today, do you?" Of all the responses from owners and general managers, three had said yes, they *did* want to buy radio time. Using the worst sentence any salesman could address a client with, three people were still interested. Tom turned to his sales staff and simply stated, "If you make enough calls every day, the law of averages will take care of you."

We would discuss dress code and demeanor. Look prosperous and neat, have a smile on your face, know a smattering of the advertiser's business, and be willing to listen to the potential sponsor's problems. When possible, don't tell them why you're there until they ask. I also suggested they always have a matchbook in their pocket so that if a potential client took out a cigarette, they had the match ready to light it—all the little things so necessary to selling.

I told the story about Maurice Mitchell which I called "Mitch's Pitch". Mitch was with the Radio Advertising Bureau, and after several years he left it to become head of Encyclopedia Britannica. He was a brilliant salesman, and used to tell the story of the radio salesman who was told by a client, "I'm not interested in radio. I tested it and it didn't work for me." The salesman's reply was, "Do you occasionally enjoy a cocktail?" When an affirmative response came back, he would say, "You know, I'll bet you $5.00 you can't tell the difference between bourbon and scotch." With that, the client said, "I'm not a heavy drinker but, believe me, I know the difference." So the salesman invited him to a bar across the street from his office and ordered a shot of scotch, a shot of bourbon and two glasses of ice water. He then added one drop of scotch to one glass of water, and one drop of bourbon to the other glass of water, and started mixing the glasses. The client looked at him and said, "How do you expect me to tell the difference between bourbon and scotch when you only put one drop in each glass of water?" The salesman responded with, "How can you tell me radio doesn't work for you when you've only tested it?"

It was fun working with the salesmen, and the results those first few months were very gratifying. When we took over the station, we canceled almost all the income, which was more than 80 percent religion. After ninty days, we were close to showing a profit.

The record industry hired promotion men who would bring their talent into a market and visit each radio station to hype the stars and their latest releases. They were similar to song pluggers, and when you realize that radio stations received at least 300 new records a week, you understand how it often helped getting play on a station. Frankie Avalon, all of eighteen years old, came in one day, a handsome and very shy young man. Liza Minnelli, who had to be about the same age, came in also, and I fell in love with her. She had a look of wonder and a most delightful naivete, with saddle shoes and white socks—someone you would love to have had as a daughter.

Another day they brought in Sammy Davis, Jr. At the time, he was still with his father and the Will Maston trio, and was so poor he had only recently come off the relief rolls. I have never seen a more unattractive man—until he opened his mouth and smiled. He couldn't have been more then 5'2", perhaps 100 pounds. He was almost emaciated. He took me aside and asked if I would clear the top of my desk so he might take a nap for ten minutes. He said he had not been to bed for two days. I cleared the desk, closed the door and stood guard for one hour while his manager screamed that they had other appointments. Sammy thanked me when he left and I forgot all about it. Three years later, in Los Angeles, I was at Jilly's and, suddenly, a little man, Sammy Davis, Jr., came running up to me, took my hand and brought me back to his table where he said, "This is the man who saved my life." Then he introduced me to his friends, Frank Sinatra and Peter Lawford. We had a drink together and I rejoined the people I was with. Sammy was not only one of the most charming people I have ever met, but also one of the most talented.

The first quarter of a new year in most businesses is always very slow. Retail establishments take inventory, and people don't shop much after the Christmas holiday. It could be a tough time, particularly in radio and television. When I was traveling, however, I always found that first quarter sales could be exceptionally good, since station people were looking for ways to sell their advertisers and a new approach with fresh programming would often help. Now I was on the other side of the fence, and suddenly realized how desperately stations had to find ways of bringing in income quickly.

In a medium-size market, you would find all kinds of clocks in the windows of advertisers' places of business. On the clock would be the client's name, as well as the call letters of a station, and I always wondered why there were so many of them in the downtown areas.

There were several companies involved in this business, and most of them were unsavory. They would go to a radio station, offer to bring in their own sales staff and sell a schedule, keeping a percentage of the sale for themselves. To any general manager, this was a godsend. As there was no cost involved, he was perfectly willing to give a portion of the sale to the clock company. It was also a great way to sell one's station and call letters. But in the majority of cases, the problems for the stations after the clock sales team left the market could prove horrendous.

These high-pressure sales crews would go out and sell morning drive time or evening news time, guaranteeing that position to, let's say, fifty different advertisers. They would then make up a personalized clock for the advertiser with his message on it and the station's call letters.

After collecting the full schedule in cash, they would keep their percentage and leave town quickly. The station, having discovered what they had done, was obliged to go to each of those advertisers and find a way to work out the problem. What a mess!

We decided in January to try a different approach. Without telling our advertisers who had spot schedules with us what we were doing, we would run an extra three to six commercials a day for them. We never told the advertiser, but most of them continued with us.

In late February, we contacted Lloyds of London to insure a contest. Whoever could name the top forty list as printed by *Billboard* magazine would win $10,000. It cost us $500 to insure the contest promotion, and no one was more shocked than I to discover it laid the biggest egg of any promotion I ever ran. Suddenly, the realization hit us that no one believed us—no one would give away $10,000 as a prize in 1958.

Most disc jockeys came from other stations, many with excellent track records. We paid them all the same, $65 a week, but they made hundreds more every week doing "record hops". High schools, in particular, would set up hops in their gymnasium on Friday and Saturday nights, and the disc jockeys would work them with their top forty records, and usually their own turntable and speakers. Students would pay fifty cents to one dollar for an evening of music and dancing, and they could meet their favorite disc jockeys. They were celebrities, and a top jock could make $300 to $400 in an evening's work.

Each week we would call the music stores and rack jobbers to get a listing of the records that were selling. We thought this was the most honest way of going about it, and it took us several weeks to discover we could not trust those people. They would give us records that were not most in demand, hoping to increase their sales on over-stock. Our top forty list could not touch that of our competitor, Dick Lawrence at WBNY. We soon found that we, had to gamble on the new releases as he was doing. Soon, our top forty list became much more competitive.

Helen Powers had come to us from Baltimore and did an admira-ble job in the first few months. We found an apartment for her and loaned her $1600 to buy furniture, which she was to repay from her salary. Unfortunately, Helen had become an alcoholic and I had to let her go a few months later. Also, I had hired a disc jockey who had come very highly rated. I soon found his credentials were false, but not before I had personally loaned him $500 to get settled. I never had the opportu-nity to fire him because he took off after two or three robberies in the area. What a surprise it was when we discovered he was on the FBI's wanted list, having built quite a reputation in other parts of the country.

A year later, I deducted $2100. as bad debts on my income tax, only to have the IRS disallow it, claiming that I had to get a judgment in both cases. I wrote to the IRS stating that Helen Powers was in a hospital for alcoholics and the disc jockey was wanted by the FBI. Will wonders never cease? The Internal Revenue Service accepted it with-out judgments.

For several months I had gotten phone calls from Minna Thorne, Dick Ullman's "girl Friday," who was the Ullman Company's accoun-tant as well as secretary, and basically did any job necessary around the office. She would call and complain bitterly, saying, "Mr. Ullman is making so many bad decisions," and "the company was deteriorating." I would call Dick and have lunch with him an average of once or twice a month, and he would always tell me how rosy things were. At the time, I was too busy to really care. I figured the contracts he had before I left should keep the company financially stable for a fairly long period of time. I really didn't give it a second thought during those early months at WINE.

That first quarter of 1958 was very tough. The country was in a recession and local advertisers were not doing much business. In the middle of March, John Kluge called and asked what my projection was for the month. I gave him a figure and he said, "Marv, if you do that, I will personally fly to Buffalo and take you and your wife out for the best dinner in town." We worked our butts off and did $5,000 more for the month of March than my projection! I never got that dinner. Instead, I got a letter from John saying I was the only man in his radio group who had let him down, that I was low man on the totem pole, and I should be ashamed of myself.

Today, John Kluge is one of the richest men in the United States. His business acumen is brilliant. Through the years, one could find him late at night in New York sitting at the counter of the Brass Rail on 53rd Street, between Madison and Park Avenue, going through the profit and loss statement of a company the way most of us would read the newspaper or a good novel. He loved figuring out the problems with his companies. He once said to me he had more money than he could ever spend, and it was now just a fun game with him.

John always had a strange way of handling his executives. I know of only one man that stayed with him through the years, Mark Evans, who handled his PR. All of the others had rude awakenings and were summarily discharged.

Ernie Tannen of WEEP in Pittsburgh, called by John in Pittsburgh was told that he had sold his station and was going to take his profits and invest them for him. Ernie asked that the money be given him so that he could invest it himself. The station was sold, Ernie was transferred to television station WTTG in Washington as a salesman, and six weeks later, he was out of a job.

Harvey Glascock went from WKDA in Nashville to John's station in Tulsa, then replaced me in Buffalo, went on to WIP in Philadelphia, and ended up at WNEW in New York. Shortly thereafter he was dismissed. I know of no one, other than Mark Evans, who was ever fortunate enough, or maybe bright enough, to continue serving John Kluge.

My own personal opinion? He taught me more in a little less than a year than anyone else before or since, and I know for a fact that he made anyone who stayed with him until let go, wealthy men.

The evening following my receipt of John's letters, after the staff had left, I sat down at my secretary's desk and typed a letter back to him. I mentioned what I had accomplished at WINE, and how difficult it was having an AM transmitter that, when it rained, because the wiring was shot, the chief engineer had to hold the "on" button on because otherwise we would short out and go off the air. I mentioned the strain of trying to keep a 1929 police FM transmitter operating, and of having to go across the street to a gas station to use the johns because our offices were on a sulfur well and, if we used our running water or toilets, the whole place smelled of rotten eggs. I always had a reputation for writing "poison pen" letters, and I really spewed it out.

Two days later, John called me and said, "How dare you write me a letter like that?" I answered, "I just told you how I felt about your letter, which I still feel was uncalled for." He said he wanted me in Washington the next day. I flew down, walked into his office, shook hands with him, and handed him my resignation. He didn't expect that. He said his plans included me in something that would be breaking in the next week to ten days. It would be very exciting. But I was determined to get out, because running a radio station no longer was a challenge for me. Spending two hours with a client for a measly $300 schedule, going to Kiwanis meetings and all those other affairs which local broadcasters have to be involved in, just wasn't my cup of tea. I missed the challenge of working with top management and sales people, and meeting some of the most exciting people in the world. And I guess I'd spent too many years traveling to stay in one place.

We parted amicably, and I stayed on until early summer. Two weeks after my trip to Washington, the newspapers and trade papers were full of John Kluge's buying Metropolitan Broadcasting, which included the Dumont television stations. It was the beginning for John Kluge and Metromedia Broadcasting. Two years later, I met Ernie Tannen, who had bought two radio stations with the money from the sale of WEEP. While having lunch, we reminisced about the Kluge days, and I said I felt I had failed as a broadcaster. Ernie said, "Marv, you had that station in a higher gross position and a higher rating than anyone before you or since, and Kluge's CPA will attest to that." Looking back, I realize I never got my $75,000 finder's fee, nor 15 percent of the station's stock, as promised by John Kluge—just four weeks extra salary.

8.
Starting Over

It was early June, and my last day at WINE. John brought Harvey Glascock in from Tulsa to take over the station. It was a Thursday afternoon, and I called Dick Ullman to say hello. I told him I was heading for New York on Monday morning and had several opportunities which I wanted to explore. When he invited me to have lunch with him on Friday at the exclusive Buffalo Club, I was pleased, and never had a thought that it would be anything more than just a pleasurable get-together.

When I arrived at the club, Dick greeted me with Ed Kavinoky, a large stockholder of the company and its attorney. In all my years in the broadcasting industry, working with many attorneys, Ed is probably the most honorable gentleman I have ever met. Only one other attorney is in his category—Mil Fenster who was with Hall, Casey, Dickler & Howley in New York. Over cocktails, Ed started speaking about my coming back to the Ullman Company, and I got one of the greatest sales pitches imaginable from both of them. It ended with Ed and Dick offering to give up a large chunk of stock if I would return.

Salesmen are strange animals in many ways. I have often felt that because of our ability to sell, we are the greatest suckers in the world. I recall coming home one evening and my wife saying, "You're going to kill me," and I asked her what the problem was. She said, "I couldn't get rid of him." "What are you talking about?" "He's coming back at 8:00 o'clock tonight." When I inquired who was coming back at 8:00 that evening, she told me the man who was selling the Americana Encyclopedia. I smiled and said to her, "Watch how quickly I get rid of him." Thirty minutes later, I was signing a contract for Americana Encyclopedia, a complete list of the great masters in book form, and the bookcase to hold them. I looked at her and said, "Please don't ever do this to me again."

Dick and Ed did a good sales job, giving me the title of executive vice president, carte blanche in running the company, and a sales force as I saw fit.

I always went into the office on Saturday mornings, normally from 8:00 or 9:00 until noon. It gave me a chance to read correspondence, or catch up on what had transpired if I had traveled the week before. The Saturday after our luncheon, I went into the office and was going through several papers in one office when Ed Kavinoky arrived and sat down with Dick. Suddenly, I heard Ed screaming at Dick, "You stupid son of a bitch! You're in involuntary bankruptcy and don't even know it. You owe more money than you have in contracts." That proved to be the "starting over" of the R. H. Ullman Company. I soon discovered that we had $240,000 in loans outstanding, and about $200,000 in contracts. Putting my house up as collateral to make payroll for several months proved scary.

The week before my return, Dick had received a phone call from Stu McKay, general manager of All Canada, a station rep firm. They not only represented radio stations and, later on, television stations, but also owned several stations in the Canadian provinces. Stu was a very unusual person. He had that British-Canadian charm, was of medium height, with gray sandy hair, and there was an aura of believability about him. He had called Dick suggesting that he come up to Toronto and look at a product they were selling in Canada that could prove successful in the United States.

Dick sent one of his salesmen, Ken Kaplan, in his place. Ken wrote everything down that he heard, and brought back some tapes of some of the materials. Unfortunately, Dick didn't understand the materials, but I was very excited about its potential and called Stu back. He, in turn, suggested I call Peter Frank in Beverly Hills, who was producing the materials, known as "Big Sound". Peter was supplying the "Big Sound" stations in Canada with musical intros and Hollywood stars doing promos, such as, "Hi, this is Frank Sinatra, stay tuned to the finest sound in Detroit-Windsor, CKLW," etc. Each month, Peter would supply additional stars and would tailor stations' call letters on promotional spots. I told Peter I felt, with several changes, the "Big Sound" could be very successful in the United States, and I told him I would get back to him in a day or two.

In order to understand the potential of "Big Sound" one had to go back years ago to what were known as the transcription libraries. These libraries were normally sold on three to five-year contracts, and gave individual stations in a market all types of programming. One could make up quarter-hour musical shows with the great orchestras of the time. One could build specialty sports programs, documentaries, holiday specials, etc. Some of the libraries included Capitol, which was a division of Capitol Records, Muzak, Langworth, the NBC Thesaurus, Standard, and the most successful of them all, World.

With the exception of the World Library, all the transcriptions were supplied on 16" vinyl discs with lateral cuts. They would have a fifteen minute program on each side, and would be categorized in an index so you could find the type of music, or the type of talk show, etc., you were looking for. Stations could set up programming from their library and sell local advertisers on a daily or weekly basis.

All transcriptions and records in the industry used what was known as a lateral cut. That meant that the wider the cut, the lower the sound; the narrower the cut, the higher the sound. It became a standard in recording, and has been used for many, many years. The World Library discs had vertical cuts. That meant that the deepness or shallowness of the cut gave you your sound. It is interesting to note that vertical cuts were developed and originated by Thomas Edison. With the change in music of the rock and roll era, libraries, although they lasted for several more years, no longer gave stations the timely materials they needed.

Peter Frank was the developer of the first modern library for broadcasters. Peter graduated from UCLA, and was a very handsome young man, with dark hair, approximately 6'1" tall. He had bought a small radio station near Pasco, Washington, with very poor ratings. He decided, with his contacts in the Hollywood area, to try supplying motion picture star intros for his station to see if it would help. It proved to be very successful.

Peter had early ownership in Lassie and, although the program was produced in Hollywood, the pilot was financed by All Canada, headquartered in Toronto, Ontario. At the time, Stu McKay was general manager of All Canada, and Peter mentioned to him what he was doing at his radio station. Stu suggested he send him a tape, which All Canada presented to their stations at the Canadian Association of Broadcasters

85

convention. The next thing Peter knew, Stu had sold seventeen of their stations and Stu had named the library "The Big Sound".

During this period, Peter had formed a corporation called Stars International, and the sales to the Canadian stations were made through that organization. He was an astute business man, still in his early thirties, and was a pleasure to work with. I had met Stu McKay when Dick Ullman had approached him and given him the sales rights for Jingl-Library almost ten years earlier. Stu, now president of All Canada, had become one of the driving forces behind their ownership of radio and television stations, and was also involved in cable here in the United States. After listening to what was on the tapes, I was very excited.

The months with John Kluge running a radio station were beginning to pay dividends. I told Peter that what he had was great, but it was not enough for the American market. I told him what I felt was needed for successful selling in the States, and he asked me to talk to his producer, Will Scott. When I called, we discussed changes at length, adding stingers, stabs, musical intros, a daily Hollywood reporter, news, sports, weather, openings, and several other musical materials not available in any other current library. Within a week, Will Scott sent me a presentation tape that was sensational. How he got the materials or put them together, I'll never know, but it was exciting.

At about the same time, Lou Avery of Avery-Knodel, station reps in New York, called Dick Ullman and asked whether he would be interested in a jingle package and, if so, would he contact Rod Kinder at KGEM in Boise, Idaho. Dick asked my opinion and I smiled and told him to make the call. We were both on the phone when Rod suggested he fly in the next day. Naturally, we were pleased. All of this happened in my first week back at R. H. Ullman. Taking the company back into radio programming in the late fifties sounded very exciting.

Rod Kinder was of average height, on the chubby side, with a round and jolly face. He was a bundle of energy and one hell of a talent. He had been feature vocalist with the Johnny Long orchestra and, during World War II, with Glenn Miller's service band. He was married to a gal named Margaret, nicknamed Maji, who had studied classical music in Los Angeles and at the Eastman School of Music.

Maji will honestly admit she can't sing pop music, but "damn—I'm good at singing jingles". We listened to Rod's "W" package of fifty jingles, all instrumentally different with male vocals, female vocals, duets, trios, quartets, etc., and the music was brilliantly done. The owner of the station, Cecil Heftel, had financed the musical beds

86

for which Rod had written the music, done all the arrangements and recorded with full orchestra. I didn't find out until several months later that Rod and Maji sang all of the parts, recording and re-recording each jingle with musical tracks playing through their headphones.

I asked Rod what was the minimum payment he would accept for the whole package tailored to each station's call letters. He said, $300 a package. We made a deal on a 50:50 percentage break. We would pay all sales costs, promotion and advertising—he would do all the tailoring. We signed a simple agreement, sent it to our attorney, with a copy to Cecil, and final papers were drawn up. Within ten days, I had a new "Big Sound" presentation tape, and a fifty jingle tape from Rod, whose company, IMN Productions, had been named after radio station KIMN in Denver, which Cecil Heftel partly owned.

To this day I don't know why I headed first for Philadelphia, a 380-mile drive. I just had a hunch it was a good market to test the two new products. My first call was to Lionel Baxter, the new general manager of WIBG, a 50,000-watt station which had recently been purchased by George Storer, a multiple owner headquartered in Bal Harbor, Florida. Lionel was the perfect vice president-general manager—tall, almost white hair, and an aura about him. Not long after I met him, he ended up in Florida as a vice president of Storer.

I made my presentation of the "Big Sound" first and, still feeling my way, offered monthly releases covering music, hollywood reporter, name stars doing personalized promos, etc., and asked for a two-year contract and $200 a week. I got an immediate "yes". I then played the "W" jingle package, and the excitement in Lionel's and his program director's eyes was a thrill to see. I called Rod Kinder to tell him I had made the first sale of the "W" jingle package. When he asked what I sold it for, I told him $10,000, and he dropped the telephone. I drove back to Buffalo, and the next day, Cecil Heftel called, not believing the price Rod had told him.

My next step was not a pleasant one. I fired the entire sales staff of R. H. Ullman. I had told Dick that I wanted to build a new sales staff from scratch, one that I could train myself and, preferably, one that had no broadcast experience. Among Dick's salesmen, I had found one man who was supposed to be in Birmingham, Alabama, in bed at home. I then discovered he was buying airline tickets all over the country and cashing them in, never leaving Buffalo. The other Salesmen just weren't delivering. Bear in mind, we still had *Colonel Bleep* and several other properties.

The first salesman I hired was Herb Berman. Herb was 5'8" and as wide as he was long, weighing about 260 pounds. He was a graduate of George Washington University, and had played fullback for the Washington Redskins in the days when they paid $75 a game. He had been with Columbia Pictures as a regional rep, and had opened up a car leasing company that he sold at a good profit to Greyhound. He then opened up a tire and servicing store, and went broke within a year. Herb was one of the few great salesmen I have known. People loved him.

Herb had a wonderful sense of humor, but he could embarrass the hell out of you. In taking me to the airport one afternoon, he escorted me to the gate, kissed me full on the mouth, and ran off shouting, "See you soon, sweetie!" Try getting on a plane after a scene like that! He also had his faults. He was a compulsive gambler and we saved his house, his car and his family several times. He also was lazy. If he made two sales by Tuesday, he went home and took the rest of the week off. Still, he was a phenom.

I took him out to train him, and we hit Rochester, Syracuse and Albany, making sales of both "Big Sound" and the "W" jingle package in each market. On my first night with him after our first sale, we decided to celebrate. When Herb ordered "Chateaubriand for two, for one", a rollicking merry-go-round of seventeen years began.

I met him a couple weeks later in Springfield, Massachusetts, and watched him make a presentation to three men, all with flowing black beards. Being short and heavy, when Herb made a presentation, he perspired profusely. The three bearded men, all sitting next to each other on a couch, hadn't asked a question or changed expression, and just sat there. In the middle of the pitch, Herb stopped, pointed a finger at one of them and said, "Which one of you Smith Brothers is going to sign my contract?" They broke up in laughter and signed on the spot, even though he had only gone through half his pitch.

After he had been with us for about a month, Herb asked if I would hire his brother-in-law, Harry Sanger, who lived in Miami Beach. Harry, in his mid-fifties, had been a song and dance man on the vaudeville circuit in his early years. He was of medium height, with a round, red-cheeked face and thinning hair. He had charm and an infectious personality. He would be wonderful in the south because of his easygoing nature, and for years had been a salesman for a tobacco company. He was never very good in the major markets until the barter years, and we had to spend several weeks with him hitting the major cities.

Throughout the years he was with us, however, he did a very fine job in the small, medium cities in the south.

Barry Winton proved to be one of the most unusual people ever to work for us. Barry, for years, had his own society orchestra and played in the Rainbow Room at Radio City Music Hall. He was an accomplished violinist, comparable in popularity at the time to Lester Lennon and later, Peter Duchin, but Barry tired of the night life.

He was a very handsome man, about 5'9', with black hair graying at the temples. Women loved him, including Hildegarde, the chanteuse, who was never quite able to catch him, although she tried for years. When Barry covered the Maryland-Virginia-West Virginia-Carolinas territories, wherever he went, girls jumped up, hugged and kissed him. We used to say Barry Winton was the only man who sold "from confusion". Strangely enough, he never really knew the product he had, but he sold it, and I have never met anyone, man or woman, who wasn't very fond of him. During the time he was with me, he and a friend bought a radio station in Charleston, South Carolina, but Barry did not manage it himself until several years later.

A few months after he went to work for us, he asked me, as a personal favor, if I would find a spot or territory for his son, Fred. I suggested he bring Fred into the office, and I would be only too happy to discuss an opportunity with him, thinking at the time it wasn't a bad idea. The following week, Fred arrived with his wife, Vy, and the three of us went out for lunch.

Freddie was a six footer, handsome like his dad, but about seventy-five pounds overweight. His wife, Vy, although very attractive, had the same weight problem. Fred owned a seat cover company, but he was not doing well, and his father was looking for a better opportunity for him. When we sat down at the restaurant, Vy took over, and for over an hour I was cross-examined, the likes of which I had never endured before.

I got through the lunch but I knew there was no chance of Freddy ever working for us with a dominant wife like that making a damn fool of him. She was a very strong-willed woman, very clever, and had been in the jewelry business for years. But there was no way I was going to get involved with her and her husband. Poor Barry was very upset, and several weeks later offered half his salary if I would let Freddy work with him. We finally agreed to a tryout at a lower salary, and several weeks later did find a territory for Freddy with the full understanding that his wife was not to be involved. I took Freddie out for a week and never got over a 260-pounder driving a Volkswagen Beetle at 75 miles an hour. I found him to be a different guy without Vy around, someone who really loved the job.

Charlie Grood was my next trainee. He was of average height, dark-complexioned, and one of the few "voyeurs" I have ever known. He loved the ladies, but I can honestly say, except for the conventions where he always found hookers, he played it straight with me. He had had dozens of jobs, and had a great deal of sales experience but, for one reason or another, was never able to make it until he joined us.

Then there was Gene Daniels, 6′3″, very good-looking, charming, who had been a salesman working mainly in women's specialty stores. Gene always did well in major markets, but never had the ability, or the personality, to get down to the level of small-town people in the medium markets. He had quite a chip on his shoulder, and one year, when I worked with him, he was number one in sales. He tried to belittle the other salesmen, and the following year I left him alone and he went from top to bottom.

We had a sales meeting one day and Gene was discussing how he was going to buy some record playing equipment, but couldn't make up his mind whether he should buy "stereo or mono-rail". I told him he should get out of the railroad business. From that moment on, he came off his high perch and I did start to like him.

My last choice was Bernie Edelman. He was a Damon Runyan character—a six-footer, 50 pounds overweight, hair always askew, tie cockeyed, shirt always hanging out under his jacket, sweating profusely at all times, a chain smoker. With it all, everybody loved him.

Driving on the road with him while training, Bernie kept making strange statements, like "There's a marble orchard" and "There's a gopher". I soon figured out that "marble orchard" was a cemetery, but I finally had to ask him what a "gopher" was. Bernie explained how, years earlier, he had been a door-to-door salesman. When he saw aluminum awnings on a house, that meant "they'd 'gopher' anything". I got quite an education training him.

After working with him for several days, I decided we would place him on the west coast. He left his wife and two sons in Buffalo and drove out by car. Three days later, I received a phone call from him. He was just leaving Phoenix, Arizona, having made his first sale of the "W" jingle package, and was so excited he could hardly talk.

The next day, the manager of the station in Phoenix called asking for Chuck Goldstein's telephone number. He wanted to make sure that

90

Chuck and his wife, Paula Kelly, would be singing his call letters in a special way. I had to tell him that the Modernaires were not our vocal group. Fortunately, I managed to save the sale. Nevertheless, everyone that Bernie called on was crazy about him. He proved to be a real natural.

Picture, if you will, this nucleus of a sales staff in the broadcasting industry, with no experience, no know-how nor background. They had no friends in management, sales or programming at any station. They didn't know the difference between a spot announcement and a tag, but *God,* were they salesmen! It was a rough year for me because I was working with somebody every week. It also was one of the most enjoyable of times, getting Richard H. Ullman, Inc. out of near bankruptcy and into a profitable position.

9.
Barter

Broadcasters used the barter system all the time. They would give the local newspapers radio and/or television time so that they would print their schedules and advertise special programming highlights. They would go to the car dealers and trade for automobiles for their sales staff and executives, giving the dealers time on the air in lieu of cash. Restaurants traded food for advertising, while stations traded time for billboards. I have seen a small radio station owner in a northern Florida market trade the food on his table, his clothes, rent and entertainment.

The first big broadcasting pioneer in barter was Matty Fox, a brilliant and I might add, honest, businessman from New York City. He was unattractive, short, bald and very overweight, but his prowess in making the impossible and unusual deal became legend. He had a penthouse apartment at 445 Park Avenue, and he used his bedroom as his office. Sometimes one might find him parked in a limousine in front of one of the famous 6th Avenue delicatessens, while his chauffeur ran in and ordered corned beef sandwiches. He married a former Miss Universe and surprisingly, a few years later, was found dead in bed with a hooker at the Drake Hotel.

Making a deal with Howard Hughes in the mid-fifties was considered nigh unto impossible, but Matty managed to negotiate the purchase of Hughes', RKO library consisting of 746 features. At the time, with the freeze on television having been lifted, stations were going on the air throughout the country in large numbers, and the movie companies were not yet heavily involved in selling their features to the new media.

There was a shortage of programming, and television needed product, especially movies. Matty sold the 746 features as a library to Playtex, one of the largest undergarment manufacturers in the United States, for the unbelievable figure, at that time, of 21 million dollars. His idea, incorporated into his pitch to Playtex, was for them to offer the library on a five to seven-year contract to individual television stations taking commercial time in lieu of cash. It was the first major barter deal ever negotiated with broadcasters.

Each station received its 746 RKO features, and for the next several years gave up so many spots in daytime, both morning and afternoon, and in prime time, which in those days was from 7:00 p.m. until 11:00 p.m. As opposed to "ROS" or "run of schedule", which means that stations can put an advertiser's spots in at any time during their schedule of broadcasting, with fixed positions for thirty-five spots a week (and not thirty seconds as we know it today, but full sixty second spots), the stations guaranteed Playtex the time positions in which their commercials would run.

One could understand why stations jumped at the opportunity to have over 700 first-run features, but no one at the time realized how truly powerful television would become. Here was an instant response media, one that became so powerful overnight that sales staffs in many markets never had to leave their offices. Clients were placed on waiting lists for commercial buys, and the best time periods were sold out. It wasn't long before those television stations which purchased the RKO features would have given anything to have those thirty-five minutes available again on a weekly basis. The value of the commercial time Playtex was able to generate from the deal was worth in the neighborhood of 250 million dollars.

Shortly after the Matty Fox-Playtex deal was completed, barter companies sprang up, many in New York City, like Atwood Richards, Regal Advertising and Jeffery-Martin, to name but a few. Atwood Richards, currently owned by Morton Binn, is still a very successful agency, although barter in the nineties has no resemblance to its original form.

Jeffery-Martin was formed by the father of one of the principals, and his son David Edell. The operation was run by Marty Himmel, and the name of the company was derived from the first names of Marty's sons. Marty eventually bought out Dave Edell and his father. In addition to buying time for programming, they traded merchandise. Marty would buy a product in fairly large quantities at 25 cents on the dollar, trading it to broadcasters on a dollar for dollar commissionable basis. He then found himself in the pharmaceutical business producing one of the early sleep products, Compoz, and later a tooth-whitening solution called Porcelana. When one tried to do business with Marty, it was difficult to know whether or not you had a deal because, being a very tough negotiator, he often would sleep on the offer overnight, coming back the next day with a lower figure.

Once, I told Marty I was taking a cruise from New York. That afternoon, a package arrived for me from his office. It was a note wishing me "bon voyage," with an 8-millimeter color camera. After using 500 feet of film, I returned from the cruise and found on my desk a bill from Marty for the camera. I returned the camera to him with the 500 feet of film, all black. The camera had been defective.

Marty Himmel, after having made millions, would drive to the Food Fair Supermarket in Short Hills, New Jersey, behind the wheel of a new Rolls Royce, wearing a black derby hat, and send his wife into the store to buy a loaf of bread while he stayed behind, with the engine running, waiting for her.

Regal Advertising was founded by Garson Reiner, president of Exquisite Form Brassiere Company. I guess Garson, knowing the story of Playtex and the RKO library, had to get his company involved. Garson was a piece of work. He had been in the numbers racket and somehow escaped from the mob without a "concrete jacket". He was a short, thin wiry man, and one hell of an operator. Charles Wiegert, Sid Barbet, Sid Honig, and Stanley Grayson were principals in running the company. Sid Honig had a law degree, and was one of the few truly honorable men I met in many years working with barter agencies. He personally came to my rescue many times when I needed him.

Stanley Grayson was one of the strangest men I ever knew. He had gone to prison years earlier for a securities fraud and owed a fortune. He was brilliant in his dealings, but crooked as hell. He had to pay the government back for the rest of his life, but he never made more than $300 a week, so Uncle Sam never got more than a small portion. The big money was always paid to his daughter.

Barter companies were somewhat unsavory in their early years in the broadcasting industry, but they cleaned up their act over the years and proved saviors to many independent program producers trying to get a foothold in television.

I had originally met Sid Barbet in Baltimore where he was working with WBAL, the Hearst station. Having discovered he was now with Regal Advertising in New York, I went up to see him, walking into an office in such disarray that I couldn't help but wonder how this company could be successful. People were yelling into telephones, paper all over their desks and on the floor. Others were having arguments. There was so much noise and confusion that I wanted to walk out and forget the whole thing.

Sid came out of a small office in the back of the hall and took me in to meet Charlie Wiegert. They shared a small office, about 10x12, with two desks and a couple of metal chairs. I took an immediate liking to Charlie, who had such a quiet authoritative way about him. Sid, although charming and a delightful friend, was very flighty and could never make a decision. Charlie had a coolness about him. They were opposites, but for years these two totally different personalities were inseparable in business. While talking with Charlie, I suddenly had a great idea. Here was a company running off in every direction in a horribly disoriented office, doing many thousands of dollars of business in television barter. If it worked so successfully in television, why not try it with radio?

I made the suggestion to Charlie, and a strange expression came into his eyes. I had the feeling that maybe there was a chance. We discussed it further, and Charlie said he would broach the subject to Garson Reiner and get back to me. The following week he did just that, and I flew back to New York to meet with Charlie Weigert and Garson Reiner to work out an agreement between our two companies. We initiated a sliding scale for the sale of radio programs or jingles on the following basis: the top fifty markets in the United States would pay us on a 3:1 commissionable ratio; the next fifty markets would pay us 25 percent commissionable; and anything below the top 100 markets would pay us 20 percent commissionable.

The agency always added 17.65 percent as a commission, giving them 15% of the gross, when placing a schedule. For example, take a top fifty market like Cleveland, Ohio. I sell them a $10,000 program, and barter it at 3 to 1 commissionable. My contract will say $30,000 at 3 to 1, and then I will multiply that 30,000 by 17.65, getting a total 3 to 1 commissionable figure of $35,295. Adding 17.65 comes out to a full 15% when it is deducted from the total figure.

Why would broadcasters in radio or television jump at the opportunity rather than pay cash? For years, many stations would not barter, but the large majority were finally obliged to. There is a lot of airtime on a radio or television station from sign on in the morning until sign off. Using the above illustration, I have just saved a company $10,000 cash. In lieu of cash, the station is going to give $35,295 in time including commission. No station has ever been sold out. One can always find additional airtime to place a commercial, and the contract would be written in such a way that if a cash advertiser wants to buy the time that was going to be used for the barter agency's client, the station has the right to preempt without advance notice. So the only spots the barter advertiser is going to get are those that have not been sold. The station, when signing the contract, will always state that the commercial time will not be unreasonably withheld, and, with few exceptions, broadcasters made good on their barter spot commitments.

I look at it in another way. Let's say, I have a motion picture theater that seats 1,000 people, and I charge a dollar admission to see a movie. I never average more than 900 seats sold. Doesn't it make sense to sell the other 100, even if I only get 33-1/3 cents for each seat?

I went back to Buffalo with the terms of the agreement that our attorney would write up for our signatures. The contract, when signed a few weeks later, became the biggest success in the Ullman Company's history. In the next twelve months, we wrote six million dollars in radio barter. For many years, barter agencies built up an inventory of stations all over the United States. They would go into the field and find advertisers, as well as advertising agencies, willing to work with them, and became the time buyers for hundreds of products. If you were using broadcasting, and could save fifteen percent, you would have to investigate it. It was very easy to save a client fifteen percent, and make fifteen to fifty percent on that 3:1, 4:1 or 5:1 barter deal.

Time buyers of barter companies became familiar and very friendly with sales managers and general managers at the station level. They could throw extra business to stations who helped them place schedules at less than 100 cents on the dollar. The first quarter of the year, January through March, always proved a bonanza for the barter agencies, since in many, many instances, with this quarter being a slow one, the stations loved large schedules, even if it was at fifty percent of their rate.

Strange things happened, particularly in the large markets. The barter agencies would not have enough inventory of time, and would attempt to make their own deals with the stations. When this was unsuccessful, quite often they bought time on a cash basis. Sometimes, agencies would place additional cash schedules through the barter company when the client still had money available in certain markets. A major problem ensued for anyone selling his program or product to the stations on a barter basis. The better agencies had more than enough inventory in several of the markets, and although you had a sale of your product, the barter agency could not buy the additional time. This forced us to work with several additional barter companies, leading in some instances to "shopping around". By far the largest agency in the late fifties was Atwood Richards. With them, and with Jeffery-Martin and several other companies, we always found ways of selling the additional time when Regal could not handle it.

Other forms of barter quickly came on the scene. Hotels in Las Vegas became available to us, and we had the opportunity to buy directly from stations. If a Vegas hotel, through their advertising agency, bought $100,000 in radio time in Los Angeles, New York, Boston, etc., the agency would get the 15% commission for placing the time, and the station would get the hotel credit. The time would be in run of schedules chosen. We, in turn, would go to the stations and buy large portions of the hotel credit for thirty percent of its value, giving the broadcasters a cash profit on their time. The stations, after reserving whatever their needs were in hotel accommodations, were happy to oblige.

Las Vegas hotels were very tempting because their deals included hotel, meals and drink. I recall a general sales meeting we had in Vegas when we ordered magnums of French champagne for breakfast since there was no other way we could use up our credit. The Sheraton Hotel chain had hundreds of thousands of dollars in barter time, and we would buy it from stations for our sales staff, normally at thirty cents on the dollar. That meant one could stay at the Sheraton East Hotel in New York in a $26-a-night suite for just $7.80. Quite often we were able to buy at 15 percent and pay even less. The Sheraton Hotel script was only good if the hotel was not sold out, but seldom were we refused if we palmed a $5.00 bill into the room clerk's hand.

We traded cars on a dollar for dollar basis for jingle packages, and sold them to our own people for only the actual cost of talent in producing the package. In two and a half years, I bartered two fully-equipped Thunderbirds for $600 cash each, and a Pontiac for my brother-in-law at fifty cents on the dollar.

With one station in Syracuse, New York, our company traded out our product for merchandise for years on a 2:1 (no commission) basis for our people. There were fur coats, kitchen appliances, tractor lawnmowers, color TV sets, first class airline tickets overseas, to name just a few. The station would supply their time, and ship the merchandise to us. This went on for many years.

Crazy things were done with barter. I recall a station manager bartering out a round-trip, first class airline ticket, a suite in a top hotel, a doctor, and a private room in a hospital in Puerto Rico—all for an abortion. A well known general manager of a station in New Jersey came into our suite at a National Association of Broadcasters Convention in Chicago one evening and loudly proclaimed that he had a $100 call girl and traded her out. When all the salesmen got on him for being such a cheapskate, he was somewhat taken aback and said, "I gave her a damn good deal—I gave her 3 to 1" ($300 in Sheraton script).

I saw barter deals made with the networks where American Express credit cards were sent to the radio and television station managers of CBS, as an example. Whatever the radio or television station spent, the billing went to the barter agency and was paid by CBS with time on a 3:1 commissionable basis. Simply stated, the agency was placing spots for one-third the rate card, fully-commissionable, and selling them at anywhere from 65 to 85% of the standard rate card to their advertisers.

Through the years, barter changed drastically with several major advertising agencies getting involved, particularly in major markets, for their clients. When that happened, we were able to sell our products in the large markets on a 2:1 commissionable basis, and the agencies would place schedules in an entirely different way. If they wanted to buy a $5,000 spot campaign at a station, they would offer half the schedule on barter at 2:1 commissionable, and half the schedule at full rate commissionable.

Let's figure that out using a dollar a spot, for simplicity. A 2 to 1 spot commissionable came to fifty cents plus 17.65% added in agency commission. A 1 to 1 spot was a dollar commissionable, so when adding 17.65% to both deals it averaged out to about sixty-three cents on the dollar. Simply put, a 2 to 1 dollar is fifty cents; a 1 to 1 dollar is a dollar; add them together, and you have a dollar fifty for two spots, or seventy-five cents each before taking commission out, and you had extra dollars because you added 17.65% commission on the contract.

As the years passed, barter became more and more sophisticated. No longer could you trade a car on a dollar for dollar basis as the stations used to for their sales staff, but, rather, they would trade a portion of the car almost like a lease, whereby the car dealer would take the cars back every six months and sell them as demonstrators.

Years later, a man by the name of Lee Wolfman, who had his own barter company and inventory time as other agencies did, went into bankruptcy. Lee was a very bright, handsome young man. He loved the ladies, and always found time to live with one (or more) for years. He had divorced his first wife and was a playboy's playboy until one gal, thirty years younger than he, finally cornered him. His women were always unusually beautiful.

After his company's demise, we had to write off thousands of dollars in time. A few years later I was fortunate in being able to reinstate the time for my own company.

Because of his bankruptcy record, Lee had to form a new company using others as officers and giving the appearance that he worked for them. He formed Broadcast Marketing with offices on Fifth Avenue, and for years used his home on the river across from Gracey Mansion (the New York Mayor's residence).

Lee's concept was brilliant. He would go to a company, like General Foods' main office in New York near the Tappan Zee Bridge, and ask whether they had overproduced any of their products. If the answer was they had a warehouse full of frozen Birdseye corn, or green beans, or other products, he would find out from them what their actual cost was. Let's say they had three million dollars, at cost, in a warehouse, which would be there until the following year and on their books become a debit. His pitch was that he would take their three million dollars in overproduction, save them warehousing costs, and give them a three million dollar savings in advertising. The debit would come off their books, and they would have an asset of three million dollars in savings on radio, television, newspaper and magazine. He would take that three million dollars, in cost, of the manufacturer's product, and sell it for two million dollars, or whatever the market would bear, putting the money into his own account. Then working with the agency or agencies of General Foods, he had his own time buyers place the schedules. In broadcasting or print. They were able to buy the advertising at from fifty to sixty cents on the dollar, or less. If they placed a schedule for 60% of the rate card, they would credit General Foods with a 15% savings and credit themselves with the rest, making money on both ends of the deal. And remember, commission on all buys would still go to General Foods' agencies, making everyone happy. Whatever was received from the sale of General Foods' over-production was theirs, and they could take years to write off the three million dollars in savings. He would never consummate the deal until he had the product sold in advance, thus insuring himself.

The fascinating part of this type of operation is that the clients came back for more each year because it made sense, and their financial statements looked better. I've seen Parker fountain pens, cameras, radios, watches, food products, even automobiles involved. It's become so big, it's now world-wide. I don't know what went wrong with Lee's operation, but in the mid-nineties he again filed for bankruptcy after garnering millions for himself. Since the mid-eighties, barter in television has become a way of life. If one wants to buy top-rated off-network programs in syndication, he not only pays huge amounts per program in cash, but also gives one or more minutes per half hour in barter. The syndication company then sells the barter to national advertisers.

If one wants to buy feature films today, there is no longer an inventory held by the barter agency. Instead, on the first run, and sometimes the first two runs, up to half the commercial time goes to barter advertisers.

If a company wants to produce a program in television today, it can find barter sponsors as long as the show is placed in 70 to 75% of the ADI (Audience of Dominant Influence). That, basically, is the population factor in the different size markets, with the top five cities in the United States representing somewhere between 22 and 23% of the audience.

Although it is illegal as hell, the major market stations, knowing the deal won't go through without their market share, demand as much as a $5,000 cash payment to themselves. The contract, when signed, will read: "The distributor paid $5,000 for promoting the program." The station gets the program for a certain number of spots, sells the remainder and receives an extra five grand for promotion. Thus, the distributor meets his 70 to 75% of ADI, and everyone is happy. New York, Chicago and Los Angeles are normally "must" markets to achieve the percentage of audience required.

Of course, some barter deals can backfire. In television, most children's programming is with barter advertisers. I've seen independent stations with a three-hour kids block in the afternoon making little money because the cash advertisers thought to be available were now barter accounts. In the 90's, many programs in syndication are bartered in their entirety, the stations having a certain number of spots to sell locally. Barter in broadcasting today is a multi-billion dollar business.

The Fun Years

With a brand new six-man sales force, our "Big Sound" library and "W" jingle package exploded on the market. We began writing three-year contracts on our library, at prices ranging from $50 to $200 per week. Our "W" package was averaging better than $6,000 a market, and we followed it with a second and third jingle package known as the "A" and "B" series.

Peter Frank and his head of production, Will Scott, were giving us new releases every month, and the stations were pleased with what we had to offer. I was traveling constantly, working with the men. I spent almost a week a month on the west coast working with Peter and Will, and coming up with some fresh ideas.

In music, as well as in specialty items, Will Scott was an unusual talent, and his wife was one of the most breathtakingly beautiful women I have ever met. She had been in the motion picture industry, but had never been able to reach stardom. I was fascinated by the two of them when I discovered they consumed a quart of vodka a day, but it never seemed to affect their work.

Rod Kinder continued producing out of Boise, Idaho, and was delivering a wonderful product. With barter, making sales was much easier and, although the percentages in the small markets were less than in the majors, the volume of sales was there. Minna Thorne could no longer be found sobbing at her desk in the morning, and our debt was going down rapidly.

I discovered that Fred Winton, Charlie Grood and Harry Sanger worked much better in the small medium markets. I helped them in the larger cities whenever possible. Harry could never get rate card prices, and would continually call asking if he could accept a contract for 50 or 75% of what was called for. Finally, I gave him his own individualized rate card, and I don't think he ever realized why I was accepting most of his contracts. We just made him ask for more and when he got 60 to 70% of his rate card, we were happy. Bernie Edelman was a dynamo, but kept us in continual trouble with some of his shenanigans.

I received a contract from him for the "Big Sound" and a jingle package for a station in a small town in the state of Washington, and several months later, after no payments were received, discovered that the station was in bankruptcy. I queried Bernie about it, and he told me that the front door had been padlocked but he went around to the back and was able to get in. I could have killed him. He went back to another station in the market and re-sold the product, but we still had to re-do the jingle package.

Early in June, Dick Ullman and I received a phone call from the executive vice president of the Marine Trust Company (the Marine

101

Midland Bank) inviting us to lunch at their main office. We were escorted to the top floor, where we proceeded to have cocktails, followed by a salad and the first cheese souffle I had ever had. It was a delightful hour and a half, one I remember vividly because of the executive vice president asking us, "When are you going to borrow more money?" We had paid our debt off, built a sales organization and shown almost a $300,000 profit. Since our statement reflected a corporation on a cash basis, we had only to report our collections, not our contract worth. It had taken us less than one year to pay off our debts.

The sales staff was doing a magnificent job. At that time, each salesman was getting a $300 a week draw against commissions. In a five-day week, spending four nights in a hotel or motel, their costs for food, gasoline and lodging came to approximately $75.00 a week. They seldom spent weekends on the road, but if it was necessary, they were reimbursed. Their draw left them with $225 a week and with their commissions, they all did extremely well.

*   *   *   *   *

Chicago has always been one of my favorite cities. I love Michigan Avenue, unusual with its shops and beautiful merchandise. I always enjoy the landmark Wrigley Building, water tower, and walking up and down the lake front with its beautiful apartment complexes. Everything about Chicago is exciting. Midwesterners are always so friendly, courteous and willing to help. In my early visits to Chicago, the loop with the trains running overhead and the old Sherman Hotel had a special aura about it. One almost felt like the pioneers of sixty or seventy years earlier. Mayor Richard Daly was still in power, and the city was wide open, with all types of nightlife—red light districts, massage parlors, great jazz—you name it.

In those early days of broadcasting, one seldom made advance appointments. One would check into a hotel, get on the phone, and have few problems in seeing management or sales at the various stations. One that I always did have trouble seeing, however, was Sterling "Red" Quinlon at WBKB-TV, the ABC-owned station. I would call, his secretary would always be gracious and take the message, but Red would not call back. At the time, Bob Kintner was president of the network, headquartered in New York, and with my name being Kempner, I once called and slurred the last part of my name. Ten minutes later, Red Quinlon called me back. When he heard my last name, he broke into

102

laughter, saying, "For God's sakes, Marv, don't ever pull that on me again! I was sure I had done something wrong." I got in to see him without any trouble. I didn't realize until years later that Red was "Mister Broadcasting" in Chicago. In later years, he wrote several books about the early days of broadcasting, and is revered in the industry.

In the spring of '59, I took the sales staff to their first NAB convention. It was there that I think these men realized, for the first time, what the industry was all about.

I took them to NBC, which had the top two floors of the Merchandise Mart. I showed them a huge room with over fifty color television sets in it, all tuned to Channel 5, their network station. Two men starting on opposite sides of the room, did nothing but go from one set to the other readjusting the picture. By the time they got back to the first set, maybe ten or fifteen minutes later, it had to again be fine tuned. It was an interesting sight to watch, particularly in those early days of color TV.

There was a famous club in Chicago called the 6-6-6 Club, located at 666 Lakeshore Drive, a striptease joint. The girls would come off the stage, look for men in the audience, sit on their laps, and have them buy champagne cocktails for them at hugely exorbitant prices. It was really ginger ale the girls were drinking, and men would run huge tabs from which the girls received a percentage. Sitting at one table with a beautiful blonde on his lap was Ben Strouse, general manager of WWDC Washington. Ben was one of my favorite people and we had become very good friends through the years, but I had never seen him in an environment like that. He saw me, motioned me over, and with a twinkle in his eye said, "Marv, I've never had so much fun in my life without getting into trouble." It's the only time I ever saw Ben tipsy. I took him back to the hotel later that night and helped sober him up at the coffee shop.

Several months later, I walked into Ben's office in Washington and found him with dozens of telegrams on his desk. He was laughing and told me a very funny story. WWDC was one of over 400 Mutual Network affiliates, and carried Fulton Lewis, Jr.'s news commentary every evening. Fulton, one of the top commentators in the country, had his own studio facility in his home, and they would just patch into his mike for the evening newscast.

Fulton Lewis had one terrible habit. When they broke for a commercial, he would never come in on time, so the station always had a public service announcement available for their network announcer to use. This had become routine, and no one thought anything about it until, one night, when they broke for commercial, Fulton, as usual, did not come back on time, the announcer used a public service spot, and the red light in the studio went off, indicating that the studio was now "dead". What no one knew at the time was that the red light had simply burned out. The studio was still "live", and the announcer's "Some shit!" echoed over the entire Mutual Network.

Ben had to go on the network that evening and make a public apology and fire the announcer (which he did by getting him a job at the CBS affiliate and, I believe, re-hiring him thirty days later). He also had to send a written statement to the FCC explaining what had occurred. What Ben was finding so amusing were the dozens of telegrams he had received, many agreeing with the announcer. One in particular I remember: "Truer words were never spoken." The telegram was signed by the publisher and editor of the *Atlanta Constitution*.

On another occasion, Ben told me the story of Richard Eaton, a successful broadcaster who became owner of stations in Washington, Baltimore, Cleveland, New York and Detroit. Eaton had been crippled by infantile paralysis as a youngster. He was very bright, but had a bad reputation from his business dealings. To upgrade their signal in Washington, Ben had built a new tower for WWDC. Ben told me he had always heard unsavory stories about Eaton, but never believed them until, as he stated, "The son of a bitch dismantled and sold *my* old tower." I never did ask Ben what he did about it.

* * * * *

In early 1960, Rod Kinder called with an idea for a new jingle package. He wanted to take the great song hits, copy the original talent, and build a new series. That would mean copying the voices of Perry Como, Bing Crosby, Dinah Shore, the Andrews sisters, the Pied Pipers, Paula Kelly, the Modernaires, etc., and by using several bars of the original orchestrations, copy the arrangements.

He put together what became known as the "G.E.," or "Golden Era," package. He never recorded anything without first writing to or calling the publishers and offering to pay royalties. Interestingly, Rod Kinder never paid more than $25 for the rights of any song he copied. The publishers must have figured, "What the hell can a guy from Boise Idaho afford?" If a song were unavailable, or the price too high, it was not recorded. We now had more than 425 sales of the "W" package

104

and close to 300 sales of the "A" and "W" packages, and "Golden Era" was given to the salesmen—with sensational results. In February of 1960, I called Harry Sanger in Miami and told him to plan a ten day trip with me to Texas. At the same time, I called Lionel Baxter, formerly of WIBG in Philadelphia, and now at the home office, and asked him if he could get the Storer boat for a day while I was in Florida.

For years, George Storer kept a 40-foot yacht, with captain and First Mate, across the street from Storer Broadcasting headquarters in Bal Harbor, Florida. Broadcasters could call the Storer office and use the boat. Many of us took advantage of it when it was available. Lionel gave me a date, and I planned my trip so that we could take the boat out for a day and go deep sea fishing before heading to Texas.

Captain Eddie and his first mate gave Harry and me a very special, memorable day. It was a perfect time, out on the ocean with a first mate baiting your hook, a gin and tonic in one hand, fishing pole in the other, turkey, ham and roast beef sandwiches, cold beer, and not a care in the world. We tipped our captain and mate after a successful and exciting day catching lots of fish and having a wonderful time.

George Storer gave all broadcasters the opportunity to take the boat out with no strings attached. It was his way of saying "thank's" to the small fraternity of those working in radio and television. Never was it a payback for services. His stations were probably the most successful of any in the early days of the industry and whether or not you worked with or sold your product to them made no difference. The boat was available for the asking. Several months later, an FCC commissioner was given the boat to go fishing, someone reported it, and our Storer fishing days were over. Knowing George and his people, I am sure it was never meant to garner special favors of any kind.

Harry and I headed for San Antonio, Dallas and Houston. Prior to making the trip, Peter Frank had requested that while I was in Houston I do a simple survey, required by the FCC, to prove the need for an additional broadcasting facility. This required basic interviews with people in and around stations' management, and even with people on the street. Peter was filing for a construction permit requesting to build a daytimer in the market.

We called on Dave Morris at KNUZ, and two or three other stations, as well as Jack Harris of KPRC. Jack was president of radio and television, both NBC networks. The station was owned by Oveta Culp Hobby's family, who also owned the *Houston Post* newspaper. Although the television station was making big money, the 50,000-watt

NBC radio station had not switched their format in any way, and was losing a lot of money. Harry and I sold Jack Harris two packages, totaling $29,000 and Jack took us out to lunch. We were fortunate to make a couple of other sales on the trip, and than I headed home.

Stars International and the Peter Frank Organization

In April of 1960, we headed for the NAB Convention at the Conrad Hilton Hotel in Chicago. The sales staff, having been to the convention the year earlier, was well-rehearsed. Our suite was directly across from one of the top national rep firms, and traffic in sales was brisk. It was my first opportunity to get to know Cecil Heftel, who had hired Rod Kinder at KGEM in Boise. I had heard many stories about Cec and his background, plus I had many dealings with him through the years, and I still look upon him in awe at what he has accomplished.

Abe Glasman headed up the Intermountain Network, with headquarters in Salt Lake City. Their stations were throughout the northwest, and he owned the Ogden, Utah, *Standard Examiner* newspaper. Abe had two daughters, one of whom married George Hatch. George was a very bright, well-educated young man, who looked like a banker. He wore glasses, was prematurely gray, and always appeared to be doing other mental tasks while you were talking to him. One could never get close to him in a personal way—at least I couldn't. He became president and CEO of Intermountain, as well as the owner of several radio and TV stations.

Cec Heftel married Abe Glasman's other daughter Cec was short and stocky, with a round face and boundless energy. If he got three hours sleep a night, it was more than he needed. One could find him wide awake in a hotel room at 4:00 a.m. watching a movie. Originally, Cec and his wife owned 20% of KGEM, George Hatch 14%, and Abe and the newspaper the rest. Having made a success of KGEM, Cec formed a company with Rod Kinder, IMN productions (their jingle house), and proceeded to sell packages regionally prior to our taking over on a national basis. Abe Glasman, seeing the ability that Cec had, sold him KIMN radio in Denver, Colorado, for $400,000, which included approximately 400 acres of land on West Colfax Avenue. The deal was consummated for $20,000 down—and those 400 acres on West Colfax became the big growth area in downtown Denver!

Several years later, Cec and his father-in-law bought KGMB radio and television in Honolulu. The AM radio station was, by far, number

106

one in the market, with a morning man who became legend in his time. His name was Aku Aku and as I recall, was paid the unheard-of salary of $200,000 a year, most of it going in alimony to his several ex-wives.

The television station, a CBS affiliate, was the "dog" in the market, behind in ratings even to the foreign language station. Cec flew to New York and talked the network brass at CBS into allowing him to reprogram the station. At that time, there were no satellites. Programming would be brought over by plane or ship, normally being broadcast one week after the mainland stations. Cec then proceeded to take the prime-time programming and broadcast it in entirely different time periods. He programmed that TV station similar to a radio operation, with its own distinct personality.

His promotions were brilliant, including the slogan "Colorful Nine". He programmed the station on a twenty-four-hour basis, with movies and contest gimmicks running all night long. Before long, KGMB-TV represented more than fifty percent of the audience unheard of in television. It became, by far, the #1 station in Hawaii.

If Cec wanted to do something, he set his mind and made it happen. One time, he decided to take up golf. He arrived at the golf course dressed in the latest knickers, very stylish at the time, ready to tackle a new challenge. Before long, he was playing an excellent game. His next conquest was to be elected to the House of Representatives from his district in the Honolulu area. Anything he set his mind to was successful. He took a nondescript FM radio station in Ft. Lauderdale, WHYI at 100.5 megahertz on the dial, promoted with big money give-aways and changed the call to "Y-100," and again proved his unlimited talent. Today, after selling most of his original broadcasting facilities, he owns nine Spanish-language stations. He recently took his company public, using the funds raised to buy other properties and add to his station list.

I always found Cec a very tough, but fair, businessman, and I had many dealings with him. When going to Honolulu, I would wire all the stations to make appointments well in advance, and they would either wire back or send letters with appointments for me. Cec always waited until the very last minute, but I would get my wire and have a 7:00 a.m. appointment on the given day—a compliment, I guess, because he always saw me first. (Many stations in Hawaii would start by 8:00 a.m. because of the five-hour time difference between Honolulu and New York, and the two-hour difference from the west coast.

I arrived at 7:00 a.m., and Cec was not there. I made my presentation to his general manager, made out a contract, and, as his manager, pen in hand, was poised to sign my contract, Cec arrived. I had to start all over again with the presentation and then got Cec's standard response—he couldn't afford my price. I came down about 20%, and the general manager, in Cec's presence, signed the contract. I have always suspected that Cec knew that I always raised my price by 20 to 25% because I knew he would always find a way to bargain it down.

I once spent from nine o'clock in the evening until after two in the morning sitting at the bar of the Brown Palace Hotel in Denver, Colorado, with Cec. His competitor, Don Burdin of KICN, had turned Cec in to the FCC because a disc jockey at 10:00 one night had used the sound effect of a flushing toilet. In those days, that was enough to lose a license or be heavily fined by the commission. (Remember the Jack Parr episode on the *Tonight Show* when he was taken off the air for using the words "water closet"?)

Don Burdin was one of the most unscrupulous broadcasters in history, and one of the few that eventually lost all of his licenses. He figured this was a way to get rid of his top competitor. Cec sat at the bar with me and must have consumed a bottle and a half of bourbon straight, with water chasers, while I, not being able to keep up with him, switched to cognac and water. Cec Heftel could drink anyone under the table; alcohol seemed to have no effect on him. Fortunately, nothing happened with the Commission, but Cec was very worried. In retrospect, that was the last time I ever saw Cec take a drink. If you met him at a bar before dinner, he would never order anything but iced tea.

During the convention, I had an opportunity to finally really get to know Cec Heftel, and I recall a brief conversation Cec was having with Peter Frank. At one point, he turned to Peter and said, "I have never before seen a sales staff that knows nothing about broadcasting, but *man* can they sell." Another evening in Chicago, I had dinner with Peter Frank, who was complained bitterly about Dick Ullman.

Dick disliked rock and roll, and never truly understood his own products. Peter was thoroughly disgusted with him. He said, "Marv, I am going to take $100,000, build a new sales staff and take "Big Sound" away from the Ullman Company. Why am I giving away 50% of the gross when I can build my own organization and do it myself?" I looked at Peter and said, "I think you're making a mistake. From my experience years ago with the Louis G. Cowan organization, and Dick Ullman, it isn't that easy to build a sales staff that will be successful

108

immediately. I think you would be wiser to buy the Ullman Company."
I got back to the hotel that night after spending a few hours with the
men nightclubbing, and went to bed. At 5:00 a.m., the phone rang. It
was Peter Frank, who said, "I can't sleep. Meet me down in the coffee
shop. I want to buy the Ullman Company." I met him downstairs and
we sat discussing his proposal until 8:00 o'clock, when we called Dick.
Dick asked him to call back at 10:00 because he wanted to talk to our
attorney, Ed Kavinoky. In the interim, Peter offered me what, at the
time, seemed a wonderful opportunity. I would move to New York and
run the company for him, with a large increase in salary plus a percentage of profits. At 10:00 it was decided to meet in Las Vegas two days
hence and work out the particulars. I declined, having made reservations
to meet my wife and children in Ft. Lauderdale for ten days, and told
Dick and Ed that whatever they decided would be fine with me. The
deal was consummated in Las Vegas, with Peter Frank buying the corporation effective July 1st.

With my stock in the company, I was about to see more money
than I had ever dreamed of. When I got the news in Ft. Lauderdale, I
was very excited. Another new chapter was about to start for me, and
I was going to the Big Apple!

Peter Frank

Getting back to Buffalo after ten days in Florida, I sat down with
Dick and Ed and discussed the terms of the sale. It was a standard 29%
down, with payments on a graduated schedule, the total dollar value
being the contracts in force effective July 1st. That meant that if we
could add several hundred thousand dollars to our contract valuation by
July 1, we would be paid several hundred thousand dollars additional. I
was given the job of getting as much out of the salesmen as was humanly
possible. And I still had to sell my wife, who would not be happy about
leaving the Buffalo area, selling the house and finding something in the
greater New York area.

New York, with all its problems, is still the most exciting city in
the world. As someone once said to me, "London reminds me of a
virile man, Paris is a beautiful woman, but New York is the most alive,
fascinating and exciting city in the world."

I devised a plan for the sales staff with a contest paying additional
commissions and other bonuses. For sixty days, May and June, we gave
them some leeway in rate card, and told them if they could not get cash

109

to take barter. I drove them unmercifully in those two months and the salesmen hated my guts. I once overheard them discussing me. They called me a son of a bitch, but in the next breath I heard one say "but he's fair".

I had been a salesman and worked with salesmen for many years, and I had learned that you never kick a man when he is down. If he is having a tough time, work with him, pat him on the back. By the same token, when he's on top, flying high, that's when you kick him to get him angry enough to keep doing the job. It always worked for me and, whether they liked me or not, they always respected me. I never believed in house accounts.

When we went to a convention, every salesman knew that whatever was sold would be split equally among the entire sales force, so I gave away a lot of money that might have been mine. But I have always said, "You can't take it with you, and you can't say you won't go. If you could, it would burn."

At the end of May, we started having severe problems with our basic barter agency. Unbeknown to us at the time, Garson Reiner of Exquisite Form had concocted a most unusual scheme. He would take the full value of the barter time, and use it in getting Exquisite Form on the New York Stock Exchange. Having sold the top markets on a 3:1 basis, and the small markets at 20%, he had a little less than four times his actual cost of time. He tried to cut down his costs by refusing to pay the full value of his contracts with us.

Having just sold the company, we were in a very precarious position. If we instituted suit against him, we would eventually collect, but it would jeopardize the sale of the company. We finally compromised, and Garson ended up with close to a quarter million dollars in cash savings.

Stanley Grayson, a most unsavory character, was instrumental in talking Garson into the scheme. At a luncheon about a year later, he bragged about how he had screwed Dick Ullman and the company, not realizing that I had been involved. I let him know what I thought of him in no uncertain terms. I discovered during that luncheon, however, that if we had gone after Garson he would have backed down.

With almost four times the money which he allocated his worth of the Exquisite Form Company, Garson brought it out on the New York Stock Exchange. He went to prison later, on a stock fraud deal. I have learned through the years most devious people get their just desserts.

That June, our last month under the R. H. Ullman banner, proved to be the biggest sales month in our history, and for months Peter Frank couldn't figure out what happened. We just got lucky, and we worked damned hard.

On July 1st, I started commuting between Buffalo and New York. I set up an arrangement with American Airlines that, unless I canceled, I had a 7:00 a.m. flight to LaGuardia on Monday morning and a 7:00 p.m. flight to Buffalo every Friday evening. Peter had arranged office space at 666 Fifth Avenue through his brother-in-law, Ed Tishman, since the building was managed by Tishman Realty. Our offices were to be at the Time Life Building on Sixth Avenue but as it was still under construction, and was not ready for occupancy. Even when we finally did move in, it still wasn't finished. Someone forgot to put telephone lines in, so workers were drilling holes above our ceilings for weeks. I would leave the office with my black shoes almost white from the dust that filtered down.

I introduced Peter to Charlie Weigert and Sid Barbet in New York, and I suggested we form our own barter agency. Peter formed a new company, Dellwood, with his brother-in-law, Ed Tishman, and Charlie and Sid set up shop with the Ullman Company at Time Life. We could now make incredible savings in that Dellwood made deals for hotels which we could buy at 15% of cost, and, since it was a new company, Dellwood was taking 100% of all barter that we could generate. Peter would come into New York an average of one week a month, and I would normally spend a week a month in Los Angeles. The company prospered under Peter's stewardship. Dellwood's staff continued to grow, and I met many unusual personalities who worked closely with Charlie and Sid. One of them, a pure delight, was a man by the name of Jason Darol. Jason's mother was a countess from England, and had taken very good care of him. For years, he lived at the Essex House off Central Park in New York, until one day his mother decided it was time he made his own way in life and his allowance was discontinued. His first job was as a time buyer for Dellwood. He had a charm about him that was infectious, and although he was gay, quickly made friends with everyone. He was thin, with sandy hair, eyes full of mischief, and a bundle of energy. He had one of the greatest senses of humor I've ever known.

Charlie and Sid shared an office with two large desks on either side and a couch between them. One day, Sid called Jason into the office and started giving him holy hell about a time buy he had made.

Jason was leaning against the doorway when he suddenly excitedly pointed his finger at Sydney and yelled, "You're nothing but a Homo Sapiens!" Sydney, trembling and turning crimson with anger, jumped up from his desk, pounding it, and screamed, "You stop that—that's how rumors start!" We laughed about that for weeks, and Jason became one of our favorite people in the office, someone you had to like.

Peter Frank's office was on Melrose Avenue in Hollywood, next door to Paramount Pictures and an independent studio. We often had lunch at one of the commissaries and watched the starlets taking a break. I also got a kick out of seeing extras taking a break from filming, dressed as cowboys or German generals.

Peter was a very unusual man in that he could juggle half a dozen things at the same time. He would be working with Will Scott, the motion picture recording stars doing intros, checking out financial statements of RHU and Dellwood, talking with Rod Kinder and Cec Heftel about a new jingle package and other projects, all at the same time. His mind was a kaleidoscope of action. He was interesting to watch because he never lost his cool under the most stressful conditions. Few men I have ever known have had as an inventive a mind as Peter Frank. He was brilliant as an idea man, and was also able to bring most of his ideas to fruition.

He invested in an idea to bring out a west coast version of TV Guide, eventually selling it to Walter Annenberg of Triangle Publications. His Peter Frank Organization was the parent company of Stars International, each star representing a different company, including IMF Productions, Richard H. Ullman, Dellwood, Omar Music and Frank Enterprises, which dealt with the purchase of radio stations. He also ran his own advertising agency and produced television specials, all from his office in Hollywood.

What caused Peter many problems through the years, was his naivete and softness in dealing with some of his executives. Years later, he admitted to me that one of his few weaknesses was picking the wrong men to run several of his operations. I met some very interesting people through Peter who became fast friends. Mann Scharf and Lloyd Bleier, two opposites in appearance and personality, had been childhood friends while growing up in New York City. Mann was a short stocky bundle of energy. He could talk faster than any man I ever met. He was a chain smoker, was always on at least two telephones at the same time, and was a very successful public relations man.

112

Lloyd Bleier, tall, thin and graying at the temples, was the quiet introvert, totally lost in any business enterprise such as public relations. Lloyd and Mann having both been divorced for several years, decided to build a home together overlooking one of the canyons outside of Los Angeles. They designed it with a central entrance foyer, large living room, dining room and kitchen with a distinct wing on each side of the house, each having its own entrance. In each wing was a bedroom, sitting room–office and bathroom. Thus they had total privacy whenever they wanted it, but sharing a kitchen and living room let them enjoy social activities together. I guess opposites do attract.

Through the years, their hobby of collecting Wedgewood china became almost a second business for them. Together they amassed one of the finest collections in the world, which was shipped to galleries all over. I have seen Wedgewood china many times, but never like the plaques, figurines, sculptures, etc., that these two had found.

Mann introduced me to many of his clients. One, Vicki Carr, had made it big on the charts with the song "It Must Be Him." She was a charming, adorable girl, very attractive and extremely proud of her Mexican ancestry. She had married a "do nothing" guy who decided to go back to college, with Vicki paying the freight. He was taking one or two classes a semester, and Vicki finally wised up.

I met another beautiful young lady, Mitzi Gaynor, through Mann. She had supported her family as a dancer since the age of twelve, and finally made it big when picked for the lead in the motion picture *South Pacific*. She met her husband, Jack Bean, when, as a CBS page, he was chosen as her escort for the opening night festivities for that picture. After their marriage, Jack became her manager, the only other job he ever had. He would place an annual ad in the newspaper selling Mitzi's Cadillac, since they bought a new one each year. He got more than top dollar for it because the buyer could say he bought Mitzi Gaynor's car. To me, Jack was a conceited horse's ass who latched onto a good thing (Mitzi) and made a career out of it. Mitzi, however was always a doll. One would find her at her home in blue jeans, where she would take you into the kitchen to grill hamburgers, and find her a down-to-earth, fun-loving, all-American girl. Then there was the public Mitzi, an exotic, gracious, charming, beautiful movie and theatre star.

Calling one day at my hotel, Mann asked me if I would take a cab out to the CBS Studios and meet him at Art Linkletter's dressing room. When I arrived, I was introduced to Art, and Mann asked me my opinion about a company that Art was buying. It was a barter company

113

with upwards of two million dollars in barter time. Looking at the list of stations involved, I turned to Art with a smile and said, "This time is literally worthless." The list was made up of the smallest markets in the country, with no major stations. I said it was a very bad deal for the money. I left, went back to my hotel, somewhat surprised that a man of Art Linkletter's stature would have such little business acumen—or maybe he just didn't understand what the barter business was all about. Shortly after I got back to the hotel, Mann called and told me how thrilled Linkletter was that I had saved him a lot of money.

Ben Strouse had become president of WWDC in Washington, and had become involved with an equipment manufacturer, Spotmaster that had designed and built one of the first tape cartridge machines. They had developed a unit whereby stations could reproduce their own commercials, jingles, promos, etc., on a cartridge, getting on the air quickly, saving both time and space. With materials on individual cartridges, it was easy to quickly play a jingle or commercial. Jack Neff, an engineer, had developed the unit and broadcasters loved them plus they were not too expensive.

Peter and I suggested to Ben that we be given the sales rights since our men were always out with the stations. We could barter them, and their company could get cash that much faster. The idea jelled for both companies, and sales of libraries, jingles—everything—soared. We got commissions on every one we sold, and—stations would take two or three units with every contract. Our business continued to flourish, and it helped, in many ways, to sell our other products.

The Changing Tide

Hal Neal had been vice president and general manager of WXYZ, ABC's O&O in Detroit, and I had worked with him and sold him many products. He was named vice president/general manager of WABC in New York, a station that was doing poorly at the time. I went to see him to congratulate him and, naturally, to also see whether I could find a way to sell him in the big city.

Hal told me he had no money. He was very upset with the network in giving him a minimum budget to work with. He was in the process of taking WABC into the rock and roll era, and I suggested a new jingle package. I would be happy to work out a barter deal for him. Hal jumped at the opportunity, and I called Peter suggesting we build a special package, one that could be sold by bragging about a major New York City station.

114

In broadcasting, it is not what you're selling, but who bought it. It is a follow-the-leader business and, if you look at the eighties and nineties in television you'll see that nothing has changed. We decided to produce a new jingle package using the Johnny Mann singers, a nationally-recognized vocal group from the west coast. The package was produced specifically for Hal, but we also did very well with it in syndication to other markets.

Hal Neal was a wonderful guy who eventually became president of ABC radio. Tragically, he was an alcoholic, and although the network did everything possible to help him, he died years later still a young man.

Being in New York had tremendous advantages, with station managers continuously coming in to work with their national rep firms. They often found their way to our office, and we were able to not only make new sales but get renewals as well.

One afternoon, Charles Buddy Rogers, the husband of Mary Pickford, came in to see me. They owned a couple of stations in Kansas, and I remember as a very young child meeting Buddy when my father brought him home for dinner. My dad headed up the Paramount Pictures Exchange for many years in Buffalo, and Rogers was appearing at the Shea's Buffalo Theater with his full orchestra. He played every instrument in the band, and with his jet black hair and pearly white teeth was one of the handsomest men in Hollywood. Meeting him over thirty years later with his steely gray hair, incredible blue eyes and wonderful smile was a thrill. I mentioned to Buddy how he had been at my home for dinner in Buffalo, and I was very pleasantly surprised when he said, "Yes, and I still remember the special rice pudding with the caramel sauce your mother made for dessert."

In the fifties and sixties, the airlines had special clubs, and the most difficult one to become a member of was American Airline's Admiral's Club. I had tried for twelve years, with little success, and even now that I was commuting with them twice a week I still got nowhere. I received a phone call from American Airlines one afternoon telling me that their flight would be delayed for two hours because they were switching from a jet to a DC-7. I was on my way from New York to Dallas and was pleased they had called about the delay. What I wasn't so pleased about was getting to the airport and finding there was no crew, and sitting there for an additional three hours. Upon my return from Dallas, I wrote to American and expressed my displeasure, mentioning that I guess they didn't want me as an Admiral and I would stop trying. A week later, a man from American came into my office and told me that in the city of New York they could only nominate twelve people a month. He gave me several passes to the Admiral's Club, said that I was on the list, and I would be given my credentials within sixty to ninety days. Three weeks later, two people from American came up to my office and presented me with my Admiral's Club card.

I maintained membership with American for twenty-six years after that, finally quitting because it meant nothing anymore. It's a shame that flying, which used to be fun, has become such a chore. Once upon a time, if you got to an airport and showed your Admiral's Club card, you were placed number one on the list in case of a cancellation. The Club would not allow anyone in without a jacket and tie, and the airlines themselves had class.

In Detroit one evening, Bob Six, president of Continental at the time, walked into the Admiral's Club with no jacket or tie. In those days, there were little nine-inch black and white television sets on the desk where the Skipper sat, and Bob Six's former wife, Ethel Mermon, was singing. Bob had just gotten divorced from her, and started swearing. The Skipper, Shirley McManus,threw the President of Continental Airlines out of the Admiral's Club for not only swearing, but also being improperly dressed. Thirty minutes later, Bob Six came back with a tie and jacket, apologized to Shirley, and then offered her a job as head of Continental's clubs.

RHU flourished and became the largest syndication firm in radio in the country. I received a call from Peter Frank telling me he was in Newark, New Jersey, and asking how long it would take me to get there from New York. He requested that I meet him on the mezzanine floor of a bank in downtown Newark as quickly as possible. I hopped a cab to Penn Station and caught a train, arriving at the bank about twenty minutes later. Peter introduced me to a vice president, said he was borrowing $75,000 and needed a second corporate signature. I said I was not an officer of the Peter Frank Organization, only of RHU, and he immediately stated that I was now assistant secretary of the parent corporation. I signed the necessary papers thinking nothing of it.

Two days later, I arrived at the office, glanced at the headline on the front page of *Radio-TV Daily* and got a jolt I don't think I will ever forget. The headline read "Morton J. Wagner Named Executive Vice President of Peter Frank Organization". For the first time in my life, the realization suddenly hit home to me that, like most people, I had one hell of an ego. I spent the 4th of July weekend in a trance. I was hurt, feeling like someone hit me below the belt and kicked in the teeth at

116

the same time. I had promised my wife and children a weekend at a resort, and somehow ended up sitting beside a swimming pool for the better part of three days.

I had met Mort in Madison, Wisconsin, several years before, and also in San Diego, where he worked for the Bartel Organization for several years. He had always left a bad taste in my mouth. From the first time we met, I didn't like him. Mort was about 5'6' tall, well-built and athletic, with black hair, flashy pocket slacks, shirt open to his navel, and an expression on his face like someone who looks down on everyone else. Mort Wagner loved Mort Wagner, and if you asked him, he would tell you what a genius he was.

He arrived in the New York office a few days after the 4th. He let everyone know that he was taking over, and it wouldn't be long before "the shit hit the fan". I had two secretaries: Claire, who had been with me a long time and had become my "girl Friday", whom I trusted implicitly, and a second girl who was a delight and did much of the dictation. But Claire was number one. Mort immediately flew her out to the west coast, where she spent a full week. When she came back, she was an entirely different person.

Quite often, I would leave my house in north Jersey and drive to New York, particularly on a Monday morning when the mail was the heaviest. I would get to the office by 7:00 a.m. and spend the next two and a half hours with a dictaphone. At 9:30, when my secretaries came in, one would take the dictation and start typing while the other opened the mail, giving me an opportunity to go answer phone calls and continue with dictation. One Monday morning, my number two gal arrived an hour early and gave me some very interesting information. Any letter I wrote was copied and sent to Morton, together with excerpts of my phone calls, on a daily basis. It is amazing how one can trust someone after months of working with them, only to find out she is a Mata Hara, all because someone new was sleeping with her.

From that moment on, any letters I dictated went to my other girl, and what a darling she turned out to be! If she went out to lunch, she took any half-finished letter out of her typewriter and locked it in her desk. At the end of the day she would personally post my mail. Any personal calls I made to the salesmen were made from home.

Then, Mort took over the sales staff. Every week, for years, my salesmen got a letter from me which usually ran from one and a half to two pages long. Suddenly, twelve to fifteen page letters were coming from the west coast. My decision to look elsewhere for employment came when one of his sales letters had a line I will never forget. The last line went "If the Jew fits, wear it." Sales started to fall, and the men were not happy.

While all this was happening, my wife, who had developed diabetes several years earlier, was diagnosed with tuberculosis. Treating a diabetic with TB, even with the new miracle drugs, was not going to be easy. Bringing her home from the hospital meant making an apartment for her in part of the house where the children could visit from a distance. I had nurses around the clock, and fortunately was covered by major medical. It was one of the most trying times of my life and, in retrospect, I didn't handle it very well. I did something that, to this day, I am still ashamed of, but I probably would do it again. I made a trip to Cleveland, Ohio, by plane, checked into the Statler Hotel, left my bag there and proceeded back to the airport. I flew to Buffalo, spent an evening with my mother, flew back to Cleveland the following day, checked out of the hotel, and went back to New York. I did that in your honor, Mort Wagner, wherever you are.

Insurance companies can be strange in the way they operate. My coverage included registered nurses on a 24-hour-a-day basis, which was costing the insurance company a small fortune. I called them and said I would like to hire a practical nurse who would live in. She would charge about ten percent of what RNs were charging. I was told, emphatically, "no". I would not be covered if I did that. So I recalled the insurance company and asked to speak with the president. I told him of my plight, how I would maintain nurses around the clock, but didn't it make sense for them to cover something that would cost so much less? He immediately agreed, proving another lesson in sales—always get to the top man. I found a practical nurse, which gave me an opportunity to make short trips where necessary, but for months I did not make any extended trips.

Several weeks later, I discovered that when Peter Frank had borrowed the $75,000, it had been guaranteed by Marty Himmel, one of the barter kings, and the loan was to be paid back in bartered time. I don't think Peter ever realized that he had been taken. Dellwood had to give Marty $750,000 in top 20 market time with the top stations in the country.

I was invited to make a speech at the Mutual Networks Advisory Committee meeting in Port Antonio, Jamaica, early in September, and I accepted. Just prior to my leaving, I was asked to fly to Las Vegas for a meeting with Peter and Mort. When I arrived, I discovered that Peter

118

was not coming and spent the two days with Mort. He did everything possible in those two days to force my resignation. When one is under stress, one seldom thinks straight. I wanted out so badly, but I didn't realize that my major medical would continue as long as my wife was ill, even if I left my job. I remember vividly walking the strip in Las Vegas all night long, going back to the hotel, showering and shaving, and going on to the next day's meeting.

The following morning, I finished my meeting with Mort. That afternoon, I headed to the airport to fly back to New York. Peter, with Marty Himmel, had traded out a suite at the Plaza Hotel, which Peter would use when he came to New York. Marty would entertain his guests there as well. I arrived back in Manhattan about midnight and took a cab to the Plaza, having been given the okay to use the suite that night since I had a 7:00 a.m. flight to Kingston, Jamaica. I was escorted up to the suite by a bellboy, who opened the door only to find Marty Himmel in bed with a hooker. The embarrassment of the hotel management was pure delight to me. They found me another room, and I left early the next morning.

Arriving in Kingston, I was picked up by one of the executives of Mutual and we drove for three hours in a driving rain on a two-lane winding road around the mountains. It was one of the wildest rides I have ever encountered. The driver would turn his lights off when he came to a hairpin turn and, if he didn't see a reflection, he kept going full speed.

We made it safely and checked into a hotel that was owned by Errol Flynn. The hotel was an experience in itself. It was old, had slanted doors to allow air through, floors that creaked ominously as you walked on them, and yet it had a certain charm even with a musty odor about it. Each room had its own separate air conditioner that leaked on the floor. The furniture was cane, and the mattresses really sank. Outside, there were two swimming pools—one salt water, and one fresh water—and above them was a 100-foot-long bar.

I made my speech the first day of a five-day meeting, and then sat at that bar from ten in the morning until at least 2:00 or 3:00 a.m. I discovered bitter lemon, a drink that had not yet been released in the states. By drinking bitter lemon and rum, one could literally drink all day, get a mild glow on and forget one's troubles.

I left a day early and drove by limousine back to Kingston, where I stayed at a Sheraton Hotel that had just opened the day before. It was also the first day of Jamaican independence from England, and there was a wild celebration going on in Kingston. I flew back to New York in a much better frame of mind, determined to be patient and plan my future in a sensible way. I had taken the Ullman Company and made it the largest in the country, with more than 1500 accounts. Mort Wagner be damned.

Another Beginning

A few weeks after my return from Jamaica, I received a call from a Milton Herson, a man I had met briefly with Peter at Music Makers, a company owned by a Mitch Leigh. Peter was looking for another contact to do some of the music for the several libraries we now had developed and sold. At a meeting, Milt mentioned that Peter had sent Mort Wagner up to discuss the details of adding to their music library, and that both he and Mitch had taken an instant disliking to him. I just smiled at the time, but I felt good knowing I wasn't the only one. I asked him what his ideas were, and he suggested we have dinner with Mitch later that week.

Milt and Mitch were unusually good businessmen, although I eventually discovered they were not always honorable. Milt was about 5'10", with a mouth full of capped teeth and eyes that never could quite look you straight in the face. He was an attorney by trade, and somehow, for some unknown reason, Mitch thought he was a genius. He was money hungry, and always took credit for anything that turned out well, while blaming others for mistakes. He was a terrible hypochondriac and a whiner, and one learned quickly that he would do anything for a dollar. He had a certain false charm about him, but one was never quite comfortable around him. You just didn't feel you could trust him.

Mitch Leigh's father was a tailor in Brooklyn, and Mitch's real name was Irwin Mitchnik. He graduated from Yale University as a music major in woodwind instruments, with the bassoon his main instrument. Years after, his cousin came into my office one day and told a delightful story about Mitch.

He had sent a limerick, or music jingle idea, to one of the agencies in New York, and they called him stating they were interested in buying it. He borrowed ten cents from his father and took the subway into Manhattan from Brooklyn (in those days a nickel each way). He vowed to himself that he would not take less than $25 for the jingle. When they offered him "seven fifty", he didn't have the guts to turn it down, and the agency handed him a check for $750.

120

It was the beginning of Music Makers, which Mitch founded with one or two partners. He became the king of the jingle world in Manhattan, and did just about every major commercial for several years. If an account executive wanted the best jingle for his client, he went to Music Makers and Mitch. Among their clients were Benson and Hedges, American Airlines, Volkswagen, Chrysler and General Motors. Sara Lee in the nineties, is still on the air with Mitch's jingle. He had a great talent for putting the right people together, always hiring top musicians and writers.

In a recording session, with the client and account executive in the control room, Mitch might do six or seven takes until the account executive and client would call down and tell him which take they wanted. Mitch had a wonderful flair for doing five or six *more* takes, then looking at the account executive and playing back the spot he had selected. Then Mitch would play the spot *he* liked. His famous line was, "This is what you bought, but here is what you take," and the superiority of Mitch's selection was immediately recognizable.

Mitch did a jingle once for Delta Airlines. The vice president in charge for Delta was a nut about Gilbert and Sullivan music. He had picked the song he particularly liked, and wanted us to sing it with new lyrics, changing only those lyrics that were absolutely necessary. Mitch did the session, and the materials were sent to Atlanta. A few days later, a tape arrived from the vice president, and it was hysterical.

The vice president announced on the tape that he had made some changes in the lyrics, like changing an "a" to a "the", because it read more like the original. He said he was sitting at the piano with his wife early in the evening, having a martini. He then proceeded to sing his changes, and he was obviously tone deaf. By the end of the tape, he was so drunk we could hardly make out what he was trying to say.

Mitch suggested we form a new company with ownership to be on a 50:50 basis, so that I at least had negative control. He immediately would set up recording sessions to do original music, and I would work with his staff of writers on what should go into our first package. His engineer, Bill Schwarthout, was the best in the business when it came to mixing and editing. The corporation was to be called Mark Century, and our first production, very aptly named by Milt, was called "Radio Ala Carte".

Prior to leaving the Ullman Corporation, I made one last trip to the west coast and found, to my delight, that every office had a full-size portrait of Mort Wagner on the wall. With the help of a couple of the boys working in the office, we managed to re-hang all the pictures up-side down.

On Thanksgiving weekend 1962, I mailed my resignation to Peter Frank. I was somewhat surprised on Monday when Peter called me and seemed sincerely upset, as were Charlie Weigart and several of the boys at Dellwood. But another exciting episode for me was about to begin.

10.
Mark Century

Early in January, with my "Radio Ala Carte" tape in hand, I headed out on my first trip under the aegis of Mark Century Corp. I planned a two-week trip, and decided to drive rather than fly since I wanted to go into Washington, Richmond, Nashville, Cincinnati and Pittsburgh. I was not too pleased with my original presentation tape. Something seemed to be missing, but I could not put my finger on it. Making this trip by car would give me the opportunity to stop in several other smaller markets to get a feel for what the problems were with "Radio Ala Carte," as well as get some idea as to its potential.

I spent almost an entire day with Ben Strouse at WWDC in Washington, and I firmly believe he bought the product because of me. I got some answers in Richmond and Roanoke, and then decided to go into Knoxville, where I also made a sale. I went on to Nashville and saw another great buddy, Jack Stapp at WKDA. I had known Jack from his days at WSM, where he headed up Grand Ole Opry for years, and there were many nights I spent back stage with him at the Ole Opry House, meeting some very talented and wonderful people. Jack also bought the product, but instead of going on to Cincinnati or Pittsburgh, I headed back to New York for a meeting with Mitch.

I still could not tell what was wrong with the tape. The music and the materials were excellent, but the presentation just didn't flow. Mitch was very excited, what with $78,000 in contracts in less than two weeks, and he asked me if I had any suggestions. I wanted to call Ev Wren, a brilliant producer in Denver, and see if he would come into New York and re-do the tape presentation. Mitch said to go ahead, and Ev arrived three days later. I told Ev that basically the presentation just didn't flow. Here was a man about six feet tall, with sandy hair, very handsome and a womanizer, but a great talent when it came to modern radio programming.

Ev went to work Friday night, and on Monday morning came into my office with a new presentation tape that was incredible. The music, the voice overs, and the presentation of all segments suddenly fit, and I now had a tape that did the selling for me. We hired Ev on the spot, and he came to work with us in New York for several months.

When I returned from my first trip, Milt Herson told me that he had hired a secretary for me, something I was quite upset about because I like to pick and choose myself. She was to start the following Monday. Realizing he had done the wrong thing, Milt suggested I give her a chance, and if she didn't work out I could find my own secretary.

Monday morning Barbara Cordell came into my office. She was tiny, about 5'2", with jet black hair, an incredible figure and strikingly beautiful. As I was dictating a letter to her, her hand came up and I recognized that as a sign that I was going a bit too fast, so I continued at a slower pace. When she handed me the dictation a few hours later, it was perfect. She had a very classy way about her, and was as beautiful inside as out. We became very close personal friends. Weeks later, she admitted to me that she had been terrified on her first day of work because she didn't take shorthand. She had learned her own method of speed writing, and it proved to be incredible.

I will always love Barbara, even though it was purely platonic between us. For the eight years she was with me, I never called the office, ever, without her first words being, "How are you?" She married after six years with me, and left two years later. We managed to keep in touch these many years and, when in New York, I occasionally have lunch or dinner with her and her husband, Sid.

With Ev's new presentation tape, and Mitch and Milt overseeing the production, "Radio Ala Carte" became a standard of quality in the industry. I concentrated on hitting the major markets, with great success.

For years there had been a group of stations that called themselves the A.I.M.S. Group, which stood for Association of Independent Metropolitan Stations. This group held two meetings a year somewhere in the United States or Canada. Owners and owner-managers would get together to discuss programming, promotion, sales ideas, etc. Hearing that one of the meetings was about to take place, I called Dave

Morris, president and general manager of KNUZ radio in Houston, asking him if there was a chance I could make a "Radio Ala Carte" presentation to the group. Dave had bought it a few months earlier, and he called me back telling me the hotel and city where the next meeting was to be held, and then sent me a personal invitation to make a presentation.

Dave Morris introduced me to the group, many of whom I already knew, and then made the statement, "This the first time I have ever bought a product that delivers more than it promises." After my presentation, I sold every A.I.M.S. station in the United States and Canada, with the exception of Richmond and Baltimore which were already sold.

As a member of NAB I wanted to try something new with Mark Century. I contacted one of NAB's officers and arranged to have a breakfast seminar sponsored by Mark Century. We were given a 7:00 a.m. period during the convention, at which time we would serve a full breakfast and invite speakers. Seventeen general managers appeared, and I acted as moderator, a task I thoroughly enjoyed.

For eight years the breakfast seminars were held. Our speakers included F.C.C. commissioners, presidents of broadcasting groups, and even Mitch Leigh of Music Makers. Mitch proved to be a total dud. When he speaks in public, he uses a lot of words, but says nothing. We were now a must for broadcasters, with more than 600 attendees, and we were heavily covered by the press. When that meeting ended, after Mitch had spoken, one reporter came up to me, and with a smile on his face and a twinkle in his eyes said, "What the hell did he say?"

At one memorable seminar, our guest speaker, the president of Lin Broadcasting, cost us the whole show. He stood up after being introduced and said, "I just heard President Johnson is coming and is expected in a few minutes." I never saw a place empty so fast in my life.

We continued these seminars until 1971, when NAB took our time from us. It was the beginning of the end for program people at the convention. We were treated like third cousins twice removed, there being much more interested in equipment manufacturers. We, and most other syndication companies, resigned as NAB members.

In the spring of 1963, I received a call from Peter Frank telling me that I was going to be subpoenaed to appear in Washington at the FCC regarding the construction permit for a radio station in Houston he had applied for a year and a half to two years earlier. I had done the necessary, or what I thought was the necessary, leg work in research which was required for filing for a CP. I told Peter that a subpoena was unnecessary, just let me know when I had to appear before the commission. It was a few weeks away.

The Oveta Culp Hobby family owned the Houston *Post* newspaper, KPRC, a 50,000-watt radio station, and KPRC Television, an NBC affiliate. The president and general manager, Jack Harris, and the Hobbys must have decided to fight a new station in the greater Houston market, and the FCC had set up a hearing. The claim was we were incompetent, and had not been truthful in our filings. Although I was not in any way connected with ownership, nevertheless, the information compiled by me should be disallowed.

Jack Harris was of average height with a demeanor of superiority. He had a conceit that was hard to fathom. He thought he had all the answers. My opinion, particularly after the FCC hearing, was that he thought he defecated strawberry ice cream. Nattily dressed in his gray-striped Brooks Brothers suit, and taking the oath to tell the truth and nothing but the truth, he proceeded to state he did not know me and had never met me. In short, he said that I was a liar.

I have nothing against people like that, having dealt with them for many years, and, admittedly I can call many of them friends. But after completing his testimony, he came over to Peter Frank's attorneys, looked right through me, shook their hands, and then left. One doesn't have to like me, but don't ignore me. I have never forgotten that moment.

I spent six hours on the witness stand. Never having been involved in an FCC hearing, I admit I was frightened and nervous. The attorney for the Hobby group started by asking several questions regarding broadcasting and how I would operate a radio station. Since I had managed one, I had little trouble with this line of questioning, in fact, I even started to relax a bit and enjoy responding to the questions.

After about an hour, the FCC examiner stopped that line of questioning and stated for the record that I was to be considered an expert in broadcasting and the operation of a radio station. I was fully relaxed by then. The questioning from their attorneys, the examiners and Peter's attorney continued.

For years I maintained a record on a Memindex. It is a system which comes with a box of 365 cards, one for each day of the year, together with an alphabetical index. I always put my appointments, names, addresses and telephone numbers on the front side of each card, which measures about 5 x 3. On the reverse side, I would keep my trip expenses on a day-to-day basis. At the end of each week I would be able to quickly show my telephone calls, hotel, entertainment and cab expenses. After a week or two, I would replace the cards in my Memindex box in the month shown. Since I normally maintain travel records for the IRS for up to seven years, I had a complete record of who had been seen, dates, etc., with expense records on the back of each card.

At the end of the calendar year, I would pull all the cards out, put a rubber band on them and keep them with my tax return. If Uncle Sam wanted to audit me, in addition to having receipts, I could throw these cards at them and they could readily see day-to-day expenses.

When I was asked whether I knew Jack Harris, my answer was affirmative. The next question was whether I had ever done any business with him, and when I again answered affirmatively, I brought out one of my Memindex cards to show that I not only knew Mr. Harris but he had bought $29,000 worth of product from me and, on a given date, had even bought my lunch.

By then, I was having fun. When the day was over, I was scheduled to appear the following morning for additional questioning. The next morning, I was asked many questions on how I would program the station and the number of people needed to do so. I felt my answers were not only honest and forthright, but would be taken as from one who knew and understood broadcasting. When I was excused, the attorney for Peter Frank came out into the hallway, hugged me and told me that my time on the stand had been brilliant.

I still have the FCC examiner's findings, which state that Mr. Harris had a very poor memory, that Peter and myself were truthful, and that the FCC should grant the license. The construction permit was granted, but after going through all of that, Peter and his partners never did build the station.

"Mr. Titan"

I received a call from Dick Ullman and discovered he had sold his home, moved to Ft. Lauderdale, and was doing consultancy work for Bob Buchanan and Jack Schleu of Soundac. They had produced a new cartoon pilot and offered me first crack at it. The idea was great, and with the help of President Kennedy, who had established a fitness program for the youth of America, it tied in beautifully with the current fad for fitness. Mr. Titan was a space character who did exercises for children and adults. Bob and Jack had produced an eight minute animated cartoon that could be run on television on a daily basis. Each morning Mom and the children could do exercises along with Mr. Titan.

Having met Ed Metcalf at CKLW in Detroit when I had sold the RKO television group, I called him and made an appointment to meet him. Ed was a very interesting person. He had spent four years with Spike Jones playing tenor, alto sax, clarinet and flute. As a vocalist, he was a "straight" singer on "Cocktails for Two," "Laura," "Black Magic," "My Old Flame," etc, while the shenanigans went on all around him.

Ed was one of those people in the broadcasting industry one would classify as a leader. He could make decisions; if he liked something, you got an immediate response. After viewing the audition cartoon material on Mr. Titan, Ed helped set up a buy for all of the RKO television stations. Although it did not give us a profit on the 100 cartoons we produced, it did pay a large portion of the production costs.

I sold several other major markets and then, on a hunch, called Mann Scharf in Beverly Hills to see if he might set up a meeting with Art Linkletter. He called back a few days later, and I flew out to see Art and Jack Bean, Mitzi Gaynor's husband, to present the program. I talked about the fitness program backed by President Kennedy, and the type of promotion we could do. Art and Jack were very excited. After several additional meetings, they decided to buy Mr. Titan, and the attorneys were to draft the necessary papers. As I was with Mark Century, I was quite pleased to get out at this point, since I felt it would be difficult to do both radio and television, being in such different arenas.

A few weeks later, our attorney called and said that there was no way we could go ahead with the Linkletter-Bean operation since, unbeknown to us, they had set up a paper corporation. What that meant was that Linkletter and Bean would not be responsible if the product was not successful. In other words, their money had not gone into the company, and would not, unless they saw a very profitable venture.

Although Soundac continued to sell the program themselves, and were able to produce the entire package, very little profit was ever realized. I was somewhat upset, but it was just another good lesson in how some people operate.

Mark Century's Early Years

In early 1963, Peter Frank sold the R. H. Ullman Company to Mort Wagner, and that wonderful sales staff we had built either quit or got fired. I received a call from Herb Berman in Buffalo asking me to come to a meeting with the salesmen. I flew up there and landed amidst the snow and ice, something I had finally left for good.

We met at the old Sheraton Hotel, and I found that the boys had a wonderful idea. They were going to form their own company and build a product similar to the "Big Sound," as well as jingle packages. I suggested that they had to pick a leader, but was told quite bluntly that they had had enough of me, and they all wanted an equal say in running their company. In telling them I was not interested in joining them, I added that they had little chance of success unless one of them was picked from whom the rest would all take orders.

It's funny how salesmen, as great as they can be when making a presentation, or knowing when and how to close, don't always have a great deal of business acumen. They formed a company which lasted sixty days, and most of them went on into other fields of endeavor.

Shortly after their company's demise, I rehired Herb Berman, who worked very well in major markets, keeping him in the east and midwest, and Fred Winton, who did very well in small medium markets, in the south. At the time, my itineraries were set three weeks in advance and, except for flying home on weekends, it was becoming a bit of a chore. Herb helped greatly, and I made him call me from wherever he was on a Wednesday morning to make sure he hadn't gone home early. Fred was never a problem, and I worked with him on an average of once every four to six weeks when we would hit the major markets in the south together.

Mitch had written two or three jingle packages for us and, with "Radio Ala Carte" doing exceptionally well, we hired two more men. Bernie Edelman, our "Damon Runyan" character, asked to come back, primarily because he loved the work so much. Since his family still lived in Buffalo, we would fly him out to the west coast for two to three week trips, then he would come back and spend a week with his family. We also gave him several weeks of work in the midwest. One couldn't help but love him and I only wish he had taken better care of himself. He was a chain smoker, very much overweight, and we lost him to a massive heart attack at age forty-six. It shook us all when it happened. With all the crazy problems he created and all the mistakes he made, he was still one of my favorite people.

In the spring of 1963, I received a call from Lou Avery at KYA radio in San Francisco. Lou had sold his Avery Knodel rep firm and become manager of the radio station, located in the lower lobby of the Mark Hopkins Hotel on top of Nob Hill. The station had become involved in a promotion that had sold in Los Angeles and San Francisco, and Lou felt we might be interested. I flew out to see him heading for

129

my favorite city. San Francisco should not be visited alone. Its beauty and charm makes it a "lover's delight".

The Mark Hopkins Hotel brings back many nostalgic memories. During World War II, we would go up to the Top of the Mark, a glass-enclosed room overlooking all of San Francisco. At night, one could go up there and watch the fog roll in covering everything in a milky white, powdery mist.

We were in the Air Force stationed nearby, and although outnumbered one-hundred to one by Navy personnel, we always enjoyed the ambiance of the room and surrounding area. We would go to Fisherman's Wharf, have lunch at Giardelli Square and an Irish whiskey in one of the many bars. Or we would drive down old Route 101 to the Monterey Peninsula, with its sea cliffs and wildlife.

Having arrived the evening before, I turned on KYA while shaving the next morning. I almost flipped! A very talented disc jockey in the morning drive time had made himself the "Emperor" of greater San Francisco. He had written some of the funniest lines and craziest concepts for broadcasting I had ever heard.

This was the idea Lou had called me about. They would supply me the scripts on a monthly basis for sale as a promotion to radio stations all over the country. The Emperor, as the morning man was now known in Los Angeles and San Francisco, would ask his "subjects" to do some of the craziest things—mostly nonsensical, never hurtful—and his "subjects" (listeners), complied. In one promotion the Emperor set up a parade in downtown Hollywood with an army tank painted pink and the turnout was tremendous. This material was hysterical, and couldn't miss if it was presented properly. I made a deal on the spot, and took several tapes and scripts back with me.

I had worked out a deal on a 50:50 percentage break. I would be supplied twenty days of material each month, covering a Monday through Friday morning man. We, in turn, would supply brochure materials, stickers, billboards, mats for newspaper, promotional spots and do all the sales job. Anyone with a sense of humor at a radio station could not turn it down, knowing it would add ratings to their morning show.

I went into Chicago and called on Ralph Beaudin, the vice president and general manager of WLS, the ABC-owned station. Ralph wouldn't let me out of his office until he had called New York and Detroit, the two other O&O stations that were still available.

For years I have teased Harvey Hudson of Richmond, Virginia, who was the morning man and made a career out of being the Emperor:

"How the hell did you ever get those stickers in the ladies rooms in all the hotels and restaurants that said the 'emperor was here?' " Harvey, for 34 years the morning personality on WLEE is a legend in the Richmond area. We've been life-long buddies and continue close even today. His background covers radio, television and advertising. One can still hear him on his nostalgic programs 2 to 3 times a week in southern Virginia.

Everyone had a ball selling the Emperor, and the next six months were great. We were selling one year contracts until the realization finally hit us that no man could be funny forever, and the material started to get a bit stale.

As compensation, we offered to add six months to the stations' "Radio Ala Carte" contracts, a six-month credit if they bought a jingle package, or a credit on our next property which would be forthcoming shortly. We didn't lose a sale. It was nice to know those in broadcasting trusted us to make it good.

About this time, Peter Frank came to New York and announced that the Ullman Co., although they would continue to fulfill all their current contract obligations, would soon be out of business. Mort Wagner was finished, and he has never held a position in broadcasting since.

In late spring, Milt Herson hired Frank Beck to aid in taking over the production of our monthly releases, jingle packages and new products. Frank had been with one of the top agencies, and for years had been involved with television programming. Bess Myerson, a former Miss America, was one of the talents that Frank had worked with in television. Milt asked me to take him on a trip, but hadn't given me any real background on him. He was a bundle of nerves and was at the bar each morning consuming two or three bloody marys for breakfast. It took several months before he straightened out.

His story was tragic. Frank was very much in love with a young lady who became pregnant but refused to have the baby. A friend of his found an abortion doctor, but during the procedure, the young women died suddenly from anesthesia poisoning. Both the doctor and Frank's friend went to prison, and Frank had to live with himself. It took a lot of time and patience on our part, but he eventually did straighten himself out and became a valuable member of the staff.

We continued to add more sales people, and Mark Century was doing very well. Mitch would take two or three musicians, mostly brass (such as trumpet and trombone), fly to Munich or London, pick up some string musicians, and record several hours of music. With the AFM

131

(American Federation of Musicians) scale, we could record in Europe for about half the cost. That continued until AFM finally stopped us.

Few people realize that, even with the union scale in New York, musicians working theatrical shows, recording sessions, weddings or Bar Mitvahs were lucky to gross $15,000 a year. But with the stringent rules passed by the union, it was the end of the big band era. If a big band came into a town that had an AFM chapter virtually all major cities), a standby orchestra had to be paid full scale, making it impossible, in most cases, for the band to make a profit. The only feasible way was for the name band leaders to take three or four lead musicians with them, and hire local talent to fill in. It's still done that way today.

Two or three of the jingle companies in Dallas got together, contacted musicians and offered them a guarantee of $15,000 annually to do their music sessions and recordings. When the union tried to stop it, their members revolted, since a guarantee gave them a fixed income they could rely on. We were thus able to get much of our music done in Dallas. Although many of its rules continue to exist, the action in Dallas hurt the AFM immeasurably.

Mitch Leigh

Mitch had studied with Paul Hindemith at the Yale School of Music. Mitch's company, Music Makers, was enormously successful in commercial production, and he had won every major award for radio and television commercial music. He also wrote the incidental music for *Too True to be Good* and *Never Live Over a Pretzel Factory*. His dream was to produce a broadway musical, and ever since his days in high school he had been fascinated by Don Quixote.

Mitch used to tell me that in order to be successful writing music, one had to spend at least eight hours a day at it, which he did for many years. In his spare time, he wrote music about the life of Cervantes and his fictional creation, Don Quixote.

He began working with Dale Wasserman, who had been professionally involved in show business since the age of nineteen. Dale had written more than forty works for the stage, television and motion pictures, but this was to be his first musical for broadway.

The musical was to open in summer stock at the Good Speed Playhouse in Connecticut, a theater with a very narrow stage, but acoustically excellent. It was the beginning for Mitch of his "impossible dream" and the musical known as *Man of La Mancha*.

With Richard Kiley playing the lead, Irving Jacobson at seventy-six years young playing Sanchos, Joan Diener as Aldonza and Robert Rounseville as the padre, it was an instant hit. They brought it back for a second run during the summer. The New York critics were asked not to review it, and all but one complied.

John Chapman, in the New York *News* Sunday edition, gave it a wonderful review, calling it "the finest and most original work in the music theater since *Fiddler on the Roof*." Then, at the end of his review, came the *coup de grace*. He hoped they would not bring it to Broadway because the critics would destroy it.

Raising money for a broadway play or musical, as my attorney once told me, is riskier than buying stock in an oil well where no oil has ever been found. He used to enjoy investing $250 in a play. He would get opening night tickets, and figured the investment made for a delightful evening. To aid Mitch, we all invested much more than we should have, but in order to open on Broadway, we had to raise $200,000 (today, that figure would be in the millions).

On November 22, 1965, *Man of La Mancha* opened at the Ante-Washington Square Theater in the Village. It was a theater in the round, with seating in a 360-degree circle and the stage in the center with no curtains. One could change the settings on the stage with all lights turned off on that area. It was a fascinating way to see the show, and it was breathtaking. The finale was so spectacular that there were few dry eyes in the audience, and everyone jumped to their feet applauding. It was an evening I'll remember forever.

We all headed out for the cast party at the One Fifth Avenue Hotel and, while waiting for the newspaper reviews, put on NBC. The reviewer was Edmond Newman and I have never felt more destroyed in my life. He said the music was copied from other things he had heard, the rape scene was disgusting, and he knocked *Man of La Mancha* throughout his review. What a letdown! The newspapers gave it a mixed reception, with some brilliant reviews.

In the first thirty days, *La Mancha* lost $200,000, but an amazing thing started happening. Word of mouth brought people in, and those that saw it came back a second, third and fourth time. It suddenly became the hottest show in New York. I have seen it many, many times, but I could see it again, particularly with the original cast.

Mitch once said to me he felt the show was not a musical play, but "Seventh Avenue Opera". I always felt it was an adult *Peter Pan*. We wanted to believe, and emotionally got very much involved.

133

The morning after we opened, my attorney called and said he was sending some papers over for me to sign. He said that, although it might be a gamble, he felt I should take my investment in *La Mancha* and give it to my children. In doing so, I could save a lot of money in taxes. As it turned out, both of my children got their college educations and their first automobiles from the twenty-two times my investment was returned.

When La Mancha closed, almost four years later, it was the third or fourth longest running musical in Broadway's history.

After *La Mancha*, Mitch changed drastically. I believe he stopped spending much time writing, because when we at Mark Century asked for some fresh music, what we got from him, in most instances, was garbage. He handed me a piece of music one day and said, "Marv, this is pure genius." I said to myself under my breath, "If it is anything like the last few pieces of music, it's probably pure shit," and it was.

Several weeks after *La Mancha's* opening, Mitch was hailed by Yale University and was to conduct the Boston Pops. Picture a man who had become quite portly conducting a large orchestra, not in tuxedo or tails, but in a navy blue, velveteen jump suit.

He went on to Europe and produced *La Mancha* using Jacques Brel, the big musical star of France, and theater companies were springing up all over the world. His income from *La Mancha* was in seven figures, and Mitch became a very wealthy man.

He has never had another hit on Broadway, but I can attest to the amount I lost in *Chu Chem*, which closed in Philadelphia, *Cry for Us All* or, as I called it, "Cry for All of Us", and one or two others.

A few years later at a cocktail party, I was introduced to Stephen Sondheim. Someone brought up Mitch's name and I was quite disturbed to hear Stephen Sondheim, in a loud, clear voice say, "Mitch Leigh has no talent". I do not believe that, having worked with Mitch, but maybe the key is his remark to me about having to write eight hours of music a day. He was no longer heeding his own work credo.

Music Makers continued to write music for the many commercial jingles being recorded. In New York, Herman Edell, Mitch's sales manager, left to form his own company. He was a very charming man, and a damn good salesman. He had a great love of skiing, so he set up his new company in Aspen, Colorado. I never found out whether it was successful, but Herman certainly was becoming mayor of Aspen.

Several writers remained with Mitch and did the majority of the writing for him. Mitch was busy with the show on Broadway, as well as helping to set up casts for the different road shows. *La Mancha* companies opened in Paris, Brussels and London, with similar success. At the time, I was president of Mark Century Corporation and had full reign. In the next couple of years, we not only released several additional jingle packages for radio stations, but also two new libraries—"Formatic Radio" and "Festival".

Since we always gave a thirty-five-mile exclusive in a market, it made good sense to have one or two additional library properties to sell in the same markets. All of the materials in the other libraries were completely fresh and quite different in their makeup. "Festival" originally was designed for smaller markets. It could be sold at lower prices since our costs were not as high. Strangely enough, "Festival" sold as well in the large markets at comparable prices to "Radio Ala Carte" or "Formatic", and our gross sales annually were well over one million dollars, and should have proved very profitable.

They were fun years, and I learned to live with the eccentricities of Milt Herson and Mitch. Milt was always dying of some mysterious ailment, and in any crisis would totally fall apart. He called me one Sunday morning terribly ill, and asked me to call my doctor in New York and beg him to make a house call. I obliged and several hours later the doctor, who was a close personal friend of mine, called me and asked me not to do him any more favors. There was nothing wrong with Milt; he was a very sick man, but not physically.

Mitch made daily visits to his shrink, which was very much in sync with the times. Maybe that's what finally made him take off his sunglasses and become more the astute businessman I felt he was.

When I first formed Mark Century with Mitch, our offices were at 6 West 57th street, formerly occupied by Sid Caesar. Like most talent, Sid's ego was tremendous. His office was totally mirrored so one could see himself at any angle at any time.

We then moved over to 3 East 57th, and then to the Warwick Hotel at 54th and 6th Avenue. We had the penthouse on the 33rd floor, and only one of the three elevators went up there. My office was a large suite with bathroom, separated from Mitch's by a kitchen, and one could enter either office from the hall. We also had doors on each side of the kitchen.

I had a queen-size couch that opened into a bed, and many times when I would catch the red-eye, leaving Los Angeles for New York at eleven o'clock at night, I would call my secretary, Barbara. She would call housekeeping, and they would make up my couch in the late afternoon or evening.

Flying from the west coast to the east coast quite often was less than four hours with tailwinds, and I would get to the hotel between 6:30 and 7:00 in the morning, take a shower and go to bed. At 10:00 in the morning, I would be awakened by Barbara, handed a cup of coffee, shave quickly, change clothes, and work straight through until three or four in the afternoon.

In the lobby of the Warwick was the Sir Walter Raleigh Room, a delightful place for breakfast, lunch or dinner, and directly across from it was the famous Warwick Bar. Every evening, Howard Cosell would come across the street from the ABC Studios at 54th and 6th, and do his show live from the bar. It was the early days for Howard, prior to his making it so big with NFL football and other sports, but the bar would be ten deep.

The hotel was a delight, and a wonderful place to have an office. Having been in offices at 666 5th Avenue, the Time-Life Building, and 57th Street, my years at the Warwick were my favorites.

I recall flying back to Buffalo to see my mother before going on to Chicago. Here was a woman in her late seventies, as modern as any twenty year old until her death at eighty-seven, who grew continuously with the changing times. I mentioned to her that, after having lived in the New York area a couple years, that I often thought how nice it would be to come back to the smaller city.

She said, "Son, there is something you have to learn about life: you can never go back". Not being able to go back because things could never be the same was a great lesson in life. My dad, who had taught me that if you start something, you must finish it, taught me another lesson I never forgot.

Early one morning, I received a phone call from John Chancellor and we arranged to have lunch later that week. At the time, John was heading up Voice of America and was interested in using several bars of a jingle package as an identification. I thought it would be a great idea, great PR for our company, and took the suggestion to Mitch and Milt. Milt thought it was wonderful, if we could get a $25,000 deduction on our taxes in lieu of payment for the rights (something that was impossible). If the request had been for a lot less money, I think John would have gotten it. Unfortunately, that was not the case, and the idea was dropped.

11.
Colorskope

Early in 1966, I received a call from Bob Buchanan of Soundac asking if I might be interested in selling a new television idea Soundac was developing. At the time, computer animation was still in its infancy. It showed signs of future success in its development, but was still very primitive.

For the average television station, the cost of producing special movie openings, news, weather, sports and specialty promos was expensive, so few stations did more than use slides with music backgrounds to open their local programs.

Soundac had developed an animated series that would supply a television station with dozens of news openings and closings, sport specialty openings, weather (afternoon and evening), motion picture openings and closings—almost anything the TV station could use.

Soundac would supply complete, color storyboards with full instructions, giving each station the opportunity to supply tailoring information. Soundac, in turn, would lay the beds of their animation call letters and, sponsors. The station would be given actual film footage of how this could be done, and full instruction for programming, or the art departments could order so many on a monthly basis.

I was excited. I asked Mitch Leigh to fly down to Miami with me to work out details whereby Mitch would do the musical backgrounds and we would work on a 50:50 deal handling all sales. Mitch grudgingly agreed to go down only after he realized that Steve Lawrence and Edie Gorme were appearing nearby and he had an opportunity to spend a weekend with them. Not realizing that this was President's Weekend, which at the time was George Washington's birthday weekend, I drove around Miami in a rented car until 5:00 in the morning, finally finding a closet at the Hollywood Beach Hotel that they put a cot in for $100 a night. I got two hours sleep before our meeting at 8:00 the next morning.

We made the deal and flew back to New York. Several weeks later I had a presentation reel and brochures, and was anxious to make my first presentation. Having made appointments in the New Orleans area for a couple of radio sales, and working with a new salesman, I decided that was as good a market as any to get my feet wet.

Since I hadn't been involved in television since 1958, it was going to be quite a challenge. Not knowing those involved in the market in television, and being unknown, it is tough sometimes to reach the right people, but I've always found it much more challenging going in cold. Very few salesmen feel at ease doing this. I found it more fun, and in many ways easier, than selling friends or those you have known for years.

I was able to make appointments with program directors at the CBS and NBC affiliates, but I never got past NBC's WDSU-TV, the number one-rated-station in the market. Before I could even put my film on, the program director ran for his general manager, A. Louis Read. I had a sale of Colorskope in a matter of less than half an hour, and was told it was one of the great program services ever offered television up to that time.

Lou Read was a most unusual man. He was a bundle of energy and one of the sharpest men in television know-how. His complete understanding of the media made him special, and he was too talented to stay forever in the New Orleans market. As I recall, he eventually ended up in a much bigger position in the New York area. There's a story about him that became part of the folklore of broadcasting.

Having the number one station in the market, and doing a great deal more volume than its nearest competitor, WWL, it bothered him that his net figures after taxes were so much less than WWL, which was owned by the Jesuits. Consequently, WWL paid no taxes, and Lou was reprimanded for writing a letter to his Holiness in Rome complaining about the situation.

Colorskope was an instant success with television broadcasters, and to my knowledge no one was ever able to copy it. It taught me

138

something about television broadcasters that stayed true until the late eighties.

Regardless of how great a property was, one quickly discovered that the stations themselves left much to be desired. One could produce something for a station that was brilliant, but one could often not get that station to actually use it. For some unknown reason, stations would have products just sitting on the shelves. If it meant a little extra work or effort, it just sat there. I honestly believe the average television station in the late sixties and seventies could have found on its premises enough programming and other materials that it would not need to buy any new product. It was heartbreaking to go back to stations, having sold something that you truly believed in, only to find it sitting on the shelf.

We were able to sell Colorskope to several groups and stations throughout the United States and Canada. Our dollar volume at Mark Century soared, and those few stations that used it properly were very happy.

Milt Herson came in one day and discussed the possibility of hiring someone new to handle radio, suggesting I work full time in developing new products for television. Unbeknown to me, he had talked at length to Herb Mendelsohn and felt he would be a natural.

I knew Herb, having met him at WKBW, a 50,000-watter in Buffalo, where he was vice president and general manager of the Capitol Cities station. Herb was a six-footer, on the portly side, almost bald, but a bundle of energy, and he had spent several years with the ABC network in New York. Capitol Cities had hired him and sent him to Buffalo where he had done an outstanding job.

He was a true New Yorker and never seemed comfortable in the smaller city. Unfortunately for him, he made a wrong decision, leaving Capitol Cities and going back to New York as general manager of WMCA. Like so many other managers who left Capitol Cities, he never made it. As I said earlier, the manager doesn't make the station, the station usually makes the manager.

Herb and I sat down with Milt and discussed his joining us as head of the radio division for Mark Century. In many ways it made sense to me because it is almost impossible to wear two hats in broadcasting, and I was excited about getting back into television. Herb was a good salesman and had strong background in the industry. If he succeeded, everyone would benefit in the coming months.

Herb joined us a few weeks later, and I planned a trip to California with him to help familiarize him with our product and help him in any way possible. We flew out to Los Angeles and worked the southern California area all week, ending up in Fresno, planning to fly back to Los Angeles and catch the red-eye back to New York.

Unfortunately, both airlines that serviced Fresno-Los Angeles canceled, and there was no way for us to get back and make our plane. While I was trying to figure out what to do, Herb excitedly came running back to me, having talked to three men who claimed we could rent a private plane that would take us back to Los Angeles, with the fare split up among us. The idea sounded great and, having made the arrangements, we were taken in a station wagon to a small, single-engine Cessna which proved to be the funniest-looking plane I had ever seen. Its fusilage had a large belly that looked like a portly man lying on the runway.

The pilot introduced himself and then asked each of us what we weighed. Herb was over 260 pounds, the pilot about the same, the second and third men were well into the 200-pound range, and two of us were 150 to 160 pounds. The pilot suggested that one should sit in the co-pilot seat, while the other two sit directly behind him, and we, the skinny guys, would bring up the rear.

We stowed our luggage and the plane taxied out to the runway. It seemed forever before that little Cessna got off the ground. As we lifted up, I fell into the baggage hold since my seat had never been bolted down. The boys helped pick me up and we proceeded to L.A.

There was only one problem—the plane was overloaded and we couldn't climb above 300 feet. Fortunately, Fresno is not far from L.A., and our pilot assured us there was no problem. We would fly through the pass and just follow the highway below us.

We got to talking with the pilot and discovered that he and his partner ran an undertaking business. The plane's belly held caskets.

When we arrived in L.A., still at 300 feet, our pilot didn't understand the tower and we proceeded to fly directly into the flight pattern of incoming and outgoing aircraft. The screaming from the tower to "get the hell out of there!" was terrifying. The pilot finally got instructions to land on one of the runways. As we came to a halt, he apologized with a remark I have never forgotten. He said, "Normally I'm not the pilot—I'm the undertaker." He was whisked away by officials as soon as we landed, I vowed I would never contract for a private plane again unless I knew a pilot, and not an undertaker, was behind the controls.

After returning to New York, I gave Herb *carte blanche* with the sales staff and the operation of our radio division. Herb had asked me to stay completely out of the division and give him the opportunity to use his expertise and know-how without help. I concurred but said that I reserved the right to check sales on a monthly basis and make any suggestions I felt would aid him.

Some people's egos can get in the way. Herb had been trained in a big city and worked for a network, so "little ole me" didn't know what the hell I was doing.

Four months later, Herb made his first sale to the ABC-owned and operated radio station in Houston, Texas. All of our contracts were written on a three-year, non cancelable basis. When I saw Herb's first contract, I exploded. His first and only sale was made on a three-year basis, with cancellation at any time upon thirty days prior written notice. I was livid, and suggested that he find other employment since syndication was obviously not something at which he would be successful. We parted company on a friendly basis, however, which I find is always the best way. I had no idea what a mess I was about to encounter because Milt Herson had kept the monthly radio sales figures from me, telling me during that time all was fine.

The Family Crest

Radio sales were down $140,000 from last year's figures, so I scheduled a meeting with Milt Herson and Mitch Leigh. Milt could never take bad news and had his paper bag available for hyperventilating. He was a "fair weather" type, and any business setback caused him terrible anguish.

I had an idea, given me a few weeks earlier, that I thought might be something that would prove to be a potential successful promotion. We had been offered the opportunity to sell coats of arms over the radio, discussing how people got their names, what they stood for, and how names originated.

In medieval times, the church in western Europe was all-powerful, and deemed that teaching the public to read and write would prove troublesome. Instead the church decided to give them stories from the Bible in art form, particularly in the churches and cathedrals. Consequently, very few people could read or write in western Europe. One had to go to the Byzantine Empire in Turkey or further east, before one found higher education levels.

In Europe, with its high levels of illiteracy people were given names in a most unusual manner. If one lived at the bottom of a hill, he became known as "the man under the hill," or eventually, "Underhill." If he lived on the other side of the hill, his family became "over the hill," or "Overhill." A manufacturer of barrels was a cooper, thus the name "Cooper." "O'Conner" was the son of Conner. "McConner" was the illegitimate son of Conner.

To identify members of a family, trade group or royalty, crests or coats or arms were designed and became a form of identification. To this day, one can travel throughout Europe and find these coats of arms dating back hundreds of years. I loved walking through the Grande Place in Brussels, Belgium, where crests or coats of arms are on almost every building, or going through the meeting halls in London with hundreds of them displayed on the walls.

The idea for the radio show was to take a family name, describe its crests and history, followed by inviting the public to send $10 to receive their own coat of arms. For years, newspapers and magazines had done this successfully. Today it has gone one step further. Companies offer to research and send you the complete history of your family name.

One thing we discovered soon after making the decision to go ahead with this scheme was that many people never had a coat of arms, including the Jewish race. The people who had brought me the idea were less then honest, claiming everyone would get a coat of arms.

After several days of researching the potential, I told Mitch I was going to try it. He was totally against the idea, but we went ahead—and then the fun began.

Radio stations loved the idea and, since we were producing the entire series, paid substantial money for exclusive programming rights. We had no idea how long a promotion of this type would last, but we sold one-year contracts. In addition, we were to be paid a percentage of all coats of arms sold, so that if it was successful we had the opportunity of making money on both ends—the sale of the programs and the sale of the crests.

When our presentation tape was completed, I flew to Memphis to see Harold Krelstein, president of Plough Broadcasting. Harold, famous for his Plough format in radio, was a tall handsome man. In his early years he had been known as a playboy, but after one or two marriages he had settled down. As a salesman, and having been involved in the early syndication of programming, he was a dominant factor as head of a seven-station radio group. Harold bought the idea of the show for his markets, including Chicago, Memphis, Baltimore and Atlanta, and demanded that I send him his own coat of arms. A few weeks later, he called me, laughing, and said he just got his coat of arms, featuring a chicken.

Sometimes one gets lucky with a crazy idea that comes down the pike. This one more than proved its merit. In sixty days, we not only made up our $140,000 shortfall in sales, but far exceeded it. I have no idea what the total sales of coats of arms were, nor do I believe the people handling it were very honest in their monthly statements. I do know, however, the product was a godsend for us at the time and made me a hero.

The show had about a six-month run, after which stations started becoming somewhat disillusioned. Once again, we gave them a credit on other Mark Century products, which proved a bonanza for us. We allowed cancellation after six months by giving the stations a six-month credit towards another product and wrote three year contracts for our libraries and, occasionally, one-year jingle packages.

Going Public

In 1967, after months of discussion, it was decided to consolidate Music Makers and its subsidiaries with Mark Century, and go public.

When Mark Century was formed, I had demanded, since the corporation was equally owned by Mitch Leigh and myself, that my attorney handle the company's affairs where my interests were involved. I had picked Mil (Milford) Fenster, who years earlier had helped me (*Colonel Bleep*) while at RKO, and had become a close personal friend. As a Harvard Law School graduate, he had joined the firm of Hall, Casey, Dickler and Howley, heading up their broadcast legal department.

I had set up a retainer fee basis with him, which was in effect for more than thirty years. We would meet at least twice a month for lunch, and occasionally dinner, and his guidance through the years kept me out of trouble.

We would be going public with Music Makers, their music library, and a dubbing company which took foreign language films and dubbed English voices for release in the United States—a thriving business in the sixties. Can anyone forget the "spaghetti westerns", all made in Italy?

We also had approximately twenty motion picture theaters with multiple screens that Music Makers had bought or built in the New Jersey-Connecticut markets. By consolidating all of these companies, our plan was to go on the market under the name Music Makers.

I discussed the plan with Mil Fenster, who warned me that I would lose control of Mark Century. He also felt it was not a good idea for me because, with all the companies combined, Mark Century had 55% of the cash flow. After several more weeks of deliberation, against the advice of Mil, I decided to go ahead. I was not naive, or so I felt. Mitch had gambled on my reputation years earlier and put up the many thousands of dollars for Mark Century to go into business.

In retrospect, I probably would do the same thing again, and for a few years after the merger and going public, it seemed my decision was the right one. In the ensuing months, while all the mechanics were being worked out, the company continued to make its projections. The sales staff was growing, and Milt Herson continued to be the fair-haired boy for Mitch with his supposed genius.

Early in 1968, the company went on the market at $10 per share. At the time, I was the third largest stockholder with 50,000 shares, 13,000 of which I sold to other inside stockholders. Milt and Mitch had about 100,000 shares between them. Within a few months, Music Makers stock was selling for $18 a share, and most of us were ecstatic.

I was president of the Mark Century Division and vice president of Music Makers, as well as being a member of the board of directors. Mitch was chairman of the board, and Milt, his attorney, president of Music Makers.

Our first acquisition as a publicly-held company was a toy manufacturer that produced yoyos, another big feather in Milt's cap. The thorns did not appear on this purchase until after Christmas, when it was discovered that all stores that had purchased the yoyos had the option of returning those unsold. What a mess! It was a several hundred thousand dollar loss for us.

The company continued building or buying multiple screen theaters, and when it was discovered that the candy concessionaires would pay $200,000 for 50% of the concession, we quickly went into the candy business supplying our own theaters.

My father, who was one of the founders of Paramount Pictures in the early 1900s, had taught me a bit about the industry, including two things I will never forget. There is more money to be made in the sale of candy and popcorn than there is in tickets to a fully-packed house, and, although the motion picture people will tell you their exhibitors get 50% of the gross, that is only true on a standard movie, or what we fondly call a "box office flop." When the industry has a big hit on

144

their hands, the motion picture exhibitor normally gets 10% of the gross. He has to rely on his concession sales to make a profit. How many people realize that when they buy a box of popcorn the box costs more than the ingredients?

Now shackled with both radio and television projections to meet, I was too busy to check our monthly and quarterly statements. It was a stupid mistake on my part to not realize for several months that our statements were not "kosher".

Frank Beck was running the production end of Mark Century, with Milt Herson overseeing all of the company's growth. My sales staff was writing four to five times the volume of business against our costs, and I was led to believe that the other companies were also all doing well. Mitch, with *La Mancha* doing well and foreign companies being formed, was spending a good part of his time in Europe, leaving Milt to run the day-to-day operation of the parent company.

I was doing less traveling and spending more time with my wife and children, but unfortunately, my marriage was beginning to fail. My wife was a beautiful woman, but she did not like people, had few friends, and pretty much wanted to live alone. She trusted no one, and had a knack for finding something wrong with everyone she met. Many times she said that the only reason we remained together was that I traveled and wasn't home much.

I finally talked her into getting psychiatric help, and for the next several years tried to find a way to help her. She had done such a wonderful job with our son and daughter. Perhaps going back to work might give her a different outlook. She was an R.N. and did a marvelous job. For a time, working part-time in private duty seemed to help.

* * * * *

In 1968, we decided we should start looking for broadcast properties that made sense and were reasonably priced, with an eye to buying a radio station.

A 5,000-watt, full-time facility was available at a good price in the Manchester, New Hampshire, market. The city, not far from Boston, appeared to us to be a market we could do well in. Papers were signed and an application was made to the FCC for transfer of license. For me, it was exciting, having management experience and a pretty fair knowledge of the industry. The fact that I did not have to run it, but could oversee a management team, pleased me no end.

145

We received notification from the FCC that the transfer of the license would take place on a specific date, and I flew up to work with the manager and staff to oversee the takeover.

Manchester is a beautiful city with a small-medium market charm. The country club, in which one could become a member for very little money, was beautiful. It included a golf course and tennis courts, as well as a lovely clubhouse with dining facilities.

The downtown area of Manchester is pure New England delight, and I always found the people a pleasure to work with. They are down-to-earth, frugal, and conservative as hell, but honest, hard-working, industrious people.

Milt had hired a manager, and I was to work with him checking out the staff and attempting to maintain most of their jobs. I was also going to change the station's format to one that was more up-to-date and commercial in scope.

I flew into Boston, and was picked up by the new manager and driven to Manchester and radio station WFEA. About 11:00 in the morning, a telegram was received from Washington confirming the switch in ownership to Music Makers, and then the fun began.

Having never been in the Manchester market, or at radio station WFEA, I presumed that the equipment was not only operable, but in good working order. To my dismay, I found that half the turntables were either inoperative or off-speed, and most of the equipment had to be replaced. We were in somewhat of a cash bind and did not want to lay out a lot of additional money, but if something wasn't done quickly we would not be competitive. Our signal and sound had to be modernized right away. No one had been made aware of the situation, or of the immediacy of the problem.

The first thing I did was contact the equipment manufacturers and make dates for them to come up to Manchester and give me some idea of what costs would entail. Most of them had offices in the Boston area, so appointments were made for them to come in in a day or two, and the thought occurred to me I might have a way of replacing the equipment with little or no outlay of money.

I had worked with every major barter agency in the New York/Boston/Chicago area for several years, and I felt that, with a little persuasion, most of them would help me work out a trade for equipment, giving them time on the station. They, in turn, would pay the costs of my needs to the suppliers in cash, and I would guarantee to honor their advertisers' commercial spots.

146

One, a major problem, was that Manchester was a small market. With the top fifty cities in the United States representing over 90% of the population, getting an agency to take more than a few thousand dollars in time could be difficult. Through the years, however, I had always delivered to the barter agencies what I promised, and my reputation helped me immeasurably.

By begging, conjoling, and even promising to make it up to them if it didn't work, I was able to make some incredible deals. My only problem was that I was committed in the future to supply major market bartering with top stations, but I believe in the months that followed that I kept my word. I was able to trade out all new turntables, tape decks, even microphones, and, surprisingly, no one turned me down.

My next step was to find a way to trade out the down payment and the first year's cost of a new transmitter. At the time, RCA, GE, Continental and Gates were willing to work with me, with minimal down payments which would be very satisfactory.

Looking back, I took a tremendous gamble, but it proved to be a first in the country, one that paid off handsomely for us.

A company I had never heard of had, somehow, through the grapevine, discovered we were in the market for a transmitter and, unannounced, sent a rep in to see me. He told a glowing story of his new company, which had placed transmitters in Africa. With the rain and humidity, they continued to operate flawlessly, even when the cabinet doors rusted off.

What intrigued me was how this transmitter had been built. It was completely transistorized, with no tubes to burn out, and, in its day, was state of the art. Normally, one would buy a 5,000-watt transmitter and since the FCC required inspections weekly, have to go off the air Sunday night at midnight for servicing and inspections, returning to the air early Monday morning.

Here was a company offering me two 2500-watt transmitters that worked in parallel. If there was a problem, only one of the transmitters would be involved. One would still have half power, and could remain on the air. It also meant that the engineers could do their inspections without ever going completely off the air.

Even with half power, one only lost fifteen miles of their signal. I was fascinated by the potential and decided to be a guinea pig—it was the first dual transmitter ever purchased in the United States. Two of the barter agencies split up the cost of my down payment and the first year's scheduled costs.

Years later, I discovered that all transmitters were now being manufactured in a similar manner. In a ten-day period, radio station WFEA had all new equipment, the transmitter was on order, and I hadn't spent one additional dollar. It was a feeling of great accomplishment.

Commercialskope

Once again, I got a phone call from Bob Buchanan and Soundac. With Colorskope doing so well, and radio sales on the libraries and jingle packages being maintained, Music Maker's was doing nicely. Everyone was overjoyed. Now I was looking for a new challenge. Bob had an idea and wanted me to come down to Miami and discuss it.

I always loved going down there and having the opportunity to see Dick Ullman and his wife, as well as the crew at Soundac. I also was fascinated by Bob's apartment in Dania.

A full-size tiger skin, which he had purchased at an auction, with its menacing head looking up at you, centered his living room, with overstuffed couches and lounge chairs surrounding it. The lighting was fluorescent and could be very subdued or bright, depending on the mood.

Every piece of furniture was like a museum piece, and the art work on the wall, including Remingtons, gave forth a feeling of masculinity and power. I always thought that any girl brought to that apartment would have an impossible task protecting her honor.

His den, or enclosed porch, had been designed like the interior of a cabin cruiser, including ship controls that actually operated. The master bedroom was as close to immorality as one could get while still maintaining beauty and taste. I have been in some beautiful apartments and homes, but never a pad like this designed for a bachelor continuing to play the field. He had a fully-equipped bar with blowfish lamps above, and a kitchen with every modern appliance.

The Soundac staff was busy developing dozens of storyboards, animated openings and closings, and inserts for advertisers. The basic idea was to supply a television station with an indexed series of storyboards, and the sales personnel at the television station could then sell local advertisers a fully-tailored commercial. They could animate their logo or show their product with animation around it.

The station would be supplied with a presentation film, to go with a catalog-type folder covering all the different animated storyboards. The order form supplied would give explicit instructions on how to provide

Soundac with the requested tailoring instructions. Background music would also be included, and the client would be charged a $25 to $50 fee for the entire tailoring procedure.

Looking through the storyboards, that old feeling of excitement started bubbling out, and I could visualize the potential. Another challenge! Another product no one had ever done before! We named the service Commercialskope.

I could almost see stations taking the product away from us. Since you would only sell one station in a market, giving the standard thirty-five-mile protection, a broadcaster would have an incredible advantage in local sales. I thought we should charge the stations a license fee for three years, and allow them a maximum number of orders per year.

The $25 or $50 charged to the advertiser would defray some of the costs. Since most of the tailoring would be done in advance by Soundac, it would be a simple task to photograph logos or the client's art work. I was impressed, and I gave Bob the go-ahead.

I spent the weekend with Dick Ullman and his wife before flying back to New York. Bob had given Dick a small office in their shop, and they kept him busy. I've always believed that Dick gave them the format for Commercialskope, being such a great idea man.

Getting back to New York with some material to show Mitch and Milt, I set up a music session. One of Mitch's writers wrote the background music, which was recorded a few weeks later. I was so excited about the potential for Commercialskope that I high-spotted several markets before the product was ready for presentation. The reaction was immediate. Not even having contracts printed as yet, I signed a dozen stations with their purchase orders.

To me, there is nothing more thrilling than selling or marketing a product that is new and innovative. The challenge is so immense and, although you are not always right, when you are, there is an inner satisfaction that is indescribable.

I don't think I could ever have been successful selling reruns of television programs, or the same product over and over again. I did it for years with the radio libraries and jingle packages, working with salesmen, but it was boring. The fun of trying something new seems to pump so much more adrenalin into one's veins. The feeling of accomplishment is incredible, and I was one of the lucky ones in broadcasting to have been able to do it many, many times.

With contracts printed, brochures and presentation films in hand, Commercialskope was finally launched, with unusual results. Because markets like New York, Chicago and Los Angeles are agency cities, we did not try initially to sell them.

I was surprised when we sold the RKO group, including Boston, New York, Los Angeles, Detroit and Memphis, but soon discovered that independent stations in those markets (with the exception of Boston, which was CBS) proved very enthusiastic. Most stations we called on loved the idea, as did most of their agencies. It gave them a ready market for an animated product that was commercial, and the advertisers were thrilled with an inexpensive way of tailoring their spots. About that time, working with one of our salesmen in California, we called on Julie Kaufman, the head of XETV, a VHF in Tijuana, Mexico. For years the station had been an ABC affiliate until a UHF station in San Diego complained and was awarded the network. Julie, now an independent, made a fortune for the owners as well as for himself with a stock and percentage deal. He was diabetic and always watched his diet. Lunch hat to be on time each day. Julie had a special way about him—charming and disarming at the same time. No matter what price you quoted him, he would always offer you 25% of it, and then tell you to go out and sell other stations, knowing that the other network stations in San Diego were nigh unto impossible to deal with. I know of one sale of Phil Donahue that went to XETV for $75.00 a week—that's five hours!

Years later, they gave Julie a testimonial dinner. A local artist came up with his own interpretation of da Vinci's famous painting. "The Last Supper." In Jesus's outline there appeared Julie's face, and the caption read, "Separate checks, please."

We now had two sales staffs at Music Makers, with six men working radio only and three of us in television. I was surprised to discover that I could wear two hats, working with both radio and television. I would spend a week with Festival, "Radio Ala Carte" and jingle packages, followed the next week by television sales.

It was interesting to see that television was an instant response media, while radio was a saturation media—buying drive time and lots of spots. In retrospect, radio was more fun because your message had to react on the ear the way a newspaper headline reacts on the eye. With television, one could see the product and watch how it worked. In radio, we had to romance the listener with clever music, jingles, or good copy. I recall a limerick used on a 300,000-watt station in Mexico that blanketed the United States at night and made the man who ran the jingle quite wealthy. It was short, to the point, and still brings a smile to my face: "I don't care if it rains or freezes long as I've got my plastic Jesus riding on the dashboard of my car—one buck."

With the libraries, jingle packages, Colorskope and Commercialskope, Music Makers thrived. Mitch Leigh was in his element with *Man of La Mancha* still on Broadway and companies touring throughout the States and Europe. We even managed to keep Milt on an even keel.

My wife occasionally showed signs of coming back, and my children were pure joy. Still, though going home on a Friday night was wonderful, I just couldn't wait for Monday morning. There can't be too many people in this world crazy enough to love working as much as I did.

12.
Europe—Time-Warner and Sonny Werblin

In December of 1968, I decided to take my family to Europe for two weeks and visit my sister in Brussels. Dan, my brother-in-law, had a doctorate in chemical engineering and was on a five-year assignment for the Exxon Corporation. At the last minute, my wife refused to go, so I took my sixteen-year-old daughter and fourteen-year-old son, and flew to Europe with them.

After a few days in Brussels, where I became fascinated by the Grande Place and the *Frites* (the greatest French fries I have ever tasted), and after visiting Ghent and other areas of Belgium, we caught a train to Paris. We were on a dinner train, where the service and food were exceptional, and we had fun watching my son getting his passport ceremoniously stamped several times by the conductor.

In Paris, my brother-in-law rented a stretch Cadillac with chauffeur, and we saw the sights and had a wonderful time. Every place we stopped, we drew a crowd. Our chauffeur told us that few people saw a car that size on the streets, and people probably thought we were with General Charles de Gaulle's entourage.

Every restaurant we frequented was marvelous, including the corner bistro. We stayed in a tiny hotel off the Champs Elysee. With my sister and brother-in-law in one room, my daughter and her two cousins in a second, and my son and I in a third, we paid $22 per night for all of us, including a full breakfast.

152

We visited an ice cream parlor on the Champs Elysee, not far from the Arc de Triumphe which was built in a most unique way. It was a Renault show room, and one had to go through the display area to get to the ice cream parlor. All of the booths were automobiles with the roofs taken off. We went there to have one of the most incredible French treats—a Dans Blanche.

I was initiated into the Dans Blanche dessert while in Brussels. After a most incredible dinner, I was sipping a cognac when the chef and maitre d', hearing we were not having dessert, came from the kitchen and angrily stated we *were* having dessert. They brought out a pewter dish with the deepest yellow vanilla ice cream I have ever seen, followed by a pan filled with the darkest chocolate, boiling hot, and another pewter dish with pure whipped cream. They poured this bitter, bitter chocolate over the French vanilla ice cream, topping it with pure whipped cream. Delicious!

Flying on to London, we headed for the Dorchester Hotel in Hyde Park. I had made reservations for a suite and an extra bedroom, something my brother-in-law was a bit upset about because of the cost. As I recall, however, the entire two-bedroom suite with the additional bedroom cost only about $70 a night.

In the living room of the suite we had our own fireplace, and all one had to do was call downstairs and they would deliver additional firewood. With the cold, damp weather in London in late December, it was wonderful. We spent most of our evenings there, and occasionally in late afternoon would order tea and crumpets and hot chocolate for the children.

London is a fascinating city with Westminster Abbey, the Tower of London, Harrod's department store, the British Museum, a restaurant with fish and chips across the street, and a delightful English pub, a tiny bar along the Thames River in constant operation since the seventeenth century.

I remember a poignant moment. One evening, my fourteen-year-old son, Danny, put his arms around me, gave me a hug and a kiss, and said, "Dad, this is the greatest vacation I have ever had because you and I get a chance to have a man-to-man talk every night."

I even took them one night to the Playboy Club, which had open gambling at the time. The children were allowed in as long as they stayed away from the tables. My son watched me make $300 at the crap table in about five minutes, and I had to go back the next night to lose it because that evening he told me that he was going into gambling because it was so easy to make money. We flew back home to Short Hills, New Jersey, just before New Year's, after two delightful weeks.

The following year was a tough one. Our expenses continued to climb and, although our sales were good, being a public company put a great deal of stress on all of us.

Colorskope was no longer being sold in volume, but the Commercialskope package, as well as our jingles and libraries, were doing well. Music Makers continued to buy or build motion picture theaters with multiple screens, and having purchased a small music library to add to what Mitch had already put into our own, was doing fairly well.

The dubbing division was having a rough time because the American television viewer, as well as the television stations, frowned upon them, although the ABC network, at one time, bought every "spaghetti western" made. Most foreign films were not doing well. Still, it was a wonderful time for Music Makers and our other divisions, and my only worry was trying to maintain the gross volume in sales for the Mark Century Division.

In late spring of 1970, I started feeling physically run down. I was tired all the time and lost my appetite, but the doctors could find nothing wrong. They finally suggested I get away for a vacation, and I decided to go to Europe again. My wife would have no part of it and we were continuing to have marital problems. She just wanted to stay at home, be alone and not be bothered."

I flew to Brussels with my golf clubs, spending a week with my sister and brother-in-law. "Sis" is my twin, five minutes younger than I, and we have been very close through the years. And Dan was as close as any brother I could have had.

Through Exxon, Dan belonged to one of the "King's" golf courses. When we hit an iron off the fairway, a little girl would run from behind us with a salt shaker and re-seed the divot. I had a wonderful week with them, then flew on to London, still feeling very much under the weather. I wasn't eating, nor was I sleeping well. After a week of forcing myself to do many things that I loved, I flew home and again visited my doctor, who still found nothing wrong.

Early in August, on a trip to Los Angeles, I felt so lousy that I went to a drugstore and bought a thermometer, feeling that perhaps I had a fever and was coming down with something. When my temperature read 103°, I called the house physician at the hotel and saw him that afternoon. After examining me, he gave me several prescriptions

154

for antibiotics, telling me there was a bug going through southern California and I should spend the weekend in the hotel room. If I wasn't feeling better, or my temperature wasn't normal by Monday morning, I was to call him. Early that Monday morning, still having a 103° fever, I took a cab to his office.

When I arrived, I climbed a long stairway to the second floor and, upon arrival at his office, discovered I was soaking wet. My temperature was now normal, something neither of us could figure out. He suggested I catch an early plane home to see my doctor and, as a precaution, gave me a shot of gamma globulin. I managed to keep two important appointments that afternoon then caught the red-eye back to New York that evening, feeling miserable, still with no idea of what was wrong with me.

Two days after my return, after more blood tests, I finally had my answer. I had contracted infectious hepatitis. I was given the choice of being bedridden in the hospital or staying home completely off my feet for what turned out to be over three months. I was told how serious a liver involvement could be, and that bed rest with no physical activity was the only cure. No drugs would work; I could take aspirin and nothing else.

I had a very important meeting with the ABC network station managers, and I begged the doctor to allow me to keep that one appointment. He said that if I had a limousine pick me up at home, drive me to New York and bring me back after the meeting, I could fulfill the date, but that was the only way he would allow it. After that—bed rest.

I kept the meeting and, upon its completion, got back into the car totally drained with exhaustion. For the first time in my life, the realization hit me that I, too, was not immune to illness. Like it or not, I was grounded for a long period of time.

Hepatitis is one of the most debilitating infections one can endure. I was not even allowed to get dressed. I lay around, either in bed or on the couch, for weeks, but I kept in touch with the office by telephone on a daily basis. Even that proved a drain on my strength. For weeks, I was trapped until such time as my temperature got back to normal. I would take my temperature first thing in the morning, at 10:00, at noon, and at 2:00 p.m., and find it normal. But from 4:00 p.m. on, it would go up.

During this time, Warner Communications showed a great interest in our company's merging with them, and it was an exciting possibility. The senior vice president came out to see me, and we spent a couple hours together discussing a possible merger. Looking back, it could have been a dream come true, but Milt killed the deal, and I have always felt he was afraid of losing his place of importance at Music Makers. Not too long after, a second exciting proposal was offered us.

Sonny Werblin, who built Madison Square Garden and the Meadowlands Sports Complex, came to us with an incredible offer. He had recently taken over Johnny Carson's interests, and Carson was in very poor financial straits. His idea was to take over Music Makers and, with a large tax loss carryover, bring the Carson interests into a merger. We lost that deal as well. Looking back, it still bothers me, but Mitch thought Milt was his genius, and there was little any of us could do about it.

The End of an Era

In late December, just before Christmas, the doctor said I could start going back to work, I had to do it slowly. I could work four hours a day, but it took almost three hours a day to commute. That meant I was allowed one hour a day in the office. The thrill of getting out of prison was delicious, and I found a way to save thirty minutes of commuting time, giving me an hour and a half in the office.

My return was greeted with fanfare and a beautiful gold watch from Milt and Mitch, but something within me was missing. The drive was gone. Anticipation of daily battles with stations or salesmen didn't seem very important anymore. I would learn that an illness such as I had recently experienced would take a lot longer than a few months to get over completely.

By the end of January, I was back working full time. I was even allowed to travel, but there was so much going on at Music Makers that I needed to attend to.

I had gone to a stockholders' meeting and listened to Mitch state how he had signed a multimillion dollar deal with United Artists for the film rights to *Man of La Mancha*, and that money would all go to the stockholders. I learned how the different divisions were doing financially, and was told that Mark Century was losing money. There were suggestions such as cut the sales force and cut travel expenses, telephone costs, etc.

I would check my monthly statements and, although our total sales *were* down, not substantially, the strange thing was that I really didn't seem to care anymore. Why that spark was gone, and why I felt the way I did, continued to bother me, but I didn't know how to get out of the doldrums and, for the next couple of months, I took everything in stride and (although half-heartedly) continued to do my job as well as possible.

Early in April, having received the Mark Century statement, I asked our accountant and comptroller for the full Music Maker statement. I was told it was none of my business, and he was under orders not to produce it. Being president of a division and vice president of the publicly-held corporation, however, it was not too difficult to procure the material. When I saw it, I really got angry.

I had been told that Mark Century was losing money, while the Music Maker statement showed that Mark Century's payroll included all of the other companies. In other words, my payroll was paying for the music library, the theater dubbing company, even Music Makers.

The following morning, I walked into Mitch's office and blew my stack. I don't think I'll ever forget his response. He looked at me with a smile on his face and said, "Marv, that's a cop-out." The next morning, I handed him my resignation as president of Mark Century and vice president of Music Makers. Mitch and Milt had control, and there was damn little I could do about it. I didn't like some of the things that were going on, and having discussed it with my attorney he suggested I resign from the board and get out.

One thing I had forgotten when I handed in my resignation was that I was under a five-year contractual agreement, which still had twenty-six months to run. I was able to work out a deal with them whereby they would pay me half salary for the duration of the contract and I, in turn, would act as a consultant at $150 per day plus expenses. As part of the deal, I would sell Mitch my stock in Music Makers at two-thirds of its market value, something that angered me no end. Also, I was not allowed to go into the radio industry in syndication, or any other way, during that twenty-six month period.

During these conversations, I discovered that Mitch and Milt had decided to go private. They further decided to take those millions from United Artists for the *Man of La Mancha* and not sign the contract until after the Securities Exchange Commission okayed their going off the market.

Having been apprised of this, I realized that I could instigate a class action suit against them. I knew enough about some of the things they had done to cause a lot of problems. I also discovered the legal fees would probably cost me $200,000, and, even if I won, I would get nothing but satisfaction. It was an awfully tough time having to eat crow with two men like them. Mitch might be a fine businessman, and Milt a good attorney, but their greed showed their true characters. Neither was very honest.

I reluctantly accepted their terms, and told Mitch privately to watch Milt Herson, his "genius". I said he wasn't very honorable and was milking him out of a lot of money.

Nineteen years later, I received a call from Barbara, my former secretary, saying, "You remember how you told Mitch that Milt wasn't honest and he was stealing from him? Well, Mitch asked me to call you. He would like to see you and wants to know when you will be in New York." I told Barbara that I wouldn't make any special trip to New York, but I would be happy to stop in and see him when I was there. An hour later, Mitch called me himself, and when I did finally get to New York, I went up to see him.

I was greeted with a bear hug and an apology. Yes, nineteen years later, I was right—he had finally caught Milt and wanted to know about some of the deals that had gone on so many years earlier.

I haven't the slightest idea how Mitch resolved matters with Milt Herson, but I can't help smiling at the fact that Milt later worked with the federal government in Washington, and his son, Mike, ran for Congress from New Jersey (he lost).

Union Fidelity

Being smart enough to keep my mouth shut and swallow hard, I left Music Makers on good terms, knowing there would be a time in the not too distant future when I would have an opportunity to more than make up for the many thousands of dollars I was deprived of in the settlement. Since I was still on half salary and to be paid a consultancy fee, I had the use of Music Maker's offices and a secretary, when required.

My marriage, unfortunately, was pretty well over, but with a daughter in her first year of college and a son still in high school, I made the best of it. It was a tough time, and I was still not 100% recovered from my illness.

For several years I had been very friendly with a man in the insurance business in Philadelphia. He was married to a first cousin of my wife, and for years had offered me an opportunity to join his company. A few weeks after I left Music Makers, I drove down to have lunch with him. I did not want to join him full time, but he asked if I would consult for him on the broadcasting industry. He would pay my full expenses plus a guaranteed $30,000, giving me an interesting challenge with lots of free time to pursue other ventures.

Harry Dozor was a tall, handsome man, well-built, always watching his diet. He had a charming personality, was well educated, with a law degree, and owned his own insurance agency. Using his law background, he would personally draw up his own corporations, and had done exceedingly well in the insurance business.

Philadelphia has many large insurance companies located in suburban and downtown areas. Harry had formed a company known as Union Fidelity with his own health insurance plan. The largest company in the country, National Liberty, was located first in Philadelphia, then moved to the Valley Forge area. Harry, at every opportunity, tried copying their advertising style. After all, his company was the second largest I knew of at the time.

For some reason, the early weeks in January and July gave insurance companies their biggest results from advertising, and they would buy one page, or double truck ads, in all the major newspapers in the country. Most ads started out with "$600 tax free when you're in the hospital". Later, they went as high as "$1,000 tax free when you're in the hospital". This advertising brought in large volumes of mail. Kits and applications were sent to those who responded. These companies had rarely, if ever, used broadcasting, since the newspapers were proving such a bonanza for them.

All insurance companies have actuary tables to guarantee more than just a healthy return. For everyone who collects, there have to be a lot of people who never, during the life of their policies, have occasion to use them. At the time, hospital costs were, naturally, lower because inflation had not yet reared its ugly head. Still, insurance companies knew that the average stay in the hospital was three days. $600 a month, even in a thirty-day month, would only cost them $60, and the premium was $95 to $110 annually. Another consideration was that if one took out the policy and thirty days later had a heart attack, did the insurance company have the right to deny payment because it was "a pre-existing condition"?

I quickly learned that these companies spend a lot of money on attorneys in the states where the insurance examiners had thrown them out of to get re-instatement. I was learning about the health insurance industry in the very early seventies.

Harry had a beautiful wife and three lovely children and lived in one of the more exclusive suburbs of Germantown. The area around Philadelphia is one of the most beautiful in the country with rolling hills and stone homes and farms that predate the Revolution.

Harry's home was magnificent, with swimming pool and a charming, warm interior. He was a loving father and husband, and a great philanthropist. He had pictures of famous people, like Golda Meier of Israel, in his study framed with letters thanking him for his contributions.

My first few days in his office in downtown Philadelphia were a learning process. Harry had done some radio advertising in major markets to back up his newspaper ads, and I became familiar with the markets and stations he was involved in. I enjoyed it, and since it was only ninety-three miles from my home in Short Hills, I would commute using the Jersey Turnpike, or stay in a hotel for a few days to break up the 6:00 a.m. to 9:00 p.m. days.

My first inclination that something was very, very wrong occurred on the elevator one morning. It was packed with people talking about "that SOB". I discovered they were talking about their boss, and quietly started asking questions the next few days in the different departments.

Harry Dozor was a Jekyll and Hyde. Including his executive staff, he had a turnover of more than 90% annually. He had a temper that could be heard on the floor above.

His reputation with the newspapers was such that they would not accept his advertisements unless he paid in advance. If he found a "t" that wasn't crossed, an "i" not dotted, or one misspelled word, he would demand a free rerun. It soon became apparent that he was a tyrant at the office. No one could please him. He offered large salaries to top executives of other companies, and would fire them unceremoniously, sometimes in a matter of weeks.

I had lunch with him one day and he stated that he wanted to try a large radio campaign. I suggested that I could get some national talent, rewrite his commercials for radio, record them, and plan a regional campaign. I also stated I could save a lot of money in the purchase of time by working with one of the barter agencies in New York.

Where I made my big mistake was in not suggesting a test in two or three markets before going "whole hog". Harry jumped at the idea, and the following day I went up to New York and sat down with the heads of Atwood Richards, the largest barter agency in New York at the time. Knowing everyone and having done business with them for

160

years, I was able to pick up more than $120,000 in advertising in the top major markets for an out-of-pocket cost of $26,000.

Harry was thrilled, and I proceeded to go gung ho, producing the spots and duplicating them for shipment to the stations we were contracting for. Using a well-known network talent, I produced what I felt was a strong commercial. I was thrilled with the finished product. Atwood Richards placed the time for us, and we awaited the rush of mail responses.

Although we did get some response, the radio campaign was a miserable flop, and I was in the doghouse with Harry. I fully expected him to throw me out, and when it didn't happen I was quite surprised. I should have done a test and not rashly spent $26,000 of his money, and I really felt badly about it. I know that he had had some success with radio when tieing in with his newspapers ad campaigns, but I should have moved much more slowly than I did.

A few days after realizing that we had not been successful, Harry came into my office and left a huge pile of invoices. As he was walking out, he said, "Settle these bills at no more than fifty cents on the dollar." When I went through the bills, I discovered that most of them were six months to a year delinquent for money owed to stations. These people for years had bought my products, and some were close personal friends. They were about to be shafted, and I got angry.

I fully understood the $26,000 outlay with such poor results was a mistake on my part, but in no way would I use my name to settle his overdue bills. In any business dealings I have ever made, I expected to fully pay my bills and, by the same token, I expect others to pay me in full on any contractual agreement.

I walked into Harry's office, handed him the invoices and told him how I felt. I was sorry that the test did not work out, and perhaps it would be better for both of us if I left his employ. Surprisingly, he nodded assent, we shook hands, and I left.

Ten days later, I received a call from the president of Atwood Richards telling me he had received a letter from Harry Dozor claiming that I had taken money under the table in making the purchase of time from the agency and he was refusing to pay the bill. When I asked what they intended to do about it, I was told they were immediately instituting a lawsuit. I requested that since they were suing, I wanted to be included, charging defamation of character.

An attorney's letter went out to Union Fidelity Insurance Co. announcing the lawsuit and including me as part of it. The bill was paid in full within a few days. I have not seen nor heard from Harry Dozor since.

Although a little knowledge can be a dangerous thing my months with Union Fidelity proved an interesting adventure. Meeting and working with people in a completely different kind of business made me come to the realization of just how exciting and fascinating the broadcasting industry had become. Although I did continue doing home consultancy work for music makers, they weren't about to use me too often at $150.00 a day plus expenses. Strange how, for the first time in my life, I would see an airplane in the sky above and wish, no matter where it was going, somehow I would be on it.

13.
M. A. Kempner, Inc.: A New Challenge

Early in July of 1971, on a Friday evening, I received a phone call from Ed Kavinoky, our attorney and stockholder from the old Ullman Company days. He was in New York and wanted to know if I would come into the city Saturday morning and have breakfast with him.

I met him at his hotel about 9:00, and we proceeded to the coffee shop. We discussed the old Ullman days, what I had been doing since, and small talked about the many people we both knew. It was a very pleasant meeting, and one that changed my life.

Ed asked me what my plans were. I told him how unhappy I had been the last several months at Music Makers, and that I was thinking of forming my own company, finding or producing one or two products for television since I could not go back into the radio industry for several more months.

Ed looked at me and with a small smile on his face remarked how he had known me for many years, had always made money in any endeavors he was involved in with me, and that he would like to have a piece of the company I planned on forming. He said, "I want you to have complete control, and I will take a minority interest." I could almost feel tears welling up in my eyes. I told him there was no one that I would rather go into a new venture with, and how pleased and thrilled I was to think that he had that much confidence in me.

Ed then did something that has never happened in my lifetime, before or since. He took a blank check out of his wallet, signed it, and told me when the corporation was set up to fill out any amount that was needed, but to make sure to call his secretary in Buffalo so she could cover it in his account.

He then suggested that I call his law firm and have them set up the corporation in his absence. When I asked him where he was going, he said, "I am making a six-week tour of Europe and Yugoslavia. By the time I return, the company should be formed." We walked back into the hotel lobby, and he put his arms around me and said, "Good luck, Marv—I'll see you in six weeks."

Early on Monday morning, I called his office and made an appointment with one of the attorneys to set up the new corporation. I had decided, since I was well known in the industry, to take advantage of my name, calling the company M. A. Kempner, Inc.

I walked around with Ed's blank check in my wallet for six weeks, vowing that I wasn't about to just fill in any amount of money. When Ed returned from Europe, I flew to Buffalo to discuss how we would proceed. I returned his check with warm thanks, and as we were discussing some details we were interrupted by a phone call.

I didn't pay any attention until I heard Ed remark, "I have an old friend of ours in the office who I was helping set up a new corporation in which I'll have a small minority stock interest." When he mentioned my name, Ed laughed and said, "Here, you talk to him."

I picked up the phone, and Dick Ullman from Ft. Lauderdale was on the line saying, "Marv, can I have a small piece, too?" With all his faults, Dick was one of the most honorable men I have ever known. He was also a great idea man, and as long as I had full control things would go well.

I stayed in Buffalo a couple of days waiting for Dick to come up from Florida so the three of us could formulate plans and decide how we might get started. It was a fun reunion, and nice to be working again with honest people who you could trust in every way. I knew it was going to be a fairly long period of time before I would have enough product to start hiring any personnel. I didn't need a great deal of cash and, since Dick and Ed wouldn't be drawing any salaries, I started up with about a $15,000 treasure chest.

In my home in Short Hills, I had a completely furnished basement and had built myself an office in one section of a paneled playroom. My idea was to find small office quarters in Ft. Lauderdale where, once things started to roll, we would have an office for mail, telephone, shipping materials, etc. I would hire a part-time secretary in New Jersey who could come in on Saturday mornings to take my dictation and do any paperwork, contracts, etc., that had to be done.

With my leaving Music Makers, the television division had collapsed. I was able to take over Soundac's Commercialskope. When Bob Buchanan at Soundac requested return of his products, it helped me get my first salable material for the new company. Milt and Mitch were confident that there was little to lose if they gave back Colorskope and Commercialskope, but there still was plenty of life in Commercialskope, and I knew it. All contracts written at Music Makers would remain theirs, while I could take the product for the new company. We had done a hell of a selling job at Music Makers, but there was still a lot more that could be done.

Music Makers was now off the market as a publicly-held company. They had a couple of class action suits against them, and were retrenching, staying heavily in motion picture theater acquisitions and the music library. Milt decided to cut way back on monthly releases of the Mark Century product, going so far as re-releasing five-year-old materials. They put less and less into the product, cut way back on the sales force, and it was just a matter of time, with little or no direction, that Mark Century would be closed down.

I found a former executive secretary, who was married with two children, who was delighted to work with me on an hourly basis. She would come in at 8:00 on a Saturday morning, working with me until 1:00. She would take the dictation home and return it for my signature.

Dick Ullman went back to Ft. Lauderdale and found a one-room office just off Las Olas Boulevard across the street from the Governor's Club Hotel, at a rental of $30 a month. He opened a bank account in Ft. Lauderdale and ordered stationery and printed contracts.

Shortly after Labor Day, I hopped in my car and headed for Pittsburgh. The steel city, having totally rebuilt the business area around the river front, was one of my favorites, except for the 50,000-watt Westinghouse station where, I guess, God lived. One could get in to see any management easily, except at Westinghouse. I always hated that station. One could seldom get an appointment with someone who could make a decision, and management always had a chip on their shoulder. Although I spent several days in Pittsburgh, I did not make my first sale under the new company.

It took me three weeks to finally strike gold, and it happened in Boston where my first $25,000 contract was signed. Although I had been in the city dozens of times, I had never had the occasion to visit

Harvard University. I made a hotel reservation at the Sheraton in Harvard Square and, suddenly, realized what an incredible institution it is. Harvard takes one back to colonial days with its early architecture. In the early evening, just sitting on a bench in the square and seeing students of every color and race was an education in itself.

That first sale, made to the CBS affiliate in Boston, kind of took the pressure off. From there on, life became simpler in that the next dozen sales started a monthly income.

I found a little motel five or six blocks from our office in Ft. Lauderdale, and spent a week with Dick. Off season I could get the full week for just $75, but beginning the 15th of December it went up to $75 a day, so I made arrangements to stay at the Governor's Club Hotel.

It was old and falling apart, having been built some time in the early twenties, but it had a singular charm about it and a restaurant that was fabulous. In talking with the manager, I was always guaranteed a room for a week, a month, or more if necessary, at almost the price of the motel. The only drawback was that the motel had its own kitchen, living room and bedroom—much more enjoyable than four walls and a ceiling.

I had always known the first year in business to be the toughest, but with no new product I found the second year of MAK the most trying. It was tough being on the road almost every week, but I wasn't traveling by car anymore. The company could pay my expenses, and there was more than enough left over for a part time secretary for Dick in Florida. Somehow we managed, had money in the bank, added to our contracts (although very slowly at times), and kept our heads above water.

Dick Ullman was a great tennis enthusiast, and loved playing at the public courts in Ft. Lauderdale where he befriended Jimmy Evert, Chrissy's father. Chrissy, at the time, was in her early teens and just beginning her run of fame and fortune. One of Dick's ideas was to see whether he could find a way to handle Chrissy, but Jimmy, the wise father that he was, had other plans.

One day, Dick asked me to watch Channel 4, the CBS affiliate in Miami. He said they had a very attractive gal, Jane Chastain, as a sportscaster, and wouldn't it be a great idea if we could build a half-hour television show with a woman sportscaster. The idea was very appealing, and he made a date with Jane to have dinner one evening.

Jane was a beautiful girl about 5'2", blonde, with an beautiful figure, wonderful, warm personality and a lot of charm. Her husband,

Roger, was an automotive design engineer who gave up a very promising musical career because of his love for engineering. In his earlier years, he had his own band. He had a beautiful singing voice and played a very mean guitar.

Jane had been brought up in North Carolina where she worked for television station WRAL in Raleigh. They gave her a crack at sports, and called her their "Girl Friday". She would be brought in by the sports announcer during the 11:00 p.m. newscast on Fridays, and give her picks each week for the big Saturday college football games, as well as Sunday's NFL. She was more accurate and had a higher percentage of winners than anyone else.

At the time, one of the news commentators at WRAL was Jesse Helms, who went on to the U.S. Senate and continues to drive everyone crazy with his conservative ways. Still, he happens to be a very fine gentleman.

Jane went on from Raleigh to Atlanta, where the CBS affiliate hired her. She continued to successfully call more winners than the experts, and her "Girl Friday" was well-received in Atlanta. After marrying Roger, Jane moved to Miami and was soon a fixture on the 11:00 p.m. news on WTVJ doing the daily sports commentaries.

We decided to go to NATPE (National Association of Television Programming Executives) with storyboards to see what interest, if any, we could get for a half hour, or even a fifteen-minute television show, using Jane Chastain. In those early days of NATPE, we all had individual suites at the hotel and flagged down those we knew (as well as others) in the attempt to see what reaction we might get prior to going into production. There were a few interesting comments, but nothing earth-shaking, and the cost of doing a pilot didn't seem worthwhile.

The Jane Chastain Show

A few weeks later, while in Ft. Lauderdale, Jane and her husband invited me to their home for the evening where I met Paul Nagle and his wife, Marge. Paul was a professor at the University of Miami in the Communications Department. He was of average height, balding, with a most unusual talent. He taught writing for television, radio and motion pictures, and he was also an accomplished actor. For years, whenever Paul Newman made a movie in southern Florida Paul Nagle was always called upon for acting roles. He wrote and appeared in dozens of commercials, did a great deal of work in local theater, and was unmatched in talent.

167

Years later, he was honored in Los Angeles because his students not only were successful in writing for the motion picture studios and networks, but some ended up as president of major film studios. Paul was a legend in his teaching. He had an incredible, dry sense of humor, and I took to him immediately.

Marge was a commercial artist, and she did many brochures for Las Vegas hotels and other national, advertisers. She was a very attractive gal and full of fun, with a great sense of humor that had one laughing all the time.

Sitting on the floor while Roger sang and played the guitar proved to be a most enjoyable evening. We got to talking about a show for Jane, and Paul came up with an idea that seemed to gel in my mind instantly. Paul had written the short five-minute radio show for several months for Jane, and had an idea to do an insert for sports that could be produced fairly inexpensively, a format idea that had never been done. We all decided to follow up quickly, do some research and see whether or not it was feasible.

After a couple more meetings, we made the decision to build a pilot of three programs that would run approximately eighty-seconds in length, allowing for a ten-second commercial tag that could easily be placed in the sports portion of a television newscast.

Paul and Marge had come up with a delightful title, "Everything you always wanted to know about sports but were afraid to ask". It was getting exciting and, although no one knew of its potential, we all thought it was worth pursuing and producing the three shows.

I took the idea to two production companies, one in North Miami and the other in Ft. Lauderdale, to get some idea of costs. One company was ridiculously overpriced, while the other, Tel-Air Productions, headed up by Grant Gravitt, looked very promising.

At a meeting with Jane, Paul and Marge, Grant, Dick and myself, we worked out a plan of action. Tel-Air would produce the three pilots, and Paul would write and direct. Although the idea was great, we couldn't judge whether we had a successful program or not, and I wanted to defray as much of the cost as possible.

Marge, with Grant Gravitt's staff, would work out a studio set and locations in the field (basketball court, baseball diamond, football stadium, etc.), and we would pay only the actual out-of-pocket cost to Tel-Air. Paul and Jane would donate their time at no cost, but if we went ahead in production they would be paid scale, including the initial three shows.

168

We discussed residual payments, and I suggested if the show was a hit that I would rather give them a piece of the action, a percentage, feeling that, if successful, they would make much more money that way. It was a gamble, but it was fair to everyone involved.

Grant Gravitt and Tel-Air would be paid their actual cost of production plus 10%, and would end up with a percentage of all profits. Paul would be paid full scale for writing, as would Jane for starring, and both would receive a percentage of profits. Everyone felt it was a good gamble. With the exception of Paul, agreements were formulated with Ed Kavinoky's law firm doing the necessary paper work. Paul wanted his own attorney, who at the time was president of the Southeastern Screen Actors Guild, to write his agreement. I proceeded to have meetings with Mel Karl, who was very fair. He made certain that every "i" was dotted and "t" crossed before his contract for Paul was signed.

Through the years, Paul and Marge have become very close personal friends. Every product we produced since has included Paul's writing and Marge doing our brochures and advertising layouts. The next product we produced, Mel Karl wanted another contract, but it never happened. When I make a promise, it is kept, and all my subsequent dealings with Paul and Marge have literally been on a handshake, with trust on both our sides.

While production problems were being worked out and Paul was writing, I hired my first salesman, Herb Berman, who had been with me from the Ullman days to Mark Century and Music Makers. It was good finally having someone out there and I wanted to be around the shoot in Florida.

The decision was made to do 195 eighty-second programs. When doing an insert to be placed in a sports segment of the news, or any other portion of a station's schedule, one had to be very careful in deciding on a studio set because some stations have elaborate newsrooms, while others use only a background and a desk. We wanted to be certain that the viewers felt that Jane was part of the local station's staff. Because we planned to do about 25% of our shows indoors at the studio, it was necessary to build a very simple living room with couch, easy chairs, coffee table and lamp, something that would fit into any television station without being too elaborate. It proved to work well for us. In later months, stations would receive phone calls from viewers asking to talk to Jane, thinking she was a member of the staff.

Because Jane was our star, we needed glossy photographs, all types of newspaper mats for advertising purposes, filmed promotional spots, everything possible, in short, to give our stations a way to promote a special feature.

Our first shows included explaining the "pick" in basketball. We could show it on the court, as well as in a supermarket using food baskets. For baseball, we did a sacrifice play, with as much tongue-in-cheek humor as we felt it would bear. We did not want to be cutesy but Jane, with her outstanding charm and personality, whether she acted as a referee in a football game or as a coach at the bulletin board with X's and O's, worked surprisingly well.

Our schedule included everything from soccer and swimming to horse racing. We even made plans to fly the crew to Athens, Greece, to do half a dozen shows from the very earliest site of the Olympics.

It took us about three weeks to complete production of our pilot shows. We decided to do the series on 16mm film rather than 35mm because of costs. Most stations had both 16 and 35mm equipment. We did not have a choice in the early 70's, since tape, as we know it, was not available.

Paul did a brilliant job of directing the pilot shows, and all of us had a hand in doing something on location or in the studio to keep our costs down. The more I saw of what we were attempting to do, the more I was sure we had a real winner.

While shooting, we took dozens of still photographs of Jane, of baseball, basketball and football teams, as well as studio shots surrounding Jane with all types of sports paraphernalia. Marge gave us our first brochure, leaving a blank segment for us to print a list of stations and markets as sales were made. (As I said before, broadcasters are like sheep. It's a follow the leader game. The object was to get those leaders. Once they have purchased it, a flood of followers completes the cycle.)

With three sets of 16mm presentations of our pilot, I headed to New York with that uneasy feeling one always gets with a new product. Was I right, or had I let my imagination take over? There is always a time when one can't help but have doubts about his decision. And yet I had to be right.

Everything You've Always Wanted to Know About Sports But Were Afraid To Ask

In the early 70's, there were only the three major networks: NBC, CBS and ABC. The Federal Communications Commission did not allow anyone to own more than five VHF stations and two UHF

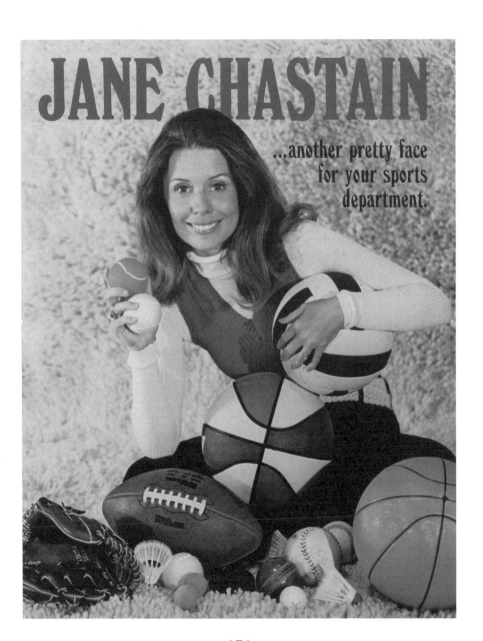

JANE CHASTAIN

...another pretty face for your sports department.

facilities, which I always thought was a good thing. No one group could control the air waves, and it gave syndicators and program producers many more avenues for sales. UHF at the time was of little interest to the big three, and we didn't think of them in O&O terms.

One of the things I learned quickly in the syndication of programming was that if you were fortunate enough to sell one of the network's owned and operated groups, that literally meant 25% of my costs, and once I had an O&O sale, it made it that much easier to sell other affiliate stations of that network.

At the time, NBC owned New York, Chicago, Los Angeles, Cleveland and Washington. CBS owned New York, Chicago, Los Angeles, St. Louis and Philadelphia. And ABC owned New York, Chicago, Los Angeles, Detroit and San Francisco. A sale to any one of those three would more than start the ball rolling, and I wanted to try the easy way—getting an O&O buy.

Dick Ullman's son, who had been with us earlier under the Ullman banner, was living and working in New York and asked to see the presentation. I flew into New York on Sunday night and met Dick, Jr. a friend of his, Bud Greenspan, who had been very successful producing specials on the Olympics and Olympic athletes. According to Dick, Jr., Bud was considered to be an expert.

We had a few drinks and I put the presentation film on Dick Jr's 16mm projector. This was my first pitch and since I supposedly had an expert in sports production, it was a good way to get my feet wet, as well as get an initial response to the program idea.

Including an opening presentation, three programs and a close, the Jane Chastain pilot took about fourteen minutes, and I was truly pleased with the way it flowed.

Bud looked at me with a smirk on his face and told me it was probably the worst thing he had ever seen. Egged on by him, Dick Jr. agreed. They both felt it was unsellable and we were wasting our time. Although I was very angry, I kept my mouth shut.

As I headed for the hotel later that night, I couldn't help but remember Edwin Newman of NBC and his initial response when reviewing *Man of La Mancha*. Still, it placed several doubts in my mind and gave me a very uneasy feeling.

My first presentation Monday morning was to the vice president and head of advertising for Schaefer, a regional brewery. Not knowing what to expect, I pitched the Jane Chastain show quite vehemently and, being ushered into a small screening room, handed my film to the projectionist and sat down.

After the opening and the first program, the vice president jumped up and told the projectionist to stop the film. My heart was in my mouth. I thought our show had bombed and that was all he was going to watch.

Instead, he brought in ten or twelve more people. We started the film again, went through it in its entirety and when finished, I was escorted back to his office. He looked at me and said, "I want the top twenty markets on the east coast, and I will pay 20% above the station's rate card if they will add 'The Jane Chastain Show brought to you by Schaefer Beer.' "

Going back down in the elevator, I admit to having tears in my eyes, knowing full well this show was going to be a winner. In the early 70's, they wouldn't give you an opening line for a client in their sportscast, but it was one hell of an entree in getting to see the right people at the major market stations.

I had made an appointment date with programming at WNBC in New York, and I got a wonderful response from them. They wanted pricing for all the O&O stations, as well as a combination buy (which meant discounts. One always had to be prepared by quoting a 20 to 25% higher rate than you expected to get so that you had room to negotiate.)

I did not go to CBS in New York. For years, many syndication people would bypass them entirely, or see them only as a last resort. Under Jim Aubrey and others, the network had treated so many of us as beneath them that it was almost a waste of time. Better to hit them in Chicago first, and let Chicago open the doors for me. Their offices on Sixth Avenue were windowless, of black stone finish "fondly" known as the "Black Rock"—a perfect name for CBS at that time. Navy blue or gray flannel was the suit of the day when you called on them and, for many reasons, one never felt quite comfortable nor welcome.

I recall making an appointment with Oscar Katz, East Coast Vice President in charge of programming, on a show idea. As I was ushered into his offices, he jumped from his chair, shook my hand and, before even knowing what I had, told me he had no budget and I was wasting my time. It took a few more years before CBS was brought to its knees, with ABC taking over the #1 position in ratings.

I went to the ABC network, made my presentation, and then left for Albany to meet my salesman, Herb Berman, where we sold the ABC affiliate. I gave Herb his first presentation tape and went back to New

York where, once again, I sat down with the NBC people and Roger Lefkon, who headed up programming. I went back to Florida with the feeling that we were on our way, but knowing also that it was going to take a lot longer than I had anticipated before giving everyone the okay to go into full production.

Selling an O&O can take time. They are not in much of a hurry to give a decision, even when they realize the competitive networks are also interested. I must have called Roger twice a week for the next three weeks trying to get an answer, and stayed in and around New York waiting for his decision.

I drove down to Philadelphia and called on the CBS O&O, WCAU, and, surprisingly, management flipped. When I quoted a thousand dollars a program for 195 shows, they thought I was out of my mind and came back with an offer of $500. We compromised and ended up with $600 a show for 195 shows—a tremendous price for that market.

With CBS in Philadelphia in my pocket, I flew out to Chicago to see Bob Wussler who was vice president and general manager of WBBM. Bob went on to become president of CBS sports, followed by president of the network, and was one of the most brilliant NFL football producers of his time. I have always felt it was his first love. He was pure genius in a studio working the different cameras on the field.

Bob was tall, a little bit on the portly side, and not too easy to like. Perhaps because he had so much confidence in himself, he permeated authority. He had an ego that made you feel he thought he was better than you or anyone else. He proved to be a very bright man, but he was not always honest with people.

Bob asked for an option for the CBS O&O's, which I refused, offering a first refusal instead. He suggested I get back to him in a few days.

In calling the office in Ft. Lauderdale late that same afternoon, Dick asked me to call Jane Chastain. It seems the moment I had left Wussler's office, he had called Jane and tried to hire her for WBBM in Chicago.

Since I was still consulting for Music Makers and had use of their office and secretary, I spent a great deal of time there while trying to get an answer from NBC. One loses patience being told day after day "call me tomorrow", and it is tough keeping one's cool. It took six weeks before Roger finally said, "Come on in and let's make a deal." We sacrificed some money and brought our rate down, and contracts were signed with NBC-owned aand operated stations in New York, Chicago, Los Angeles, Cleveland and Washington. We were on our way.

A few days later, Herb Berman called me from Pittsburgh and told me he had made a presentation to WIIC, the Cox station there, and it was suggested that someone get in to see the head of programming for the broadcasting group. I flew into Atlanta to see Mike Kievman, head of programming at the home offices of Cox, which were located at WSB. Mike and I hit if off immediately and he proved through the years to be one of the great leaders I have known in broadcasting.

If he liked something, you knew it immediately. If he didn't, you were on your way just as quickly, but he always gave you the time to make a full presentation. He was a handsome and very charming man, having been one of the original salesmen for Fred Ziv, the "father" of syndication. Mike asked me to quote a price for the Jane Chastain show in San Francisco, Atlanta, Pittsburgh, Dayton and Charlotte, and when I did, he came back with a counter offer that was more than fair.

Years later, Mike, who was a severe diabetic, had a leg amputated. Not too long after, he lost his second leg. I was contacted by Cox, which wanted to throw Mike a surprise sixtieth birthday party. It cost each of us $300 plus air fare, with a cash bar at the hotel, all proceeds going to the Diabetes Foundation. When they wheeled Mike in, the surprise was so complete he broke down. The great moment that evening was when, for the first time on two artificial limbs, he stepped out of his wheelchair and walked. We lost a great broadcaster several months later.

The Cox sale, coupled with sales to NBC, Buffalo, Rochester, Boston, Minneapolis, Philadelphia, and ten or twelve more, most of them major markets, was more than enough to authorize a go-ahead in production. We would produce 195 shows, enough for a Monday through Friday insert in newscasts for nine months, with three months of reruns.

I had estimated the cost of production at $581,000, and had to find a way to finance it. I met Dick and Ed Kavinoky in Buffalo, and it was decided to use a factoring company in Indianapolis. When borrowing money from a bank, and you have, say, a carload of refrigerators, one can always borrow against that, since they are tangible. One cannot borrow from the bank on just paper contracts, so companies that take more of a gamble than a bank, known as factors, exist, and one pays them about two percent over the bank's prime rate.

Since we had not gone into production, this was the only way to proceed. Also, our start dates were in September, and no money from our contracts would be realized until that time. On a Friday afternoon, Ed announced to us that he had made the deal at two percent over the prime rate, and our financial problems were solved.

Dick and I went out that evening and drank to the success of the Jane Chastain show, but our delight in being able to work out the financing was short-lived.

At 9:00 that evening, Ed called me at my hotel and was very upset. He told me there was no way we could borrow money from that company since he was a director. It would be a conflict of interest. We met in Ed's office the following morning at 10:00.

There was little time. Somehow, we had to find a way to get into production quickly. At the Saturday morning meeting, the three of us decided to put in $15,000 each. Ed was going to try to find another factoring company, and I was going back to New York to see what I could do, with little hope of finding a way to solve the problem.

On Monday morning, I called Sid Honig at Atwood Richards, the top barter agency in New York. Sid and I had become close friends, and we would often meet for lunch. He was in his late seventies, with graying hair, and very overweight. Although he had passed the bar at an early age and was an attorney, he never practiced law. He had been with the agency for years.

I told Sid my problem, and he asked me how much I needed. I told him somewhere between $75,000 and $125,000. He said, "Will you take it in $25,000 increments?" I looked at him, mouth agape, and the germ of an idea suddenly hit. I said, "Sid, if you do that, I'll guarantee to make up that money with the top markets where bartering is concerned."

No contract was ever signed, we had nothing in writing, but Sid, through Atwood Richards, gave me $125,000 in $25,000 increments. I, in turn, repaid it with barter time on major market stations. I guess Leo Durocher's remark, "Nice guys finish last," doesn't always apply.

I flew down to Miami to get production in full swing. We had the necessary cash to get started. We did not need 195 programs completed prior to start date. We could deliver new programs on a monthly schedule well ahead of broadcast date.

The next problem was one that no longer exists in the era of tape. We had to "bicycle" our programs on 16mm film because the cost of prints was so excessive. That meant we would take one print of, let's say twenty shows, and set up a bicycling schedule with six to eight television stations. Upon receipt, the stations would duplicate on their two-inch tape machines and send the 16mm prints to the next station on the list. That always gets ticklish. If one broadcaster did not duplicate immediately and ship quickly to the next station, your shows arrived late near the end of the bicycle. The only way to alleviate the problem was to take the slow station and put them at the end of the routing. One quickly discovered who the slow pokes were. We got complaints, but it did finally work for us. Syndicators shipping film were obliged to alleviate this problem in the same manner.

We started hiring new salesmen, and I had a lot of fun trying a new approach. Each year, I would fly to Columbus and drive to Ohio University in Athens, having been given a date by the school to interview interested juniors in the School of Communications. The idea was to take them during the summer months, train them, pay their travel expenses, and give them a small salary as well as commission for a thirteen-week period. They would make more than enough money to pay for their senior year and, upon graduation, would come back to us on a full-time basis.

I was always amazed to discover how little sales experience these youngsters had, and delighted in asking them if they had ever sold door-to-door, or sold women's shoes, etc. Having done that as a youngster, I knew from experience that if any of them had, they would make good salesmen.

Crazy as it sounds, selling ladies shoes is a good training ground. Many of the students had worked at Christmas time in department stores, or worked for their parents in retail, but we would often find a few with real potential.

Many came back to us and worked for one or two years, and, I might add, successfully, before going with much larger companies. Some went on to become literary agents, sales managers or general managers in the motion picture industry and broadcasting. Some went into business for themselves and proved to be very successful.

I recall one beautiful young lady with incredible ability, whom we decided to give a chance. She lasted just four weeks, even though we told her to put a wedding band on her finger. Staying in motels was too hard for her. Her boyfriend didn't like the idea, and what finally ended the experiment was when she stopped at a gasoline station to ask directions and the man told her to follow him, he would take her there. Of course, he took her to his house, and she just kept on going.

Occasionally, one would find a salesman at a television station who was a natural, but one never hired him before checking with the stations management and getting permission first. I recall one great talent I found in Roanoke, Virginia. I called his boss, whom I had known for years, and he gave me the go-ahead. That guy didn't know what "no" meant, and did an incredible job for us. He also kept us laughing with some of his antics.

His name was Bruce Genter, and today he is considered one of the top salesmen in "television country". He called me one day and told me he was in "Bose", Idaho, and missed a sale there because it was the end of their "physical year".

I recall one time putting him in the southern territory, and I couldn't understand why his sales almost completely stopped. I flew down to Atlanta to meet him and got the shock of my life. Bruce had grown a beard and looked like, of all people, Ulysses S. Grant. After he shaved, his sales again sky-rocketed. Bruce is still a legend, and one of the hardest-working men I ever had the pleasure of training and working with.

Working Atlanta in the seventies was like visiting a small southern town. Three network TV stations were almost one too many, with the ABC affiliate changing hands every couple of years, and few radio stations did well.

It's still difficult for me to believe what happened to me there one day. While walking into the ABC television manager's office, I overheard his strange remark, "Those two men waiting to see me haven't a prayer in making a sale to us." When I asked why, his remark was, "They're New York sharpies." "How do you know?" I asked. "They're wearing blue suede shoes." Boy, how times have changed in Atlanta!

The Flight of the Bumble Bees

Our start dates in September were fast approaching. We decided to contact our major markets and arrange for Jane to do a personal appearance tour, cut local promo spots for them, and introduce herself to the public and the newspapers, to give her as much promotion as possible.

We rented an Aero Commander Shrike, a twin-engine plane, and arranged to hit twenty-six cities in twenty-three days. In addition to our pilot and Jane, we took Nancy Rosenberg to help Jane with her hair styling and makeup, and we set off in August from the Ft. Lauderdale airport. It was a six-passenger craft and, at the time, the only small commuter aircraft authorized to fly the President of the United States.

Poor Nancy had never flown in her life. On the day of departure, her mom and dad, with tears running down their faces and Nancy blubbering all over the place, said goodbye as if they would never see each other again.

Jane had her own private license, and I had flown during the war. We were really looking forward to our trip. Our pilot was a hellion, and in every city that we stopped he had to buy a souvenir, so that by the end of the trip we were almost overloaded. Our first stop was in Atlanta, followed by Charlotte, Baltimore, Philadelphia, etc.

We were greeted in every market like conquering heroes with stations sending limousines to await our arrival. There were interviews by the stations, as well as newspapers, and Jane did thirty-second and one-minute promo spots, in addition to tags for each of the stations. Jane was an unusual talent, able to ad lib a promo with impeccable timing, finishing a ten, thirty or sixty-second spot on the nose. In many instances she didn't require cue cards or a TelePrompTer.

All aircraft have letter and call numbers, and ours was WS followed by five or six numerals. On arriving in Philadelphia, our pilot announced, "This is whiskey sour #7927 requesting landing instructions," and the tower totally ignored. They didn't like the whiskey sour," which stood for WS, of course, and would not give us landing instructions. After three tries, our pilot announced, "This is white slaver #7927" and, without a second's pause, the tower came back with, "Whiskey sour land on such and such a runway."

Boston is one of the toughest sports towns in the country, and their newspaper writers are heartless. At a luncheon given us by WNAC, the CBS affiliate, the writers were all very intense. One of them stood up addressed Jane, saying, "I don't think you know anything about sports, and I'm going to ask you three questions that I expect you to be able to answer." Jane, who not only was a beautiful girl, charming, and full of hell herself, answered by saying, "Fine, but for every question you ask me, I want the right to ask you a question." It ended right there.

When we landed in Chicago, no one was there to greet us, so we called WMAQ. Somehow, they forgot we were coming and, instead of admitting it, tried to bluff their way through. It was hilarious to listen to their excuses, and even more so when it was discovered no one had bothered to write copy for the station so Jane could do her promos. Pro that she was, Jane did several spots for them on an ad lib basis, and they were intrigued with her perfect timing.

179

Jane told us that at WMAQ in Chicago she was interviewed by this "kid" who was terribly nervous and didn't even know how to talk. That nervous kid, who had been just recently hired, was Greg Gumble.

Twenty-six cities in twenty-three days can be trying, and there were many stations that we planned to go back to later in the year. It was a very successful promotional tour, one that got us off the ground quickly and properly.

Another fun episode in selling the *Jane Chastain Show* was what occurred at her station, WTVJ, the CBS affiliate in Miami. The manager, Bill Brazzil was a hard-nosed businessman who ran a very tight ship. The station had been number one, by far, in the Miami market for years. I met the entire staff for the presentation, and when it was completed, I turned to the manager and said, "You have first crack at Jane in the market. If you're not interested, I want to take it to your competitors." He exploded! He let me know in no uncertain terms that Jane Chastain was under contract to WTVJ, and when I smilingly said, "I'm sorry, Bill, but there is no contract with Jane here at the station," I almost got thrown out.

I had checked with Jane earlier, to make sure there was no contract. Management's staff scoured their files only to discover that I was right. They never apologized to me, but they bought the show a few days later.

Jane and CBS

The Jane Chastain Show was an immediate success, but there were many problems. Many sports directors, as well as viewers, hated the idea that a woman could know as much about sports as they did. Although many viewers think they understand sports, we found that very few really do.

Some sports directors put *The Jane Chastain show* in a 7:00 a.m. kid show, while others found reasons not to run it at all. Still, we did very well, and after the shows were completed, Jane made many public appearances for the stations and their advertisers. She appeared several times on the Merv Griffin and Mike Douglas shows but, strangely, Fred DeCordoba wanted no part of her for *The Johnny Carson Show*. I never could figure that one out.

We were invited to Philadelphia for a world league football game attended by 100,000 people. What we didn't know until after the game was that it was such a flop they had to give the tickets away to fill the stadium. Jane was to do color with two old play-by-play pros, and after about ten minutes, they really let her do her job. She came off very, very well.

There were several stations we had promised personal appearances to which we were unable to visit on our airline trip, including ones in Richmond, Virginia and Washington, D.C.

In January, we flew into Richmond by commercial airliner and rented a car to drive to Washington, which was only a hundred miles away. After staying in Richmond overnight and planning on leaving at 7:00 a.m. the following morning, we discovered that six inches of snow had fallen overnight. Jane, being a southern gal, had seen little, if any, snow, and was terrified when she realized that the highway, in those days known as Route 1, was closed.

But I was a Buffalo boy who had been taught how to drive in snow. We headed to Washington at fifty miles per hour on a highway that didn't even have a tire track on it. We arrived about 9:30 and immediately went up to visit Senator Jesse Helms, whom Jane had befriended while in Raleigh.

Jesse greeted her like a long lost cousin. He called in "Vinegar Ben Mizell", a member of the legislature and former major league pitcher, to his office. From there, we headed out to WRC. Once again, because of the snow, we were not expected.

No one in Washington those days drove in snow because they didn't know how. There were six inches on the ground, and that was enough to cause school cancellations and TV stations working with skeleton crews. They were delightful to us at NBC in Washington, and we did whatever was asked of us.

It is amazing the many changes in sports that take place in a short while. Basketball and football icons change the rules of play and, after the first year, we discovered that thirty or forty shows would have to be re-produced. We also found other women were being added to television sports staffs. Our program was no longer unique, and resales in our second year would be difficult to come by. We decided that doing a second year of the show would not be productive, and we would continue selling what we had by cutting the number of programs from 195 to 160.

About that time, Bob Wussler, who had been at WBBM in Chicago as vice president and general manager, had been made President of CBS sports and was now headquartered in New York. He called me and asked for permission to talk to Jane about joining CBS, something that thrilled all of us, and, shortly thereafter, Jane became a member of the network's staff.

Although we read continuously about million-dollar contracts being signed by personalities joining networks, few people understand or realize how those contracts, in most instances, are designed. Unless they are well-known personalities who have been on the network for years, most contracts are signed on thirteen-week cycles, with the network having the right to cancel upon thirty days prior written notice. Although Jane now was an established star, having been seen in better than 90% of television homes, she still was an unknown commodity to CBS, and the standard contracts were signed with the thirteen-week cancellation option.

I have always been intrigued by talent, and could never understand why so often their egos become a detriment to their success. Jane was very talented, but she had become somewhat hard to control. No one could tell her how her eyebrows should look, her hair should be done, or in most instances, give her advice on how she was to respond or do certain things.

We had been involved in personal appearances for her throughout the country. When she was asked to appear she would refuse most requests to come in a day early for promotional appearances, which caused many problems. Major stars oblige, but Jane was now a personality and very difficult to handle at times.

When we set up personal appearances for her, we never knew whether she would change her mind. There were times we had to cancel at the last minute because she just didn't want to do it. Here was a lovely, talented lady who now had the opportunity of a lifetime—to be the first woman sportscaster with a top network. Her potential was incredible.

Once, when asked at a football game to interview players' wives, she refused, claiming she was a sportscaster and interviews of that nature were beneath her. She made enemies of those working around her, and at the end of six months her contract was not renewed.

I remember one very humorous episode when the microphone lines got badly tangled as she was about to do a horse race. By the time she was able to straighten out the lines and get to her mike, the race had started. The horses went around the first turn, and Jane's voice was heard on the network with, "They're off!"

I have always felt badly about what happened to Jane at CBS, but there were other opportunities for her, and I certainly was going to see if I could help.

Jane's husband, Roger, a clever engineer, had developed units for sports cars called the Chastain Shadow, which looked somewhat like a venetian blind, only horizontal rather than vertical. They were manufactured for the rear windows of Toyotas and Datsuns (now known as Nissans), as well as Ford coupes and other cars.

I had suggested to Roger that the Miami area was not the locale to be in, California would be a much more opportunistic locale for continuing his manufacture, as it was a sports car haven. On a trip out to the coast, Roger discovered that the market out there would be much bigger, and he procured a large contract. Hearing of that, and knowing Jane wanted to stay in broadcasting, I called John Severino, who was vice president and general manager of KABC-TV in Los Angeles. When I mentioned to him that Jane was available, he asked me to come out to the coast and discuss a contract for her. I called Jane, who was already in California with Roger. I told her what had transpired, and said I would attempt to make a deal for her.

Sitting down with Sev, I negotiated a contract that I thought was an excellent one. I felt the money offered was more than fair, and I demanded the contract have a guarantee of the first fifty-two weeks, after which thirteen-week cycles could be instituted. That meant she had a minimum guarantee of sixty-five weeks at a damn good salary.

That evening, Jane, Roger and I went out for dinner, and she was delighted with the contractual arrangements. Shortly after, however, when I asked Jane for money as her agent and manager, she became very upset. I received a check from her for much, much less than my costs, and it was the end of our relationship. I heard that after several months had gone by she complained bitterly about her contract, saying that she was not getting enough money.

ABC honored her contract, but did not renew it after sixty-five weeks. She was a great gal and I will always love her, remembering the wonderful times we had in producing her show, but I have not heard from her since.

14.
Feature Films

Our Jane Chastain show had done extremely well for us, with everyone, including talent and production people, making three to four times what residuals would have given them. With the realization that producing a second series would be too costly, we started exploring other opportunities.

While in my attorney's office in New York one day, I was introduced to one of his clients, Bernie Schubert. Bernie, for years, had produced and developed many of the prime time and half-hour programs found on the networks, as well as producing motion pictures and picking up motion picture properties. He had started his career with Philips H. Lord, the largest network producer at the time (Gang Busters, Mr. District Attorney, counterspy etc). Imagine if you were doing 14 to 16 thousand dollars a week in the late thirties and early 40's. Bernie learned well and with his own company produced "Topper," "Mr. and Mrs. North," "TV Readers Digest, "Crossroads" "The Dating Game" and "Blind Date."

I was intrigued with the possibility of having a film package of his to sell, since motion pictures were major properties for television. Bernie had science fiction, dramas and spaghetti westerns, a large number of which had been produced in Italy to save on production costs. We received a complete inventory of his features, and sent one of our boys to New York to work with Bernie's staff, since Bernie surprisingly, really had no idea what he had.

Another company had been handling his sales so we had a complete list of markets that would be unavailable to us, or markets that a portion of his features already had been sold in. We finally were able to make some sense out of his inventory, sent out promo materials and lists of features to our salesmen, and thus had an interim product to work with while looking for our next production idea.

One of the many problems with features was the editing done by station personnel. If you delivered an eighty-minute feature, and the station wanted to fill a sixty-minute slot, they would edit the film down, play it, and then ship it back to you forgetting to replace what they had cut. Stations buying an eighty-minute film, that were then shipped a fifty or sixty-minute product were not amused. Sometimes we could find the culprit at the earlier station, but usually it meant making an entirely new print.

My secretary, Leta Hudson, got hysterical with laughter one time when a station program director called and mentioned they had made a mistake scheduling a feature in TV Guide as ninety minutes long, when all they received was a sixty-minute film. TV Guide also stated, "starring Leta Hudson". Fortunately, the program director had a good sense of humor and said, "Don't worry about it; we'll just run it twice."

It was time for the NATPE Convention, and Dick Ullman, who very seldom attended, requested he be allowed to join us. I would normally take just one or two salesmen, but decided if he wanted to go, why not?

I did ask him, as a favor, not to do any selling, just watch because unfortunately this dear man never knew the products we had. For a man who had been head of a company that was nationally known, it was hard for me to understand how little he really understood about the industry. He would ask the most foolish questions and embarrass you.

I was making a presentation in our suite at the hotel using a 16-mm projector. The presentation tape had just finished, and the station manager asked a very simple question: was it an optical or magnetic track? (Normally, a 35mm motion picture is a magnetic track, but in the use of 16mm, optical, which was much cheaper, was normally used.) When I said to the manager, "optical", Dick said, "What's the difference?"

The funniest thing, however, happened during a pitch on a feature film package. He interrupted to tell the station manager that the "fi fi's, fi sci's, sci sci's—oh hell, they are great adventure shows." After that, he promised not to open his mouth again, particularly while we were trying to make presentations. Dick, bless him, could drive one crazy, but honestly, honor and loyalty were just a few of his attributes.

I have seen the man buy a chocolate soda before getting on an airplane and spill it from the end of his jacket to his trousers, and it never phased him, but at this convention, he pulled one that I'll long remember.

One evening, Dick wanted to go and meet his old buddies at the PGW (Peters Griffen Woodward) rep firm from his days as sales manager at Buffalo Broadcasting. Since all of the rep firms had suites, we had no trouble finding his friends, who gave him a royal welcome. The only problem was, Dick had had a bit too much to drink. I wouldn't say he was "wobbly", but damn close.

When we finally left the suite, in a loud voice Dick said, "Where's the john?", and I had to lead him to the men's room. Dick was wearing a light blue suit that evening. I thought nothing of it when he didn't reappear immediately. Finally, going into the men's room I was appalled at what I saw. He was wiping his trousers with paper towels. They had turned a dark blue. I looked at him and said, "Dick, what happened?" With a strange expression he said, "I forgot to take it out." It was the last convention we took Dick Ullman to.

While in New York, I was introduced to a kid by the name of Richard Rubenstein, whose father, a motion picture executive, was helping get his feet wet. It was during the days of a great tax write-off scheme that Uncle Sam stopped quite quickly. Never grandfathering the new change in the law, it cost fortunes to some of the people who were producing features and television programs and getting 90% write-offs. Rubenstein had done fifteen one-hour sports shows called *The Winners*, using such stars as Reggie Jackson, Kareem Abdul-Jabbar, Terry Bradshaw, Mean Joe Green, Mario Andretti, etc. They were well done, and would showcase the star's life and background in a one-hour format. We worked out a deal to handle them in syndication and sold part of the ABC O&O's, as well as many of the major markets.

I had an idea one day and took it to the Transworld Airline people, who were very excited about its potential for use on short-haul trips (Chicago to L.A. etc) where a feature film would have been too long. One hour plus airline commercials was perfect. I received a telegram from their headquarters confirming the sale, and the money was very substantial. It was a feather in our caps—the first short running feature the airlines had ever purchased.

We never did get the final two payments owed us by Rubenstein, because of some quirk in the contract which I never did understand. It really wasn't worth suing him over. I haven't seen him since, but expect he would fit in well with the motion picture industry of the time. He wasn't one who could look you straight in the eye, and he had a strange way about him. I always wondered if he got caught with the tax law change. The money really wasn't that important to me; the sale was more a means to an end in building a company.

Corporation For Entertainment and Learning

One meets some very delightful, interesting and talented people in the broadcasting industry, like those at C.E.L. (Corporation for Entertainment and Learning). Their president and members of their staff had done a great deal of network directing, including *The Steve Allen Show* . For some reason, their president, Mert Koplin, took a liking to me and to what I was trying to do, and we discussed at length developing and producing a new program concept.

I had just gone through one of the toughest times in my life, having finally filed for divorce. The children were grown, one graduating from college and the other in his sophomore year. We had sold our home in northern New Jersey, and my wife had gone back to the Buffalo area while I went to Ft. Lauderdale. Fortunately for everyone concerned, the bitterness did not last very long, and she and I were able to remain friends.

I was looking for anything at the time to keep busy, and the C.E.L. people were anxious for us to find a vehicle. Once again, our "idea man", Dick Ullman, came up with what we thought would be a brilliant new programming idea. Within a few months the country would start its bicentennial celebration leading up to the big festivities in Washington on July 4, 1976. Why not do a "Happy Birthday USA" series with a fifty-second day-to-day countdown?

The boys at C.E.L. loved the idea. We could take slides and color renditions, together with actual photographs dating back to the Civil War, and build a story line around everything leading up to the big celebration. Mert Koplin suggested we take the production costs off the top, and work on a 50:50 basis thereafter. At the time, that sounded pretty fair to me, since the cost of doing 260 (Monday through Friday) segments could be done quite reasonably, compared to normal filming.

We signed contracts and went to work. My job was to do a color brochure, and they were to give me a half dozen finished segments on 16 millimeter presentation reels, or, better yet, 3/4-inch tape, which Sony and their Beta system had released earlier that year. (What a change that made in television! Every TV station in the country bought 3/4 inch tape equipment, giving us a much quicker and cheaper way to make presentations.)

Having estimated the cost of doing the entire series of 260 fifty-second units, with brochures and tape in hand I flew out to see Al Flanagan of Combined Communications, the ABC affiliate, figuring if he liked what I had, he would make the decision for all seven of his stations.

Walking into his new office proved to be an experience. It was the largest television office I had ever seen, and must have been at least seventy to eighty feet long and a good thirty feet wide. At the entrance were not only glass doors, but see-through windows, and there appeared to be two sets of them, with a much smaller office for his secretary between them.

About this time in broadcasting's history, every minority in the country began to make demands for specialty programming for their people, and some of them became almost violent.

In Denver, an Indian contingent arrived with loaded rifles and forced their way into the manager's office. The glass partitions that had been recently added were bullet-proof and, although Al gave the Indians a special program on a weekly basis, he protected himself and his staff from that time forward.

I made my presentation and knowing Al, did it as quickly and thoroughly as possible. One could never tell whether he liked or disliked something because his expression never changed, nor did he ask any questions. If you oversold, as some salesmen do, you could be in trouble. Upon completing my pitch, I asked him what his thoughts were.

He came back with the standard question, "How much is it?", and I gave him a quotation, after which he thanked me, turned his swivel chair around and started dialing a telephone number. Since my appointment was over, I walked out with his general manager, Charlie Leasure, who had been in the presentation, not knowing what Al Flanagan's answer was but feeling somewhat chagrined at his not giving me a response.

Charlie who liked the idea asked that I wait for him while he went back to Al's office. When he returned, he stated that Al liked the show, but he wouldn't pay more than $50,000 for the seven stations. For me, it was a quick decision. Our production costs would be paid for, I had a seven station buy in my pocket, with "follow the leader" potential for the rest of the country.

In producing any program with ideas that appear to be fresh and unusual, one never knows whether it will be successful or just bomb. "Happy Birthday USA" was one of my few true bombs, one which, lost money, and lots of it.

A company called the CBS Network had the same idea and ran it on a daily basis in their countdown every night until July 4, 1976. We all tried hard but, although we made some sales, we never did recoup our costs for salaries, travel expenses, etc. Some good ideas, even great ones, don't always make it. Oh well, we still had our other products, and a germ of another idea was growing.

Our company, having grown and made great strides, was beginning to have some internal problems that had to be resolved. My salesman, Herb Berman, who had been with me off and on for seventeen years, had become a major problem. He suddenly stopped producing. After several months, to my dismay, I discovered he was heading to Detroit every Monday morning, faking his calls to the office, and staying with a brother-in-law until Friday. I finally realized this when one of the general managers in Detroit called and mentioned that Herb called him often inviting him to the race track. When I confronted him, Herb was a very honest man.

We had saved his house by lending him money to make up back payments, and we had overlooked many of his problems and bad habits. I had signed with the bank a guarantee to save his house, and advanced several thousand dollars against future commissions to help pay his other debts.

Herb would not keep records of any nature. He was forced to accept the maximum daily traveling expense the IRS would allow without records of $35. The company was paying him $750 a week, and with his living at his brother-in-law's in Detroit, being at the track and other sporting events throughout the week and not working, it was imperative we let him go.

Several weeks later, I discovered the company was being sued for usury. The loans we had advanced him had used the current bank interest rate, which, although illegal according to our attorneys, was of minor importance.

I then discovered that, in a fit of anger, Herb had called his sister and other relatives and as a gift had given them his telephone credit card, allowing them to make any and all calls they wanted "on him". Then, to top everything off, he had found a Gulf Oil credit card and had charged hundreds of dollars against it, signing the card owner's name. The telephone company told me that since the amount was several hundred dollars it was considered grand larceny, and they would be interested in joining us in suit against him if we proceeded. I never did bother with the oil company, but with all of the above, I was angry and hurt at what he had done.

I had the choice of spending $15,000 on court fees, or settling with his attorneys for $5,000, which would be to get us off the hook with the bank regarding his house, etc. If we went to court, Herb would go to prison, so we took the cheapest way out.

About this time, my son, Dan, who had graduated from college a year earlier with a degree in psychology and wanted to save the world, called me to tell me how he could not live on a $125 a week salary. He never wanted any part of the business I was in, having stated very vehemently many times that he wanted a five-day a week job, weekends off, and annual vacations—not bad for a dreamer, but maybe he was right. I suggested he come on down and talk about his future, or maybe take a crack at his dad's business, which he jumped at. He spent five years with me, and I believe he learned a great deal before going on to bigger things.

At the time all of this was occurring, I had to make a decision on Dick Ullman. I suggested he take retirement and the corporation buy out his stock. Dick was over seventy at the time and, although I loved him dearly, the decision had to be made. Fortunately, it never affected our relationship and, for years thereafter, whenever I was in town, we would have lunch every week until he passed on twelve years later.

It was also time to find someone who could work more closely with our six-man sales force, and Jim Phillips, who had been with us for a few years, was my initial choice. He did a fine job for several months before leaving and forming his own company.

Sandy Frank

I met Sandy Frank in the mid-fifties when he came to us to handle our product internationally. He was just starting out with his own company, and since we had no representation for sales outside of the U.S., willingly gave him our properties. Surprisingly, he did make some sales. Sandy, in his own right, is an unusual story in the industry.

Years later he had made a fortune selling other people's programming, as well as his own, in a manner that I shudder to think I could ever do. It was impossible to insult him. Once he got into your station, it was hard as hell to get rid of him. I have heard stories about how he faked a heart attack on a plane because it was not making a stop in the city he had an appointment in, and then he jumped out of the ambulance that was taking him to the hospital so he could make the appointment.

There was a story at the Friar's Club that he had his own nurse. He was a hypochondriac, and if anyone sneezed or coughed, Sandy almost collapsed.

Each year, we would go to the National Association of Television Program Executives, which became *the* television convention by far surpassing NAB (National Association of Broadcasting), which had become an equipment convention. At the time, we didn't have stands on a convention floor, but rather, everyone had suites in the hotel where clients and other station managers and program directors would stop, and we would give presentations of our product in the suite.

Sandy always made it a point to drop in and say "hello". This time, he stuck his head in the door, looked at the television screen where I was presenting a program, and watched it for two or three minutes. He then turned to me, waved, and said, "Hi, Marv! Sorry, it will never sell." I was with the program director of WSM-TV in Nashville, who started to laugh and said to me, "Please don't repeat this, but I would like to tell you a true story of Sandy Frank." After all these years, I feel it should be told.

Sandy had made an appointment at WSM to make a presentation of one of his television shows. He was cordially received and allowed to make his presentation to the entire staff, after which the station turned him down. But they could not get rid of him, and after a long period of time, they bodily threw him out.

The next morning the secretary for the program director received a dozen roses with an apologetic note signed by Sandy, and the program director received a telegram apologizing for his actions and stating "letter follows". A few days later, the letter arrived apologizing for his actions and stating that his father had cancer, his mother was in the hospital with a heart attack, and he would hope they would forgive him for the way he acted.

As the program director said to me with a smile, "We forgave him." Six months later, Sandy came in, made a presentation, was turned down, and thrown out bodily for a second time. The following morning, a dozen roses arrived for the program director's secretary, and a telegram was received apologizing and stating "letter follows". The program director then looked at me, laughed and said, "Marv, would you believe it? That letter was a form letter!"

In the past few years, Sandy has mellowed somewhat. One last item that still tickles my funny bone is how, for years, Sandy Frank would introduce you to his fiancee at NATPE, and each year it was a different girl.

15.
"Time Capsule" and King Features

After the "Happy Birthday USA" debacle, I continued talking to the people at C.E.L. in the hope we could find a more successful project to work on together. For years, they had had a contract with the CBS Network supplying film footage for the news department. The news film footage they had was excellent, but was lacking in amount of material and content.

We discussed at length doing a series for television syndication, and got so far as discussing the costs of buying additional film footage and further production. But each time we discussed costs, the figures, although fair enough, did not appear to be feasible because they wanted all costs deducted before they would work on a 50:50 basis with us.

I had some ideas of my own, and wanted to see if I could find some other outfit with enough film footage and production know-how who would be interested in working with me in building a first for television, a usable morgue. With the death of a celebrity or a natural disaster, newspapers had materials that no television station or network could have possibly compiled in its short, twenty-year history.

I had some thoughts on how we would do it if I could only find a company that had the materials and the wherewithal to put a very complete package together. The Hearst Corporation, I discovered, had 60 million feet of film footage sitting in a warehouse in New Jersey from the days of the Hearst Metrotone News, which we saw in motion picture theaters for years. It was all on in 35 mm. and sounded like a natural for us. In checking, I was told to go through their King Features division.

I called Joe D'Angelo, the president of King Features, and made an appointment to see him without telling him what I had in mind, just that it was about a television program they might be interested in. Joe had such an air of superiority about him that I was somewhat taken aback. He was a good-looking, average-size man, who must have had a great deal of talent to be President of a company the size of King Features, but his manner was not to my liking. However, I thought maybe I am wrong, maybe first impressions won't last; I have a simple Letter of Agreement made up, and I might just as well take my shot and see what happens.

With men like Joe, I couldn't help but add some high pressure to my pitch. I told him that I knew of the 60 million feet of film footage and his company's newspaper background, and I had an idea that could make money for both of us.

We would take 2,000 pieces of film from their library, edit the materials down to fifty seconds by making new negatives, and then reduce to 3/4-inch cassettes. We would supply the 50-second segments with an index and cross index, whereby a television station would have its own morgue and could find anything at a moment's notice. My high pressure pitch came close to answering every question before it was asked. When I had finished, from the look in his eyes I had hit the right spot. His next words to me were classic, and still bring a smile to my face. He wanted to know how much business I would guarantee him in contracts before they had to go into production.

Now, bear in mind, in my pitch I had stated I wanted eight, fifty-second segments on a 3/4-inch video cassette as a presentation. We had to do the brochure material and, if we went ahead, the finished product would have 2,000 units. I looked at Joe and said, "Before you have to do any additional production, I will bring in a half million dollars in firm, signed contracts." Joe D'Angelo looked at me with his fountain pen poised and said, "Where do I sign?" He signed my simple Letter of Agreement, and we planned to meet with his production people the following day to work out the film segments they would use for the audition presentation tape.

In meeting with his staff the following day, it was estimated it would take from six to eight weeks to do the materials properly, and since we had a signed agreement already, I did not worry about firming up the contract until such time as I delivered my half million dollars in

194

sales. I was pleased, and wondered once again whether this idea had the merit I thought it had, but it was an exciting possibility. Strangely enough, I had not discussed it with any television management people, and I decided not to until I had something that I could show them.

It took almost three months before the initial materials were available, and I was chomping at the bit to get started.

The vice president of the ABC owned and operated television stations was a man with whom I had become very friendly. Phil Boyer was one of the sharpest program men I had ever worked with. He couldn't have been more than in his early thirties, but he had compiled a reputation and expertise second to none. In the seventies, the ABC O&O's would run features in the 4:00 to 6:00 p.m. time slots, and Phil was one of the first people to set up on computer every feature available, its running time, its reviews, and the artists featured. He was one of those responsible for making the O&O's number one in their markets, and was responsible for some unusual programming ideas. He was always available to those of us who wanted to make a presentation, whether it was for feature films, programs or fresh ideas.

Upon receipt of the initial eight stories which made up our presentation tape, I called Phil and made an appointment to make my first presentation. It was one of the few times I ever started at the top with a new product. Normally, I would get my feet wet working the smaller markets, but somehow I had to find out quickly what "Time Capsule's" potential was.

I described to Phil what "Time Capsule" entailed, how it would be delivered to a television station on 3/4 inch video cassettes, and then proceeded to play the materials. Phil immediately picked up the phone and called Al Ittleson, who was vice president of ABC news for the O&O's. Al turned out to be not only a charming guy, but one who could make an immediate decision. He was short, of medium build, and very friendly. He asked me to call him the following day and, having given him a price for all the stations, I left their office with an incredible glow.

I called Al the next day, and we set up a second meeting and shook hands on an O&O buy for a seven-year period, with payments to be made over thirty-six months. The ABC attorneys would do the initial contract and work with my attorney in working out the details. In the interim, I received a purchase order and was in seventh heaven, having sold New York, Chicago, Los Angeles, Detroit and San Francisco in my first presentation.

The following day I met Herb Berman in Albany, New York, and went up to see the general manager of WTEN television. I never forgot Mike Corkin, having known his father several years earlier in the Davenport-Rock Island area where he was a general manager. When I used to call on Mike, behind his desk on the wall was a beautifully-framed mosaic with Romanistic printing of some Latin saying. My high school Latin made me realize that it had something to do with the military or troops, since the last word was *E-militabus*. Mike explained to me that his art department had drawn and framed it for him. When I queried him about what the translation was, he said, "Marv, it's for salesmen like you: "Don't shit the troops!"

I went back to the Ft. Lauderdale office on cloud nine, and spent the next week high-spotting a few markets before heading back to New York.

Two weeks after receiving the presentation tape for "Time Capsule", I walked back into Joe D'Angelo's office at King Features with over $800,000 in firm contracts, and suggested we get our attorneys together and finalize the Letter of Agreement he had signed.

Joe may be president of King Features (and I believe he is still there), but I learned his word wasn't worth the paper it was written on. The big boss appeared to be his accountant, who let me know in no uncertain terms that they were not about to pay 50 % of the gross for "Time Capsule". I could have sued them since I had that piece of paper signed by the president of the company, but one learns that getting involved with lawyers costs tremendous sums in retainers and court fees. My attorney, who was with me at the meeting, was of little help. We finally decided to go ahead on their terms. We would be paid 40 % of the gross on the first two million dollars in sales, and 45 % thereafter, but I was very unhappy at the change in terms.

I had very little to do with Joe D'Angelo after the contracts were signed, and King Features hired a most unusual man to oversee the production of the 2,000 segments. Lee Polk, when he arrived at King Features, was charming, very bright, and well-organized. He knew production and was wonderful to work with. King Features made him a nervous wreck, however and when he left two years later, he was snow white and a pill-popper of the first order. The two of us, who worked continuously together, got along famously, and he agreed with my opinion that the president of King Features was a no-talent blow-hard. We used to laugh about D'Angelos visits every couple of weeks to the Pen and Pencil on 45th Street, a famous steak house, where he would buy

196

steaks to take home and claim them on his expense account. With Lee's hard work and devotion to the project, "Time Capsule" was a brilliantly conceived and developed product for television.

Sales skyrocketed, we quickly reached the two million dollar mark, and we continued to be successful in selling every major market in the United States. Giving the devil his due, I must admit that King Features made every payment to us, not only on time, but up to the penny. They refused to let us do the billing, but their accounting practices, honesty and integrity were commendable.

During this period, I met a man who is still legendary today. Sammy Gang for years represented King Features internationally. He knew little, if anything, about American sales in syndication, but truly was the pioneer in opening up the rest of the world for American product. At one time he had the whole world, but he was so successful in sales he finally gave up Europe and concentrated on South America and Southeast Asia. Although retired these past few years, everyone continually asks about him. In his mid-seventies, he still has a photographic memory, and his stories about people, places and product through the years can be mesmerizing. King Features' people realized what they had in this gem of a man, and they were very good to him. We meet often for dinner and we both miss the wonderful people we knew those many years. Since King Features kept worldwide rights. Sammy was able to sell Time Capsule in foreign markets.

The stations loved "Time Capsule", and many, many of them had an insert in their evening news of something of interest from their library. Many of them sold advertisers a ten-second spot, while others would compare past events to something that happened in the news each day.

The president of ABC news called me one day to apologize for something the network had done. When Elvis Presley died, ABC had no film footage in their library, but found some wonderful material in our "Time Capsule". He called to admit they had used it on the network, and said, "How much do we owe you?" I got such a kick out of it that I laughingly assured him it was our pleasure since the O&O's had it in their possession. I still wonder to this day what I could have asked for it but, at the time, it never entered my mind.

197

16.
"TV POWWW" and its Origin

In the spring of 1977, two men approached me with an idea for a television show. It had a concept that would be new to the broadcasting industry and might have a great deal of potential. These two men, one a disc jockey, the other a radio program director, had befriended Al D'Sepio, the president of Magnavox. They had presented an idea to him for a new half-hour game show using arcade games, with the possibility of stripping it for a daytime network and syndication to television stations.

Somehow, they had obtained a commitment from D'Sepio to produce a pilot at a cost of between $200,000 and $250,000. At the time, two companies had released their game shows: one, Atari, captured the market immediately, while the other, Fairchild Camera and Instrument Corp., was a new entity on the scene. Magnavox was developing their own new Odyssey game with cassettes similar to Atari, but it would not be available for at least another year. Magnavox, which owned the patents on the chip being used, was in litigation with all other companies, although many of the arcade game manufacturers were already paying royalties.

The boys had brought a game into my office, and we hooked it up to a television set. I said that it sounded very interesting, and I was quite pleased they had come to me to handle their sales and marketing. I still, however, wanted to test it with one or two top program people in television to see what potential it had.

I again called Phil Boyer of ABC and set up an appointment to see him the following week. I spent that weekend at home playing games with friends and family.

The possibilities were spectacular, but with a half-hour play, could one generate enough excitement with a studio audience participant playing against a celebrity? I had read much about Atari, and now had played several of their games, but I was still a neophyte and knew little about that industry.

I walked into Phil's office with a game under my arm, hooked up the wires to the back of his television set and watched the vice president of programming go out of his mind. Phil said he played the arcade games every night at Penn Station while waiting for his train, and sometimes put in as much as $5.00 in quarters.

He loved the concept with one very big exception. It would not play as a half-hour game show. Rather, he felt it was the "Dialing for Dollars" of the eighties and should be presented as an insert, whereby television stations could put it into their talk programming, half-hour syndicated series, etc. "Dialing for Dollars" is still used in radio. A radio personality calls a home and if they are listening they win a cash jackpot. The jackpot increases after each call made to a home that is not listening or the phone is not answering.

I did not go further, feeling that Phil was right. It was becoming increasingly difficult to find half hours in prime access periods, and there were already too many game shows being pedaled.

I reported my findings, only to be told they were going ahead with their half-hour concept. Was I still interested in handling it? At the time, I felt it a good gamble, and we worked out the percentages verbally, awaiting the Magnavox attorney to supply the contract.

In August, I was informed that the pilot would be done prior to Labor Day weekend, and they would be pleased to have me attend the shooting. They also said that the vice president and chief counsel of Magnavox would be there, and we would have an opportunity to work out the details of our agreement.

I was told of the day of the shoot, but I was not told that there had been rehearsals and dress rehearsals two days prior, so when I arrived the afternoon before the pilot was to be produced, I spent several hours with Magnavox's attorney. Oddly enough, he appeared to be in no hurry to consummate the agreement, which I thought strange since I had already been given the go-ahead and was planning a brochure and full-page ads in the trade magazines.

One has to know Hollywood and the television industry to understand what happened next. When you produce five half hours a week, you can pay for the celebrities, the people who supply the studio audience, all the prizes, the cost of a crew and the rental of a studio, averaging about $7,500 per program. You also can shoot from four to five shows in a day, so if you are going to do 195 shows a year, your programs can be produced in a little over two months.

Considering that a set had to be built, a pilot is much more costly, but shouldn't come in at $230,000. There's a very simple answer: two or three people do one man's job. Everyone has such a good time being so well paid, and they come up to the producer, the attorneys, anyone involved, continually patting them on the back with the statement, "You've got a winner."

The morning of the shoot, I went down to the coffee shop and saw the vice president and attorney for Magnavox. I thought there would be no problem sitting down and having a cup of coffee with him, which I did, but his distant attitude struck me as very strange. When he excused himself, went outside, got into his rental car and went to the studio without the courtesy of inviting me, knowing full well I was also going there, I got the message loud and clear.

I caught a cab to the studio and watched the pilot being produced for less than 30 minutes. I was so angry, I just wanted out of there. I caught a cab back to the hotel, checked out, and flew down to San Diego to spend the weekend with friends.

Through the years, one learns that revenge may not be very sweet, but sometimes getting even businesswise for a stab in the back can be so, so satisfying.

On September 6th, I wrote Wilfred Corrigan, President of Fairchild Camera and Instrument Corporation, telling him of my interest in developing a game show with one manufacturer using a variety of game cartridges for television. We could have a viewer play specific games at home electronically just by depressing the disconnect button on his telephone.

I asked him if they would be interested in developing a small black box that would recognize the sound of a voice so that a viewer at home, speaking into the telephone, could activate the game cartridge. I put my heart and soul and every sales trick I knew into writing that letter trying to whet his appetite and give me an opportunity to come out and meet him in California.

I wrote the same letter to the president of Atari, and, strange as it seems, never got a reply.

A few days later, I received a phone call from Fairchild suggesting that I call John Donatoni, marketing director of the video games divisions. In talking with him briefly, I set an appointment to see him the following week. I flew to San Francisco, rented a car and headed to the Santa Clara area where their office is, a mile or so from a Marriott Hotel.

I take a great deal of ribbing because of my sense of direction. Blindfold me three blocks from home, turn me around a dozen times, and chances are only 50/50 I'll find my way home the first time. I got up the next morning and left for my meeting an hour early. It was only a mile or two from the hotel, so I should make it on time.

Santa Clara is in the heart of Silicon Valley, and the buildings and the landscaping are something to see. Large undulating lawns, trees, shrubs, natural stone—everything is refreshingly new, clean and beautiful. The Fairchild offices were immense, and with their background in the early development of the computer chip industry, I had an awfully good feeling going into my meeting.

John Donatoni was a young man, handsome, charming and knowledgeable, and we discussed my letter to his president. He brought in several engineers, and I told them what I needed. When I asked whether it was possible to use voice activation over a telephone, the engineers felt it could be accomplished although it had not been done before.

I then asked for something else, and held my breath: is it possible to develop a box that would take the game itself off the front of the picture tube, put it through a television system and broadcast it to every home? They discussed that for a few minutes, and came back with an affirmative response, but also told me it would take a good six months to develop. John then introduced me to several other officers of the company, called in a member of their legal staff, and we quickly came to an agreement.

They wanted to build the units themselves, and we would buy them at a cost not to exceed $2500. They would develop additional game cartridges for us, which electronically would go through the television station's system and out to everyone's television picture tube at home. They would continually supply us with games.

Each game would have to be re-programmed and, in most instances, simplified for on-air use. Also, the games were on 3-1/2 x 3" cartridges, and they had to be re-designed for the game equipment that was to be built. We ended up with a cartridge that looked like a "T",

201

about three times the size of a normal game, although it still fit into their units.

They requested the right to file for patents on the voice activation and anything else they felt was warranted. I left walking on air, with games, cartridges and everything else I needed to get started. My only worry was how to make presentations. I had a couple of ideas but first I had to be sure that what I was doing would be as exciting to the television stations and their program people as it was to me.

Marketing "TV POWWW"

After returning from the west coast, I called Phil Boyer at ABC in New York. I told him what we were doing, and he reiterated that he wanted first refusal for the ABC stations, and to please keep him informed.

Strange things sometimes occur to one in business. Is it luck, or are you just at the right place at the right time?

I don't know why, but I picked up the phone and called Al Flanagan, President of Combined Communications at KBTV in Denver (now KUSA). Al would always see me, and although he was a very tough man in negotiations, he always was wonderful to me. I told him that I had a new show idea, and that I would like very much to come out to Denver to make a presentation for his seven-station group.

Al said he would not be available. He was going to Las Vegas for a general meeting of Combined Communications. He suggested that I come out to the Tropicana Hotel to make a presentation to the staffs. He said that not only management would be there, but sales and programming as well. I jumped at the chance. Al said, "Bring your wife if you like. Reservations will be waiting for you at the Tropicana". Having married a beautiful girl two years after my divorce, someone who gave me my happiest years, it would be wonderful to be able to include her in the trip. For years, my Jeanne traveled the world and charmed all those she met. I loved having her with me.

I had no presentation tape, only a Fairchild game box, several cartridges, and lots of wires to hook up to television sets. What an opportunity!

I arrived with Jeanne late in the afternoon, and while checking in found an envelope waiting for me with a note from Al: "Won't you join us for a cocktail party this evening?" That evening when I arrived at the party, I discovered over three hundred people were there—not only Al's personnel, but the president of ABC television, most of the executives of ABC from New York, as well as many advertising agencies and those involved with Combined Communications.

I also discovered, in walking through the lobby, a dozen other syndicators were there to see whether they could get an invitation. I was the only one that was invited and, boy, what that did for my ego!

When Al spied me, he came over immediately, welcomed us, and then took us aside for a moment to tell me that he had my thirty-minute presentation set up for 11:30 the next morning. I told him it would probably take thirty or forty minutes to set up, so he changed my presentation to 2 o'clock, giving me the lunch hour to set up.

The meetings were held in the nightclub area, which seated somewhere between 2500 and 3000 people and had a huge stage. I had the hotel deliver two 21-inch television sets and placed them on tables on each side of the stage. I then set up a small table in the center of the stage where there was a live microphone, and ran my wires to both television sets from the game unit. Figuring that the simpler the presentation, the better, I took a Shooting Gallery cartridge, set it up, and then next to each television set placed a telephone which was not hooked up. I was going to have to fake the whole thing and describe exactly how the equipment would be working when delivery dates were met on or about September 1, 1978.

At 2:00, with more than 300 people taking the front of the orchestra section, with butterflies in my stomach I picked two general managers whom I knew well, and asked them to come up on the stage. I then described what we were doing. We would have liked an entirely different name for the program, but we were calling it "TV POWWW" because voice activation was in its infancy and we needed a very strong sound into the telephone (or so the engineers had told me).

With the two managers holding the dead telephones, I started the game cartridge and told them to shout "POWWW" into the telephone when they felt they could hit the target. When they said "POWWW" I pushed the buttons—and all hell broke loose.

Al Flanagan jumped up on the stage, grabbed the mike, and in a loud clear voice said, "I want an option for all seven of my stations." I smiled and said to him, "Al, we don't give options," and I thought he was going to kill me. Laughingly, I continued, saying, "You have a first refusal." The excitement shown by management, programming and sales was spectacular. There I was faking a presentation with a game

203

box, two cartridges and two 21″ television sets. The fun was just beginning.

Several weeks later, I went back out to Santa Clara and discovered the engineers were hard at work developing the equipment, and were very confident they would have few problems.

I then went down to Los Angeles, having made an appointment with the head of programming for KABC, a man I had known since he was a program director for Westinghouse. John Goldhammer was about 6′2″, handsome enough to be a movie star, bright, charming, and well put together emotionally. He was very well adjusted, with an aura of success about him. With nothing more than the equipment I had used in Las Vegas, and telling him about Phil Boyer in New York taking a first refusal for the O&O's, I went through my simple pitch. He loved its potential and said he would attempt to get a meeting for me with John Severino, the vice president and general manager.

Sev was a very tough man to see, running the most profitable television station in the country, but John said he would try and would call me at the hotel. That afternoon, he called and said, "You know how busy Sev is. You've got just five minutes at noon tomorrow. Bring the equipment with you, and we will set up in engineering."

Sev walked in right on time, I made my presentation, and Sev took the equipment away from me and played with it for almost an hour. Walking out with him, he looked at me and said, "Marv, you are going to make a million dollars with that product."

Going back to Johnny Goldhammer, and figuring the equipment should be in my hands some time in March, I went for the jugular. The NATPE Convention was in April of that year, and I asked John if he would allow me to test the program during the convention. He immediately came back with, "How about *A.M. Los Angeles* with Regis Philbin and Sarah Purcell?" What a thrilling thought that was! Regis did a 9:00 to 10:00 a.m. program with Sarah, and it was the #1 rated morning program in greater Los Angeles. I was on cloud nine with the realization that we had a potentially very successful new property.

Even with the first refusal from the ABC O&O's, and the same for a seven-station buy from Combined Communications, I still had a momentous problem. There was no way I could build a presentation for the show since I did not have a working model. That meant little if any, involvement with the salesmen until such time as we could program a show, tape it and build a presentation. It would be foolish to try in writing to explain what we were doing, so the decision was made not to give

204

it to the sales force until such time as the work by Fairchild Camera and Instrument was complete.

I continued to fly out to Fairchild and work with their marketing people, as well as their program engineers, to make sure we would have enough games with the new equipment. I also went out to KBTV in Denver several times, and met with the people from KABC, who flew in to Denver from Los Angeles, to help work out some of the formats that could be used on "TV POWWW".

Everyone was excited about the new concept, and word around the industry began seeping back to us. I received calls from stations asking us to contact them when we were ready, and in many markets word of mouth was getting around.

The engineers at Fairchild were working diligently on the equipment, and they continually gave us assurance they would meet their deadline in March.

We continued to meet in Denver and, though we had no equipment to use on the air, played many of the re-programmed games which were becoming available to us from the store version of the game. All of us were very excited. Playing the shooting gallery game, baseball, and other cartridges gave us an insight into how the program could be integrated when the equipment was available.

By using a "dummy" unit that had been built, we finally produced a presentation tape to be given the salesmen at the NATPE convention in April along with our initial brochures.

Early in March, we received the news from Fairchild that they were running a little late, but they assured us they would be ready prior to the April start date of the NATPE convention. Normally, this convention, held annually, would start on a Thursday or Friday, go through the weekend and one or two days into the following week.

I wanted to be on the air the Monday prior to the start of the convention so that we could get any bugs out of the equipment and have the *A.M. Los Angeles* show with Regis rolling by the time the general managers and program directors registered.

On the planned Monday morning, at 7:00 a.m., engineers from Fairchild and I entered the studios at KABC to set up our spanking new "TV POWWW" equipment. With everything ready to go by 8:30, Regis and Sarah having integrated the contest into the show, things looked great—until we discovered the equipment didn't work! Getting on line through the system was beautiful, but the voice activation was not operational. At 8:45, "TV POWWW" was canceled for the show, and the engineers flew back to Santa Clara to continue working.

On Tuesday, they were back with several changes only to discover once again it still wasn't operational. By Wednesday morning, when we were still having trouble I was almost at my wit's end. Still, the engineers assured me it was only a simple bug, and they once again returned to Santa Clara.

By Thursday morning, with Fairchild's engineers once again hooking up the system, I had visions of never making it for the convention, but lo and behold, everything worked. Regis, with his unusual ego, didn't make our life easier, but Sara Purcell, a tall sinewy blonde, was just precious. She was delightful to work with and had a wonderful sense of humor, even screaming out "POWWW" at the wrong time to see if she could make the equipment work from the studios. We went on the air, and Regis asked viewers to pick up the phone and call to play from home.

On Friday morning, again we had no problems. For two hours after the show went on the air, the Los Angeles telephone system was badly taxed with people calling trying to be first to play "TV POWWW" on KABC-TV and asking all kinds of questions.

As in the earlier days of the NATPE convention, we registered and took suites in the convention hotel, where we would present our products to programming and management of each station. A schedule of events for the conference was set well in advance, and we were not allowed to open our suites during the meeting periods, normally held in the mornings. We then would open our doors by noon or 1:00 p.m. and the broadcasters would be allowed to visit us.

Most syndication companies would bring their sales staffs to the conference since it was an opportunity for them to meet, service their clients, present new product, and work with anyone in their given territories. As I mentioned earlier I had an unwritten law, however, that at a convention there were to be no territories. Rather, whatever sales were made would be equally commissionable and divided among everyone. I found this always worked very well at a convention. At its completion, every salesman was back on his own to close whatever deals had been started in his territory, and be given full commission thereafter.

Having been at KABC at 7:00 that Friday morning, I stayed until the end of the *A.M. Los Angeles* show at 10:00. Then I took a cab back to the hotel, and was holding a sales meeting in our suite awaiting the noon hour when we could open, per the NATPE regulations.

About 11:30, there was a knock on the door and in walked Al Flanagan with one of his managers from the Combined Communications group. I never had the opportunity to say that I was not allowed to do business until later, because Al, with a big smile on his face, stated, "I want to buy "TV POWWW" for our stations." I hadn't seen him at KABC that morning, but he was in the background watching the *A.M. Los Angeles* show.

I didn't even get an opportunity to quote a price for a seven-station buy, which included markets like Denver, Atlanta, Phoenix, etc. Al just looked at me and said he would pay so much for the group, and I didn't argue. Out of the corner of my eye, I caught a couple of my salesmen with their mouths wide open in disbelief since we had just started to tell them about the program, show them some of the materials, and present their audition tapes. It was the start of one of the greatest conventions I ever attended.

When an O&O buy or group buy is made at a convention, the news travels like wild fire and everyone wants to see and hear about it. I looked around our suite in total disbelief that afternoon. General managers were coming in, not even having seen the program, asking cost's and when could they start.

One general manager came to me, red-faced and angry, telling me he would never do business with us. When I asked him why, he said, "Your salesman has the unmitigated gall of wanting $600 a week for "TV POWWW" in my market." When I discovered the market was Wilkes Barre, Pennsylvania, I laughed, sat him down, and wrote out a contract at a reasonable rate for a small market of that size.

Although my salesmen had just received their presentation tapes, and new brochures, they already had contracts and were able to consummate many deals with start dates of September 1. I figured that from April to September we could build enough units to be off the ground and rolling.

We did not get all of the ABC O&O stations, but more than our fair share.

Since we were paying Fairchild up to $2500 a unit, we charged our stations $5,000 in advance for the equipment and a continuing supply of new program cartridges. Their billing thereafter covered the exclusive rights, payable monthly for fifty-two weeks.

While at the convention, I discovered Magnavox was offering their new game show to the trade. Nothing ever came of it, however, and rumor had it a few months later that both the president and attorney lost their jobs. I never heard from or saw anyone affiliated with that show idea again.

207

Flying back to the office at the end of the convention with the realization that we had a real success going, a show we owned 100 % of, and an opportunity to make a lot of money, was very exciting.

With start dates of "TV POWWW" fast approaching, the realization hit us early in July that Fairchild was not going to be able to fulfill our needs. They would be supplying the games and cartridges on time, but there was a problem in making each of the units operational.

Not being an engineer and knowing little, if anything, about electronics, I started looking for a bright, young engineer to put on staff, someone who could get the bugs out of the equipment and help us meet our commitments. With some outside help, we were able to find a no-nonsense, very clever engineer, who, we later discovered, was mostly self-taught. His greatest attribute was his ability as a trouble-shooter. He had a way of finding the trouble spots or problem areas quickly, a talent that must be inborn.

Bob Elder was in his early forties, a 260-pounder with a belly that protruded a good twelve inches. As we later found out, he was also an alcoholic, an incredible womanizer and in many ways, a pain in the ass, but in the six years he was with us he did some brilliant things.

In a matter of a few days, Bob had found the little bugs in the equipment that were causing the problems. We also were somewhat upset to find that the equipment supplied us was a little "Mickey Mouse", and we designed a case to put it in that gave it a more professional appearance.

Even so, I finally realized we would never make the September 1 date. I started calling our stations, apologizing and stating that the equipment would be in their hands by the middle of September and we were changing their start dates to October 1.

Having developed the presentation tape for the salesmen, done several mailings to stations, and taken full-page ads in the trade magazines, we were doing exceptionally well with "TV POWWW" and our other products.

*　*　*　*　*

When one travels so much, one finds station managers who become close personal friends. Living in Washington for a few years, I knew most of the management people up and down the eastern seaboard. In setting up territories for salesmen, I would continually work on my own or with them in specific markets, but I always protected

them in any sales I made. They received their commissions, but they had to service the accounts I was involved in.

I loved going to Salt Lake City, one of the more unusual areas of this country. It is completely dominated by the Mormon Church, with many fascinating areas including the great Mormon Tabernacle. I always loved staying at the Utah Hotel, next to the Tabernacle, with its one-of-a-kind, tiny restaurant with a dozen easy chairs surrounding a circular counter, serving only bowls of soup and home made rolls.

For years, I had been close friends with the general manager of the Mormon-owned television station, KSL, but as happens occasionally, I had made some enemies with the program people. I could always pick up the phone, make an appointment to see the general manager, and always get a contract on the spot. Los Angeles, San Francisco, Denver, Washington and Chicago were cities I also loved to visit and work in. And I used to enjoy hopping in my car in northern New Jersey and driving south, visiting friends in the business in Wilmington, then on to Baltimore or Washington, and ending up in Richmond, where Harvey Hudson, awaited. All these markets were ready to go on October 1 with "TV POWWW".

*　　*　　*　　*　　*

Having the first really workable voice activation equipment, the realization that our new show traveled at the speed of light through the television systems made it entirely new and different for the viewing audience. What happened in the first couple weeks in many markets was not only fun but hilarious as well.

Los Angeles discovered that they could not allow people to call, and had them register with postcards with their telephone numbers. WGN in Chicago was inserting "POWWW" into *Bozo the Clown.* In Washington, the station sold McDonalds with instant success. In Denver, the station hired a disc jockey, paying him $75 a show, and starting their *Six Million Dollar Man* syndicated program with the "TV POWWW" insert. That format, starting a program with "TV POWWW, added more than one rating point to the show, making it that much more successful.

KSL Salt Lake called one day to tell us that during a call-in show the telephone company, in no uncertain terms, told them they would pull their telephone lines if they didn't change immediately. It seems we knocked the telephone system out in seven states! They had to quickly change to a call-out show.

Our engineering staff had now grown to three people, and we were modifying and improving the "POWWW" equipment all the time. Working with Fairchild and their people continued, and they really tried in the coming months to give us fresh new games.

Our salesmen were having a ball, and "TV POWWW" was proving to be a monumental success throughout the country.

MATTEL

Every year the electronics industry has two major conventions: one in January in Las Vegas, the other in the summer in Chicago. Bob Elder wanted to go to the show in Las Vegas and since Fairchild would be showing there, we thought it a good idea. Just prior to leaving, I heard from the boys at Fairchild asking if we would please come in to see them the moment we arrived. Thinking nothing of it, we arranged our flight schedule and hotel accommodations, and arrived as scheduled.

With the size of some of the booths of the other electronic companies, I was somewhat surprised to find Fairchild had a very small stand. After checking in at our hotel, we went over to their space, and they requested a meeting a few hours later. Still thinking nothing was awry, we toured the convention center until the time of our meeting.

Through the years, I have seen many very successful companies set up in businesses they knew little about. Fairchild had always been one of the leaders in electronics. For some reason, they decided to go into the manufacture of watches as well, and had lost upwards of 30 million dollars. It wasn't that their product was no good, it was just an entirely different business and they had little or no marketing expertise in that field.

Although we had contracts with Fairchild, they announced to us they were immediately going out of business. We could continue using the materials which they had supplied up to that point. That was it. I suppose we could have forced some settlement with a lawsuit, but they appeared so sincere in their efforts not to hurt us, we agreed to find other means of continuing.

By now, we had several games, and they offered to send us any equipment from their shop to aid us in building the units ourselves. I knew we could continue for several months, if not longer, with what we currently had, but television eats up materials quickly. In order to get renewals, we would certainly have to have new games made available to us. Then someone with Fairchild asked, "Have you been over to see what Mattel is offering?"

Having been hit over the head with the disclosure of Fairchild's demise in the electronic game business, we ambled over to the Mattel stand and stood with our mouths open at what we saw.

Mattel had just released their Intellivision, with animation and motion one could only dream of. Fairchild's games, like Atari's, were great but Mattel's were brilliant. We spent an hour going through some of the games they were demonstrating. I picked up one of their brochures and discovered that their headquarters were in Hawthorne, California, less than a ten-minute ride from Los Angeles International Airport.

Later that afternoon, I went back to the hotel and called Mattel's office trying to find out who was in charge of the game division, and whether or not I might have an opportunity to talk with him. Someone in the president's office suggested I contact the senior vice president, although he would be unavailable for a few days since he was at the electronic show in Las Vegas. It would be impossible seeing anyone at the show, what with their appointments with major stores, electronic suppliers, etc. He was due back in the office two or three days before the end of the show, and I figured I could bide my time and call then.

Just prior to leaving the show, I called Ed Krakauer, Senior Vice President, of Mattel's Electronics Division. His gal made it tough to get through to him, as many secretaries do. I figured I had little to lose, so I tried to tell her why I wanted to see him. After a long pause, she finally said, "Let me put you through to him." He came on the line and I made as quick a pitch as I could, only to be told, "I'm sorry—I'm booked for the next several days."

In desperation, I asked him what time he went out for lunch. I said that I was out on the coast, my pitch would only take ten minutes, and I would appreciate his giving me that short amount of time. He finally said to come in at noon. When I asked if he had a television set in his office, he said no, but he would see that one would be available. I figured if I couldn't do the job in ten minutes, there was something wrong.

I caught a cab from L.A. Airport out to Mattel, a ten-minute ride, and was fascinated by what I saw there. The company was housed in a building about a city block in size with a huge parking lot. There were only a few empty parking spaces that seemed about a mile from the building. I am always fifteen or twenty minutes early for an appointment, so I had no trouble in parking and walking to the entrance in time.

Looking around, I was amazed at the size of the company. There were hundreds of employees, all very young. In the entrance were youngsters testing out roller skates, bicycles and all kinds of unusual toys. I was intrigued at seeing the freedom given these employees. I noticed on one side a huge, cafeteria-style dining room that seemed almost full of young people.

Ed Krakauer's office was a small cubicle in a huge room with dividers. There must have been one hundred of these small offices, and Krakauer's office was at the end of a long hallway. I met his secetary, a very attractive young woman who from that moment on always found a way to get me on the phone to Ed regardless of how busy he was. She escorted me into his office where someone had rolled a television set in and plugged it into the wall. I set up a Fairchild game unit to the television set, got half way through my presentation with the Shooting Gallery cartridge before Krakauer jumped up and turned the television set off.

That "ten minute" meeting lasted three days, and the Mattel people were very excited about what we were doing.

We had been having trouble buying a specific chip for the POWWW equipment. It was in short supply, and Mattel's people said they would supply them to us at cost. We would continue building the units and immediately start adding all Mattel games into "TV POWWW". There was no problem in adapting their cartridges so long as they put them into the "T" unit that Fairchild had designed.

Ed Krakauer, although a senior vice president, was (as I found out quite quickly) a con man. He could never quite look you in the eye. He was always looking for angles, whether on the level or not. I got a kick out of how he had his coffee served on china, with a sterling silver pot and tray. His secretary even added the sugar and cream for him. That kind of proved to me somehow that he was a phony, not to be trusted.

I was introduced to the president of Mattel, sat down with their attorneys, and worked out the details with them in a very short period of time. We would ask our stations for a tag using Mattel's copyrighted name "Intellivision-Intelligent Television". We would build the units for them with our own modifications, and add whatever software was needed. They, in turn, would simplify and re-program the game cartridges.

Since we had dozens of tapes from our subscriber stations showing how they were integrating the games into their programs, we were able to convey to the Mattel people what type of product we would require, and we were promised that we would receive them on a regular schedule.

213

We had re-done our presentation tape, making it a very strong sales tool. Mattel was to make the necessary changes to incorporate their games into the formats.

It looked like we had hit the jackpot with Mattel, a company that had surpassed the development of other companies in producing their games, one found much more animation and action in the cartridges, better contrast in color and freshness in their presentation. The realization that we would be working with one of the most successful game manufacturers in the world was exciting. I was certain we would be well rewarded in the coming months.

17.
Barney

While at the electronics show in Las Vegas, we passed a stand that had drawn a large crowd. It had a television set in the front showing a little cartoon character wise-cracking and talking to the audience. There was nobody at the set, and everyone was trying to figure out how this little cartoon character, moving around like a human being, could get fresh with an attractive girl going by or have a complete conversation with anyone asking questions.

He was selling electronic products, and gave us a fascinating idea for a television show. Wouldn't it be great to take this little character, named Barney, and have live television shows for children with studio audiences that he could talk to. Children at home could call him by telephone and watch him answer their questions on their television set.

He could be educational, and we thought it would be a great idea for one television station in a market to have their own "live" Barney who could go out to the schools and talk with the children. Also, wouldn't it be great for a cartoon character to play "TV POWWW" with the children.

We found the company that handled Barney in New York, Com-art-Aniforms, and made an appointment to see their chairman and president. It was an idea tailor made for television. At the same time, one of the general managers from Raleigh, North Carolina, called us claiming he was using a Barney in an afternoon segment with "TV POWWW", and both shows were doing exceptionally well.

215

There was one problem with the people at Aniforms: they had a patent, and stations buying Barney would have to adhere to their rule that they never divulge how the equipment was operated. What bothered us was that the equipment was very simple. We had the feeling that the only reason for the secrecy was that the patent was not strong enough to be defended.

It was a simple task to take a very tiny camera, conceal it, and have the talent operate the equipment from a distance. He could see and hear what was going on, and by manipulating the equipment he could animate the cartoon character and make it talk. I felt this would be a sensation in children's programming, and we quickly made an agreement to handle the syndication rights on a percentage deal.

Although we made several sales and had some limited success, it never really got off the ground, primarily because Aniforms would refuse many of the market sales for fear of their patent, weak as it was, not being protected. We continued trying for many months, and were able to make some sales in conjunction with "TV POWWW".

At the beginning, Mattel, with their Intellivision and Intelligent Television, continued to give us re-designed games that would work on television. We had Skiing, Boxing, Space Patrol, World Rockets, Astro Smash, and even Slots for the adults, which was a slot machine that worked beautifully. But Mattel was fast losing interest in their electronic game division. They were spending millions of dollars a year in developing Intellivision, but their real plans were to sell an $845 toy, namely—a home computer. At the time, they were wise enough to not use the word "computer" because it was too early for most consumers in the late seventies and early eighties. Their idea was to sell a computer with their game cartridges included. They spent more and more time on their computer and less on games.

Regardless, for a while they were very good to us but, as I mentioned earlier, Ed Krakauer was a real piece of cake. First, he wanted to buy the company, then he had a much better idea: we should pay a percentage of sales to Mattel, thus ensuring they would deliver more games to us. Promises were continually made, but never kept, while for months he kept us dangling.

I finally went to the president of Mattel's electronic division and got an apology for the shabby way Mattel had treated us. Still, there wasn't anyone else out there, so we continued to keep trying with Mattel.

We were renewing almost 90 % of our stations, and at one time we had over 100 under contract.

In Los Angeles, Metromedia came after us requesting the rights to build a half-hour show for prime time, at 10:00 p.m. Sunday nights on Metromedia's KTTV Channel 11. Their idea was to have studio contestants competing with those at home via telephone, while the television audience would see not only the game, but the contestants in the studio. They also wanted to try other games if we could supply them.

At a meeting in Los Angeles with Metromedia's attorneys and management, they asked for an option to syndicate the show on a half-hour basis and use a network master of ceremonies, Jack Clark. Jack had done *Crosswits* and other network game shows, and was one of the best-known hosts at the time.

If only Nintendo or Sega had been around during that period! All Mattel had to do was supply new games and offer some promotional aid, and we could have made them a fortune, but it was not to be. We had a thirteen-week run on KTTV with what we had, but Mattel proved indifferent to our cries of help for new games.

A couple of years later, Mattel, too, gave up, and almost landed in bankruptcy, having been wrong in their whole marketing strategy with their computer.

Still, with what we had from Fairchild and Mattel, "TV POWWW's" game concept lasted for more than 12 years. In later years, we contacted Nintendo and Sega trying to re-release the show, but they showed no interest. I still feel we could have helped them release new games on a continuous basis through television. But history has proved they didn't need us.

Around the World in Fifteen Days

My wife and I were having dinner with Paul and Marge Nagle in Miami one evening, and they mentioned a gal they had met who was interested in meeting me. She was from Australia and fascinated by what we were doing. Paul and Marge, who handled all our presentation material, as well all our brochures, advertising, layouts and copy, had shown her some material, and she felt that her home country would be a natural.

I met with her a few days later. Pamela Jacobs was a very attractive blonde, about five foot three and somewhat busty. I hoped that a strong wind wouldn't hit her from the back since she appeared to be a bit top-heavy. She was charming and knowledgeable about broadcasting in Australia, so we gave her the go-ahead. It was suggested that she contact a Max Stuart in Melbourne, who could be a natural for us insofar as representation. Several days later, after her return to Australia, she called and wanted to know if I would make a trip to meet Max Stuart in Melbourne. He would set up a trip around the world, opening up markets in Southeast Asia and Europe.

I talked to Max and discovered he had just formed a new company and needed product badly. He was honest enough to state that he did not have the funds to travel around the world, but if I would advance it, he would repay me from the commissions he felt would be made in sales. In most instances, that is a sucker's bet, but I had done some checking on Max and discovered he had been general manager of Channel 9 in Melbourne and had a good reputation. I always wanted to see Australia anyway, so I told Pamela and Max it was a go. I mentioned to Max that I would get an open round-the-world ticket with Pan American, with a stopover in Australia. He, in turn, should make our continuing reservations from Melbourne, ending up in London, where he would fly back to Melbourne and I would fly back to Florida.

An interesting aside is that Pan American's round-the-world first class fare, including additional money for Australia and with as many stopovers as one wanted, was $3900 that year. One year later, it was $9300.

My plan was to fly to Los Angeles, spend three days there, see Ed Krakauer at Mattel, and then on Friday night catch the 11:30 flight I worked most of the week in Los Angeles, then met Ed at 11:00 a.m. on Friday, again begging for additional game cartridges and listening to more bullshit, something he was very good at.

As I was leaving his office, I mentioned to him that I was catching the evening plane for Australia and had great hopes of selling "TV POWWW to one of the networks there. When Ed heard that, he became very upset and told me that he did not want "TV POWWW" sold in Australia, which I couldn't understand. In fact, he got so angry that he suggested I cancel my trip and let him know I wasn't going before the end of the business day. He was so vehement that he even gave me his home telephone number to call him that evening. There had to be some reason he did not want "TV POWWW" sold in Australia, and I was going to find out why.

I never called him, but did catch the 11:30 flight. We flew fourteen and a half hours nonstop to Auckland, New Zealand, crossing the international date line. We had a three-hour layover in Auckland, then three hours on to Sydney, a two-hour layover in Sydney, and then a short one-hour flight to Melbourne. With a sixteen-hour time differential, I had left at 11:30 at night on Friday and arrived in Sydney early Sunday morning. By the time I reached Melbourne, almost twenty-four hours later, it was about 10:00 in the morning. Max Stuart was to meet me, but I had never met the man and did not even have a picture of him.

Everyone else had picked up their luggage. I passed a man standing quietly on the side and decided maybe this could be the gentleman. I went up to him with a smile and asked, "Are you Max Stuart?", and this black-haired, mustached, very handsome Australian gentleman smiled back and said, "You must be Marv Kempner."

Max Stuart is more English than any Englishman. He is not only charming, but brilliant, and has a photographic memory, never forgetting a name or face.

We hit if off immediately, and he drove me to the Hilton Hotel in Melbourne. We had a cup of coffee and I suggested a few hours rest wouldn't hurt me. Perhaps we could meet for dinner with his wife?

That evening, being in Australia, my first meal had to be lamb chops and, naturally, with the first bite I loosened a partial bridge in my mouth. Max suggested that I see a local dentist early Monday morning prior to our getting started. He picked me up in the morning and took me to his office, where we had a couple of hours to make appointments prior to my date with the dentist. Max's office was a one-room affair and, at the time, his secretarial service was supplied by his wife, Jill, a very beautiful blonde.

Getting directions and the address from Max, I hopped a cab to the local dentist, which proved to be a most unusual and pleasant visit. All I needed was a simple bridge cemented temporarily in the back of my mouth. The doctor was charming and took the time to write a two-page epistle to my dentist explaining the type of cement he had used.

I was not prepared for the type of equipment still being used in a modern country such as Australia. Even as a youngster, I don't recall a dentist's drill being operated with a foot pedal, similar to an old sewing machine, but that was what was in his office. From the time I arrived, the dentist never stopped talking, and I discovered he was a graduate of the dental school at Northwestern University in the states. Suffice it to say, I had my bridge temporarily re-cemented and could once again order lamb chops in the country down under.

219

The city of Melbourne is beautiful. It is made up of wide avenues and beautiful parks. In this thriving modern metropolis, one could still see the old-fashioned streetcars in a city with a population of well over a million and a half. I was intrigued by the people. They loved us Americans and, in many ways, their accent is more British than that found in England. I also loved being known as "mate", and the Australians I met couldn't seem to do enough to please me.

I Arrived back at Max's office and we proceeded to plan our itinerary, ordering airline tickets and getting reservation acknowledgments in the hotels we would be staying. Late that same afternoon, we caught a plane for Sydney, the beginning of my first round-the-world adventure.

The city of Sydney reminds me of San Francisco. It is an exciting, beautiful town, and the largest in Australia. I was fascinated to find a number of houses and office buildings with tin roofs, while the hustle and bustle reminded me of Manhattan, with people not walking but running everywhere. The waterfront, where the world-famous opera house is located, is breathtaking, and I quickly fell in love with the city.

Unlike our country, no network is allowed to own more than two television stations so naturally the three major networks, channels 7, 9 and 10, all own facilities in the two largest cities, Melbourne and Sydney. Thereafter, they affiliate with the other major cities of Brisbane, Perth and Adelaide. The fourth network, ABC, for "Australian Broadcasting Company" is government-controlled, and operates similarly to our Public Broadcasting System.

Although we were cordially received by all three of the major networks, we never got an opportunity to actually make a full presentation. We were told there was no interest. At our last call, the station general manager let the cat out of the bag. Unbeknown to us, our dear friend, Ed Krakauer of Mattel, had called each of the stations and talked with management. It seems that Mattel had a twenty or twenty-five percent interest in one of the network groups, and had other plans for Mattel's games for that country. To say I was angry would be putting it very mildly. Max assured me that he would find another way, and we cut our trip short in Australia and headed for New Zealand.

New Zealand is probably one of *the* most, if not the most, beautiful countries in the world. It is made up of two major islands, the north and the south, one being of a moderate climate and the other somewhat subtropical, like Florida. There are three and a half million people and thirty million sheep. At the start of World War It, was the wealthiest country in the world, but today it is almost bankrupt. It has tremendous mineral wealth, but maintains an agricultural way of life and has been losing population for years.

We flew to Auckland since, at the time, everyone had to fly there so that the New Zealand Airline could take you elsewhere. From Auckland, we flew to Wellington to TVNZ. When saying this out loud, you pronounce it T-V-N-Zed.

Unlike Australia, which has a television network set up similar to ours in the United States, New Zealand, at the time, was totally government-controlled. There were two VHF channels and they were programmed in a most unusual manner. For example, on a Monday in prime time one channel would program all of the commercial shows, the majority being from the states including movies, comedies, detective shows, adventure shows, etc. The other channel on that day would have educational, documentary and government programming. On Tuesday, the channels would be reversed with the entertainment programming being on the other channel and vice-versa. In this manner, the stations maintained almost equal ratings on a continuous basis.

We made an appointment to see the head of programming at TVNZ, a most delightful man by the name of Des Monaghan. Des was born and raised in Ireland, and his wife was from Egypt, both having come to New Zealand years earlier. Des was one of the most charming and knowledgeable gentlemen I have met, and his programming expertise was incredible. We made our presentation to Des and his staff and immediately received a wonderful response. We did, however, have several engineering and telephone problems that had to be worked out before we could proceed with getting on the air.

In the United States, electric power is set up on 60 cycles and 110 volts. In Australia, New Zealand and many other countries throughout the world, electric power is 50 cycles and 240 volts. One has to use a converter and a form of shielding to protect against electrical surges, lightning, etc.

Another problem concerns the type of television set used in other parts of the world. In the United States, Canada, Mexico, Japan, the Philippines, and a few other countries operate on what is called NTSC standard. That means our television tube has 525 lines in it. The rest of the world uses a PAL standard in which their television sets have 625 lines. The more lines, the better clarity and quality of the picture, but our standards for years have been NTSC. A few countries use a PAL-S standard, particularly in South America, which requires a simple engineering change to convert from NTSC. Then, of course, there is the one country that always has to be different—France. They have SECAM (which a few other countries use as well).

These were the problems confronting us, but they were not insurmountable. With converters, shielding, and other equipment already available to us, we could make the necessary changes and adapt to the different equipment quickly.

Having received a verbal commitment to go ahead from Des, with Max Stuart to follow it up, we headed back to our hotel in Wellington, planning on leaving the following day.

The explorer James Cook is well known in New Zealand, where he discovered the islands and the Mauri natives. I was always curious to see the Aborigines in Australia and 1200 miles away, the Mauri people, who are descendants of the South Pacific islanders. It is interesting that the Polynesians came that far in canoes so many hundreds or thousands of years ago, while the Aborigines, an entirely different race, lagged much farther behind in development.

We stayed at the James Cook Hotel in Wellington, atop an ancient volcano. The city itself is built in an earthquake area. It was fascinating to register in the lobby and then take the elevator down ten or fifteen floors to our room. That evening the temporary cement on my partial bridge again broke loose, and I had to hope to find a dentist in Tokyo to repair it.

We landed at the old airport, which was fairly close to the city of Tokyo. I couldn't get over the city itself, having never seen a multimillion population area that was so clean. I have very little use for the Japanese in business, having had too many bad experiences working with them, but their cleanliness is remarkable.

We made several presentations to television companies, and we were assured of a deal by not one, but two companies. Since their television was the same as ours, NTSC standard, we had no problems electronically, but thirty days after leaving the country I received the standard letter (or so I discovered) from Japan: "So sorry—we are already doing it." As we discovered later, even Japanese patents are worthless.

I realized on my first visit to Japan that I had missed the boat at the end of World War II. If I had gone to Japan, I could have made a fortune printing calling cards. Everyone bows and hands you his card (sometimes more than one), and you quickly learn to make sure when you give them one of your own that it is facing right side up. I also marveled at how there aren't more head injuries in Japan. They bow and miss one another by fractions of an inch.

While in Tokyo, we stayed at the Tokyo Hilton Hotel, and I discovered that there was a dentist in the lower lobby. Both he and his hygienist spoke perfect English, and when I showed him the problem, it took less than five minutes for him to take some temporary cement and replace the partial bridge. What shocked the hell out of me was when I got a bill for 33,000 yen! Although the yen is worth about 120 to a dollar today, at that time it was 215 to the dollar, and $153 was really taking advantage. When I returned home, I wrote the Hilton Hotel and a few weeks later received a response claiming simply that that was the rate.

While waiting for our plane in the lounge at the airport that same evening, the partial bridge fell down in my mouth, having lasted about six hours.

Our First Big Strike Overseas

Hong Kong is one of the most thrilling, exciting, and fascinating cities in the world. Looking down from the top of the Sheraton Hotel at night across the bay from Kowloon to Hong Kong is an impressive sight.

The neon lights and signs, and the bay itself, are incredibly beautiful. The sheer excitement of the place is infectious. Max had been there many times. He took me to his tailor, a few blocks inland, where I ordered a dozen dress shirts with French cuffs and an extra button on the sleeve.

I made another appointment to see a dentist, but I never went. We found ourselves in the midst of a typhoon, fortunately a mild one, but with the wind and rain we could not get a taxi. I resolved to keep the bridge in during the day, and take it out at night so as not to swallow it, an ordeal that worked until I got home. After returning home, I found my dentist was at a medical conference, and his hygienist had to do the temporary cementing. A week later, when he returned, he couldn't get the damn bridge out! Such is life.

Hong Kong is 98 percent Chinese and 2 percent English-speaking, with the majority of the latter being British. There were two Chinese television channels and one English-speaking, and we made our presentations to all of them. One channel was very excited about its potential, but did not give us a clear response as to whether or not they were going ahead with it. Since Max had set up his accounting and banking out of Hong Kong, something many companies do to save taxes, he was going to follow up. The following day we caught our flight to Manila.

I had been warned to never drive a car in Manila. If you were in an accident, you could end up in jail and they could throw away the key for several days, or even weeks, until someone could get to the American Embassy. Upon arriving, the realization hit me that I didn't *want* to drive a car in Manila.

The traffic was one giant maze of horn-blowing confusion. I saw for the first time what Manila is famous for—jeepnies. There were approximately 35,000 of these vehicles, dating from World War II. I doubt that anything but the frames were left from the original jeep; they had been converted into ten-passenger buses, trucks, and every other conceivable type of vehicle.

I never did find out the significance of the horse in the Philippines, but many of the jeepnies had up to a dozen of them on the hood. Others had brightly colored fabric tops, reminding one of a surrey with a fringed top. The noise was horrendous. Our cab negotiated the streets and finally deposited us at the Philippine Plaza Hotel.

Manilla is a city of contrasts—exquisite beauty and abject poverty. The hotel was beautiful, and it had a huge open lounge surrounded by high ceiling to floor glass, where one could sit in the evenings sipping a cocktail and listening to a fourteen-piece orchestra playing the dance music of the fifties and sixties, with both a male and female vocalist. The city around the waterfront is beautiful, and I was intrigued by what I saw.

Max had made an appointment to see the head of the Manila Broadcasting Company, and to my surprise and delight, a very, very beautiful young lady by the name of Kitchie Benedicto appeared. She was in her late twenties or early thirties, 5'4" with a gorgeous figure and an exquisite face, black hair, a light sallow complexion, with bright lipstick and sparkling eyes—a real beauty.

After a few minutes of light conversation, I was given an opportunity to make a presentation on "TV POWWW," as well as Barney, and the reaction to both products was spontaneous. Kitchie asked the price, and before I could respond Max quoted a combination buy of $250,000 on a one-year contract.

Kitchie looked at me and said, "Marv, make out your contracts," and proceeded to give me her secretary to type them up. When I had completed the agreements, Kitchie turned to me and said that she would appreciate it if we would return to Manila and set up both programs for her staff. Before I could reply, she continued, "Of course, we will pay all first class airline tickets, hotel and other expenses, as well as your wife's if you care to bring her."

I mentioned I would like to bring my chief engineer to work with her engineering staff, something she had taken for granted. Kitchie then asked us to join her downstairs. She escorted us into a beautifully-decorated conference room where about a dozen men were holding a meeting. She introduced us to her father, a man I took to be in his early or mid-sixties. She told him that she had just purchased two of our products, that they were very, very exciting, and we would be back to set them up in the next four to six weeks.

Little did I learn until later that the senior Benedicto had been a school chum of Ferdinand Marcos. In the Philippines, he owned a shipping company, three VHS television stations in Manila, and several radio stations, as well as a bank in southern California. Max and I celebrated that night at the Philippine Plaza Hotel, then continued on our way the following day.

18.
Europe Here We Come

We caught a Pan American Airlines flight from Hong Kong (we had to return there from Manila) to Frankfurt, Germany. It was an experience I hope few ever have to endure. Pan Am Flight I, which was their around-the-world flight, made a stop and crew change in Delhi, India, before continuing on nonstop to Frankfurt. With a full complement of 350 or more passengers, we were herded into a small room no air conditioning and armed Sikh guards at each end. The Pan Am personnel demanded that we take all of our personal belongings with us, and that we had to leave the aircraft.

We milled around for over three hours in total discomfort, and then I began to feel personal hatred for the Indian government. They not only forced every woman out one exit and every man out the other, but strip-searched each of us and tore our hand-held luggage apart. I have never been treated that way on any aircraft and I let Pan Am know it after my return to the states. The crew even woke up sleeping babies to get them off the plane. I later learned that if anyone had refused to go, the crew would have been forced to stay on the aircraft. There appeared to be no excuse for it.

Arriving in Frankfurt, Germany, we headed for the Intercontinental Hotel, and it felt almost like home. All Intercontinental Hotels are beautiful, and although Frankfurt, itself, is not a very attractive or exciting city, we enjoyed seeing what Germany was all about.

We headed into the outskirts to the German television networks. Although we spent an entire two days, we never really got to see anyone of importance. We finally realized it was summer, when the majority of

226

the staff is on vacation and they work with a skeleton crew. It still proved to be interesting, although that first visit was not very productive.

Flying from Frankfurt to London, I started experiencing a great deal of discomfort. One learns quickly a very important lesson when traveling out of the country—don't drink the water. Whatever the cost, only drink bottled water wherever you are. In Frankfurt, I figured the tap water had to be safe, and the night before we left the city I had two or three full glasses in my room.

Flying to London was horrible. Something inside had gone wrong and I was miserable. For three days in London, although we kept every appointment we had made, I was unable to eat anything. We called on BBC and all of the other television stations there, but Max had to take over. We stayed at the Hilton Hotel in Hyde Park, and I ended up with a closet of a room, so small that I had to climb over the bed to put the television on. Unusual for England, they were having a heat wave. Temperatures were hovering in the 90's. Naturally, air conditioning in London was unheard of in most areas, and those three days of suffering remain paramount in my mind.

Max introduced me to the head of a company called Global Television Services, which wanted to handle our product in Europe, with the understanding that I would help in any way possible. Max made the deal for me, and we then parted company. He flew the twenty-six hours back to Melbourne, and I returned to Miami.

My illness could have been jet lag, but I knew enough to always get on whatever time I was in immediately, and for years after that I never had a problem. I still think it was the water, and I haven't had a glass of tap water outside of the United States since. My first trip around the world had been very exciting and educational, and the next several months would prove to be even more so.

Opening South America

While at a NATPE convention in New York City, I met Leon Darcyl. Here was a man about 5′3″, somewhat overweight, with clothes that never seemed to fit him. His shirt collars spread-eagled to the heavens, his tie was askew, and he always had the smelliest cigar in his mouth.

Leon had escaped from Germany, settled in France, and just prior to World War II he and his family went to Argentina. He adored France, and for years kept an apartment in Paris, but his home was in Buenos Aires, where he met his wife, married, and had three children.

227

He told me a delightful story about an episode with his father. His father went to the government during the Juan Peron era to see whether or not he could get permission to import French champagne into the country. He was given the paperwork, and filled out the necessary information requesting to be allowed to import 500 cases of French champagne annually.

Leon, without telling his father, added an extra zero to the number. When his father discovered what Leon had done, he was positive they would end up in prison, or worse. But the Peron government authorized it with no problems, and for years the Darcyls made a fortune being the only company importing French champagne into the country.

Leon wanted to handle our product in South America, feeling he could do wonders for us. Figuring I had little to lose, I initially offered a contract to Leon with a 30% commission, which he just laughed at. He finally said to me, "Marv, I have to pay 20% under the table in most countries just to make a sale, this is common practice in South America."

Power of attorney was drawn up, along with an agreement, and we gave Leon presentation materials, brochures, and our contracts, which we demanded he use in lieu of his. Ten days later, I received a call from Leon telling me he had made his first sale in Venezuela, for the unbelievable price of $200,000. He then notified me that a percentage of the down payment would be forthcoming in the next few days.

Sure enough, two men with an attache case walked in and deposited thousands of dollars in $100 bills, making it necessary for us to fill out a list of forms for the government. We did well with Leon for the next few years, and he proved to be a very honorable man.

Back To Manila

Two weeks before we were to return to Manila and set up the equipment for "TV POWWW" and Barney, I was to meet Kitchie Benedicto in Los Angeles to plan our trip and pick up a check covering the advance payment on the contract. One learns that many people in business have no concept of time. Although we were to meet at the Holiday Inn coffee shop at 4:00 p.m., Kitchie didn't arrive until about a quarter after 5. By that time, I was on pins and needles, wondering whether or not they were going to renege on the agreement. When she walked in all smiles, I relaxed, and we sat down and discussed our upcoming trip.

228

Kitchie told me that reservations had been made in our name at the Holiday Inn in Manila. She gave me a big grin and said, "We own the hotel."

Taking equipment into foreign countries was a very expensive proposition. I recall going into Canada once and having to hire a broker to pay all duty charges on the value of our equipment. I had to leave a check in full for whatever the costs were.

Canada had a wonderful thing going for years. You would leave an American check and, upon bringing the equipment back over the border, would be told by some smiling customs agent that the money would be forthcoming from Ottawa, the capital, within a few days. It always arrived but it was always in Canadian funds, meaning you would lose at that time as much as 20% of your American dollar. This was a problem for all companies, and the International Chamber of Commerce helped solve it with what was known as a Carnet.

Through your bank, you would deposit a percentage of the value of your equipment, and then carry Carnet forms which allowed you to transport the equipment into another country. The forms would be signed by a customs agent when entering, and then upon leaving, that country. It made it very easy for us as long as we were just taking equipment in for short periods of time. However, if we were shipping equipment for use in a given country, we were obliged to pay whatever duties were charged.

In discussing this with Kitchie, she suggested that we ship all the equipment with our luggage, and not worry about customs upon our arrival.

Bob Elder, our chief engineer, my wife, Jeanne, and I flew Northwest Orient from Miami to Chicago, with a nonstop from there to Tokyo, and then a change of plane to Manila—a long and tedious trip.

Upon arrival, as we walked toward customs a short, skinny Filipino man carrying a sign with my name on it appeared. He quickly asked us for our passports and told us to wait where we were for a few minutes. Upon his return, he gave us back our passports and asked for all of our luggage and equipment stubs, telling us again to be patient—he would be with us as soon as possible. A short time later, he appeared with two porters, all of our equipment and luggage, and escorted us out a side door to a large, black Mercedes. We were introduced to our chauffeur, Pacifico, who helped pack all of our equipment and luggage as we made ourselves comfortable in the car.

It was a beautiful, large four-door Mercedes 600, with white linen covers over the leather upholstery, which we discovered was changed every day. Pacifico drove us to the Holiday Inn and, since martial law was in effect at the time, each of us and our luggage and equipment was searched before entering the hotel.

We had flown first class from Miami to Manila, been picked up in real style, with no problems at customs, and escorted to beautiful hotel suites.

Unlike Holiday Inns in the U.S., international Holiday Inns are in many ways five-star hotels, and this one was no different. Pacifico announced that he would pick us up at 8:00 a.m. and take us to the television station. We were to make ourselves comfortable and enjoy the evening at the hotel.

At 8:00 the following morning, as arranged, our chauffeur was awaiting us, and we headed out into one of the wildest thirty-minute rides imaginable. Jeepnies, cars, trucks and taxis were embroiled in one great big traffic cauldron, with everybody blowing his horn to add to the confusion. Near misses and screeching brakes were common practicea in driving in Manila.

When we arrived at the station, we discovered armed guards and barbed wire completely encircling the beautiful white stone buildings which held the television stations and broadcast offices. Even though we were escorted to the station, anywhere we went, including the television facilities, we were searched prior to being allowed entry. Martial law meant that the government and troops were in total command. Though at the beginning it was not too pleasant, we encountered during our entire stay no real problems whatsoever.

The television facilities in Manila were mind-boggling. Three fully-equipped VHF stations were being operated out of one master control. We were flabbergasted to discover that the wiring from the master control room just lay on the floor, and if one tripped over a wire it could cause all kinds of problems.

Manila in the early fall is very hot and humid, but the air conditioning in the television facility had to be set at sixty degrees—and we were freezing.

We set up "TV POWWW" first, and had a dozen engineers jabbering away excitedly when they saw it operational. Our chief engineer, Bob Elder, was going crazy with all the loose wiring. Kitchie just laughed and said, "Don't worry about it. They'll resolve any problems."

230

It was a beautiful building, exquisitely decorated and furnished, except for the johns. I found that to be true all over Asia. It always amazed me to walk into the toilette, as they called it, to find there were only holes in the floor. I would hate to have to squat like that, and prayed it wouldn't be necessary before going back to the hotel.

When Kitchie realized I had my wife with me, she had our chauffeur pick her up and gave her a chaperone, or gal Friday, to spend the day with her. The Philippine women are probably the most beautiful in the world, and the gal that was given Jeanne was no exception. Most of the Philippine people are short, but Rexi was 5'8", with a face, body and personality the likes of which I did not expect. She took Jeanne sightseeing and shopping, and showed her around Manila every day that we were there. When I came home the first evening, Jeanne told me that if she so much as looked at something in the store window, Rexi went in and bought it for her. During the entire time we were in the Philippines, when we protested against this over-indulgence, we were told, "You are our guests."

One evening, we were invited to their concert hall, or opera house, a structure with so much glitter and gold that it made the Kennedy Center look shabby. Once again, upon entrance, we were searched. On entering the theater itself, we were searched a second time. This continued throughout our trip.

Another evening, Rexi asked if we would like to go to a real Philippine restaurant to see how the natives dined. The Americans, Spanish and Japanese have all occupied the Philippines, making Manila an international city. Going to a genuine native restaurant sounded like fun.

We sat at a table with no utensils and ate with our hands. After each course, we walked over to a water trough, washed our hands, were given a towel, then returned to the table awaiting the next course. It was a fun evening.

I finally cornered Kitchie at the station and told her we were embarrassed because she had not allowed us to reciprocate. I asked her, as a personal favor, if she would allow us to take the managers of the stations out for dinner. She suggested that we could meet that evening at 8:00 p.m. in the mezzanine of the Holiday Inn, where there was a very fine gourmet restaurant.

At 8:45, Kitchie and her entourage arrived with somewhere between thirty-five and forty people. She had ordered the menu ahead of

231

time, and after cocktails and hors d'oeuvres we were treated to an incredible feast. Dessert was a crazy concoction prepared in front of us, accompanied by much laughter and applause. It was a wonderful evening. When I went to take care of the bill, I was told the dinner was in our honor.

I don't approve of dictatorships, but being on the right side of one sure made for a visit I'll never forget. We went to the cemetery on a Sunday and watched families having picnics in front of mausoleums with life-size pictures of their ancestors. We were fascinated by the culture.

Several years later, when the Marcos regime collapsed, we discovered that Kitchie and her family were on the Marcos plane to Hawaii. The Benedictos a few years later made restitution in the millions and lost all their property, but eventually returned to the Philippines.

Since our air fare included continuing on to Hong Kong, we decided to spend four or five days there before returning home. I wanted to call on the television station that had shown so much interest in "TV POWWW." The evening of our arrival, while fooling with the television set, I came across their attempt at stealing our concept. They had jerry-rigged an Apple computer, and were using a form of shooting gallery that was so slow and so bad that it was a disgrace.

I didn't call them the following morning to make an appointment, I just caught a cab to the station, walked in, asked for the head of programming, and was immediately granted an audience. I took a contract out of my briefcase and put it in front of him. Without saying a word, he signed it. He and his station proved to be a royal pain in the butt. There were months of there screaming for new games, and we could never quite satisfy them. We did not attempt to get a renewal in Hong Kong, but the contract, while in force, was lucrative and worthwhile.

We flew back by way of Honolulu, and decided to spend a few days to rest. We stayed at a bit of paradise, called the Royal Hawaiian Hotel where one gets a feel for Hawaii as it used to be before the islands became so commercial.

It's like an oasis in the desert, a building only five or six stories high on the beach at Waikiki overcooking Diamond Head, an extinct volcano. With beautiful gardens surrounding the hotel, and an outdoor bar I loved, it's a very special place. The real estate power boys for years tried to tear it down to build a high-rise, but it has been named an historic site and remains as a true monument to Hawaii.

Returning home, we discovered the sales staff was doing beautifully. Leon, in South America, was breaking all records insofar as sales,
and everything was going wonderfully.

19.
Marche Internationale Des Films et des Programmes

The above is the French name for International Television Programming Market. We call it MIP, a convention that brings together programmers from countries throughout the world. At the time, it was held each April, and thousands attended. Buyers from the various countries were given such wondeful "perks", it is no wonder attendance was so good.

Ninety percent of all television in the world was government controlled in the 1970's and 1980's. With the exception of the United States, a portion of Canada, Japan, Australia and a few other countries, television was programmed by government. In France, at the time, it was not uncommon to have a two-hour special in the evening, in what we would call prime time, on a subject like the sex life of the snail. In England, which was just inaugurating commercial television, the number one program in the country was on Sunday night at 9:00. It was a one-hour show on antiques.

With governments controlling programs, the most sought-after were documentaries, educational films, and political propaganda programmed for those in power.

Ninety percent of those attending this international convention had all their expenses paid by their government. They could eat, drink and be merry except, for the ten percent who had to pay their own expenses. I always felt that the program people and heads of the stations received this perk in lieu of high salaries.

234

Max Stuart had arranged for us to be included with Global Television Services Ltd. of London, feeling that we could, with their help, do a big selling job in Europe and other parts of the world.

After that invitation, I contacted Vince Sotto, President of Comart Aniforms Co. which owned the Barney concept. He arranged to have talent who could speak both English and French operate the "Barney" equipment which would be several feet from our stand. Vince was going over two days early to set up, and I decided to take my wife Jeanne and find out first-hand what MIP TV was all about.

Cannes, twenty miles from Nice, is in the heart of the French Riviera, Europe's playground for well over 2,000 years. It has been under the control of the Romans, French and English, and runs for miles on the shore of the beautiful Cote D'Azure (Sea of Blue). It is an area surrounded by walled-in palms dating well before the middle ages, and was the home of Renoir, Monet, Manet, Toulouse-Lautrec, Vincent Van Gogh, Miro, Picasso, and many other revered artists, all of whom had spent time in the area and created so much beauty for the world.

The Croisette—somewhat like a boardwalk along the Mediterranean, with many beautiful hotels and incredibly expensive shops—is beautiful. Looking down the Croisette, one sees the old city of Cannes in the background, the original walled fortress, and the narrow, winding streets into the old city.

The food, the one saving grace for the French nation, is incredible. The French are arrogant as hell and are not much to my liking. They don't like Americans, and they find every way possible to take advantage of us, but they still have one of the most beautiful countries in the world.

On arrival, we went directly to our hotel, a ten-minute ride from the Palais, the convention center on the Croisette. I went to the Palais to meet Max, as well as our host from Global. Vince had already set up Barney, and it was impossible to figure out where or how they had hidden the equipment. My only wonder was how anyone could find his way around the Palais.

It was a several-story building constructed somewhat like a palace, but in terrible physical condition. The floor and walls were old, the ceilings were crumbling, and there were almost no aisles to speak of. Every corner of the Palais, including closets, had been rented to companies attempting to sell their products. The basement was full, half the stairwells had partial stands on them, and the noise around us was almost deafening.

Our stand was in a corner, but people had to turn here with perhaps two feet to spare. We had a 19-inch color TV set suspended from the ceiling, and our Barney host did a brilliant job of insulting everyone who went by. We drew such crowds no one could get through the hallway, The German, French and Italian program people were fascinated. Working from 8:00 in the morning until 8:00 at night, with all the foul-ups Global had, we estimated we quoted prices at this six or seven day convention worth somewhere between 3.8 and 4 million dollars. If only I had known the type of company Global really was, I could have saved myself a great deal of aggravation. They never followed up on any of the accounts we generated, and not one sale was ever made. It was the last time I ever attempted to have other people sell our product in Europe. It was a bitter lesson.

One man at Global had made a presentation of "TV POWWW" to the BBC in London. Any electronic equipment for the British Isles has to be cleared by British Tel-Com, and I flew over with our chief engineer in case of any problems. In calling Global, I was informed that there was a railroad strike and no one outside of London would spend the two hours on the road to London to work out the contractual agreements. The BBC was very cooperative working with us, and we signed the contracts ourselves, writing off Global as pretty much a waste of time.

Opening Up Australia

Several weeks after my return from France, Max Stuart called asking how quickly we could build "POWWW" equipment for Australia. Although he had not been able to sell Sydney or Melbourne, he had made a presentation and gotten commitments from fourteen other markets in the country, most of which were small. He had quoted a substantial price, including up front money that would more than pay for the modifications necessary. He had also been able to clear through Australia Tele-Comm (the telephone company which was under control of their form of our Federal Commmunications Commission). A meeting had been set up in the city of Wollongong, which was about 150 kilometers from Sydney.

Bob Elder, my wife and I flew to Sydney. Jeanne was going to go on to Melbourne and spend a few days with Pamela Jacobs, the gal who had put Max and me together. Max met us in Sydney, where we rented a car and drove to Wollongong.

We arrived about 2:30 in the afternoon, only to discover that all of the restaurants were closed in the city of Wollongong (population 15,000), and we had but one choice—McDonalds. Our hotel reminded me of the type we stayed in in the late 1940's. It was clean, but old and decrepit.

I managed to stay awake until 9:00 that evening. We had an all-day meeting scheduled for the following day, a Saturday. Everyone appeared excited about "POWWW's" potential, and we gave them our many success stories in the States, as well as worked with their engineers who were also at the meeting.

On Sunday morning, we went down to the coffee shop at the hotel only to find it was not operating because it was Sunday, so, we again headed over to McDonalds. That evening we were fortunate to find one restaurant open in the entire city. They were kind enough to accept our reservations for 10:30 that night.

On Monday morning, Bob Elder wanted to go his own way before returning home a couple of days later. We planned to meet him on Tuesday in Sydney, and Max and I drove back to get Jeanne. Max's wife, Jill, was joining us from Melbourne, and we were going on up to Brisbane to work with our television station there and take a few days just to unwind.

Australia is not a beautiful country. Ninety percent of it is desert, and it has a very harsh climate. Its foliage is much different than other areas of the world. Eucalyptus trees are in abundance—the only food consumed by the native koala bears. Australia's beaches, however, are outstanding, with the whitest sand I have ever seen and the clearest and cleanest water. Just before leaving for Brisbane, Bob Elder joined us and raved about his lunch at Bateman's Bay the day before, when he consumed nine dozen oysters.

We caught the one-hour flight to Brisbane, rented a car and headed for Surfer's Paradise, a beach Max and Jill raved about. We stayed at a hotel on the beach which has since become a condominium, and I was amazed to find Miami Beach in Australia, with all the souvenir shops and garbage merchandise we find in our own country. The beach itself, however, was wonderful.

While there, we were treated to something I continue to marvel at, the Currumbin Bird Sanctuary. Forty or fifty years earlier a man had rescued birds and animals that had been hit by cars or otherwise injured, and restored them to health. With a few exceptions, they were allowed to roam freely, and one quickly learned to watch where he stepped! We were charged $3 to gain entrance, and could buy food to feed the kangaroos, wallabies, etc. The wallabies, which appear to be miniature kangaroos came up to beg for food with babies in their pouches the size of my thumb. It was incredible.

The koala bear may be adorable to look at, but with a diet of nothing but eucalyptus leaves, it is always in somewhat of a drunken stupor. They are caged for their own protection, and to see eight or nine of them on one limb was fascinating. The young female attendant, wearing a very heavy woolen sweater in 100-degree heat, had taken one of the baby koalas in her arms and we were allowed to pet the bear which, surprisingly, has a very coarse coat of fur. The sweater she wore was for protection from the claws of the koala bear, which are long and razor sharp.

We saw other animals strange to us in the western world, including the dingo, a wild dog species, but the most thrilling thing I witnessed was in a pen, where if you were completely still for fifteen to twenty minutes, a platypus would come out of his den under the water.

The continent of Australia has more poisonous snakes than any other in the world, and at night the platypus pen is covered with a chain-like wiring to protect them. I loved those few days at Surfer's Paradise, and I hope some day to go back to that sanctuary. I am an animal lover, and it was one of the most thrilling days of our trip.

Max, Jeanne and I flew on to Auckland, New Zealand, and then to Wellington amid beautiful country that is still 100 years behind the times. Max and I went to TVNZ to be with Des Monaghan, while Jeanne had lunch with Des's wife. I invited Des and his wife to dinner with us that evening, but Des declined, having another date. When I returned to the hotel, there was a message from Des's wife to please call. When I did, she asked me in a most delightful way, "May I keep your darling Jeanne a little bit longer?" Shortly after that, Des called and said he had canceled their appointment for that evening. The four of us had a wonderful dinner together, Max having returned to Melbourne that afternoon.

We had heard so much about Mount Cook that we caught a single-engine six-seater plane south and spent a weekend in Mount Cook National Park at the Hermitage Lodge near the foot of the mountain.

We climbed and visited Tasman Glacier, the only glacier in the world to be found in a moderate climate. We looked in awe at the waterfalls. There were dozens of them higher than Niagara Falls, and the wild flowers growing everywhere were incredible. New Zealand, being an agricultural country, is unusual in many ways. Visiting Christ Church and several other cities, one finds its food to be simple and honestly, a bit fattening. Seems that desserts have real whipped cream atop all of them and cooking with pure creamery butter is the norm. Their fish and chips when ordered for take out always comes wrapped in the daily newspaper but proved to be a tasty evening meal. I also loved breakfast where a chef cooked your eggs to order in front of you while you watched, and then proceeded to make toast a la England style with no crust.

We flew back to Auckland, then on to Sydney and home having had a wonderful time.

20.
Telephone Poll

In late 1980, our staff consisted of six full-time salesmen on the road, a chief engineer with three engineers under him, two part-time engineers who worked an average of twenty hours a week and two secretaries. "TV POWWW" was no longer using the Fairchild Camera Instrument Corporation's patents. The electronic industry had come far and we had found easier ways of producing our interactive equipment.

After hours of meetings, it was decided to go ahead and try building a new piece of equipment that we felt would be very well received by the broadcasting industry. With synthesized voice chips now available, our idea was to build a piece of polling equipment that could be installed in a station's present telephone system. It would take phone calls from viewers and give them the opportunity to vote on current events, political questions, capital punishment anything from sports to local subjects. Bob Elder thought we could build a unit in a six to nine-month period that could be leased to television and radio stations at a reasonable cost.

At the time, AT&T was offering a polling device with a 900 number for a "yes" and a different number for a "no", at a cost to the viewer of fifty cents. We would design a piece of equipment that was automatically answered with a solid-state polling device. It would record, compute, and then present the results in running totals in percentages in a digital readout on the television screen and/or by a synthesized voice, at no cost to the local viewer.

The project meant investing thousands of dollars and man-hours to build a piece of equipment that would not cost the viewer that half a buck to voice his or her opinion. By leasing only one unit in a market to a broadcaster, we could give that station additional clout in gaining news viewers or listeners.

Our engineers were all very well paid, but what happened in the ensuing months proved thrilling and very satisfying to me. Since everyone was on salary, I never gave a thought to overtime nor, for that matter, did anyone else, to my knowledge. Our workday was 9:00 to 5:00, with up to an hour for lunch, as it had been since the company's inception.

I guess, in retrospect, I do believe that "nice guys don't finish last", because we never held anyone to a time clock and there might have been times one or two of the engineers might take advantage with an extra day off here or there, etc., but God bless all of them.

I would come in in the morning and discover two engineers were so excited with what they were doing that they had worked all night. No one in my company ever had to worry about a reward because we had set up a percentage deal on the gross, not the net, for all our people in the office. Believe me, in the long run they made much more than time-and-a-half or double-time would have paid them.

It was worrisome, but fun, watching them test and re-test this new-found miracle we were building. It also became quite funny, at times, since it was a well-known fact that if it worked with Marv Kempner running it, they had a winner! Whenever I was called into the engineering department and asked to test a piece of equipment, many times it didn't work for me although it had worked for them. When I finally had it working, they knew it would work for anyone.

Although the equipment was still not operational, we had designed a sleek compact piece of rack-mounted equipment that could be installed in a control room, or installed in a studio next to a newscaster or talk show personality. It was finished in brushed aluminum, and the initial unit, with each telephone line having its own microprocessor, could accept up to 360 calls per hour. The initial equipment would handle five telephone lines, and each line, or TIU (telephone interface unit), would answer a call automatically with a trouble-free synthesized voice telling the listener how to vote. It would instantly register the vote as it was made.

Most stations have eight to ten telephone lines, minimum, so all that was needed was to add a modular jack to each line of their rotary system at a very modest charge from the telephone company.

Each day, the engineers came up with new and fresh ideas to add to the equipment. What pleased us most was that we could, from a five-line standard unit, which included the microprocessor, supply them with additional units that could take them up to ninety-nine phone lines.

Since our rack-mounted piece of equipment was ready (although nothing worked), I called an old buddy at Channel 12 in West Palm Beach and asked if we could lease his news studio and use part of his news staff to make a tape presentation of our new project, called Telephone Poll.

I had never attempted to make a full presentation on a piece of equipment that was still not operational, but with Bob Elder behind a black curtain with wires and switches he could manipulate, we spent several hours in the studio making up a presentation tape.

It was hilarious at times when Elder flicked a switch at the wrong time, or touched a wire inappropriately and we had to start over, but eventually we finished and edited a master to be used in the sale of Telephone Poll.

What the engineers had accomplished was truly a miracle for its time. A synthesized voice told the caller how to place his or her vote. The vote was instantly registered, tabulated and recorded, and a digital readout appeared showing the running totals or percentages. With the flick of a switch, the readout could be spoken by a synthesized voice. By pushing another switch, one could go back to running totals or percentages.

Each telephone line could accept up to 360 calls per hour, with all the calls being answered automatically by the synthesized voice. Since the equipment had its own built-in character generator, a station could instantly project the results on their television screen, and its memory bank would hold onto the running scores even when the equipment was turned off or there was a power failure.

Our initial equipment would record six different responses: yes/no, true/false, agree/disagree, like/dislike, A/B, for/against. Later on, we were able to add ABC and ABCD. If there was a malfunction of the equipment, such as a connection working loose or a switch incorrectly positioned, the Telephone Poll system's check light would signal a digital readout on the equipment, helping step-by-step to find the appropriate remedy in solving the problem.

Having hired a patent attorney, we began filing for patents on several portions of Telephone Poll. Then, it was only a matter of getting some bugs out, starting to build units, and making sales.

242

HOW DOES **TELEPHONE POLL** WORK?

The TELEPHONE POLL is exceptionally easy to operate. On the right are phone panels, one for each of the first six lines of a station's rotary system. (The equipment can accommodate up to 99 lines!)

Each phone panel has an On/Off switch so you may devote as many lines of your rotary system to polling as you choose at any given time by switching each line on or off the 'polling' position. Each panel also has a light indicating that the line is operational, plus a testing system to adjust the level of the outgoing signal and another to test the sensitivity of the voting mechanism.

When you turn it on, five microprocessors go to work and the TELEPHONE POLL is able:

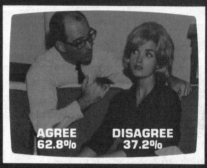

AGREE 62.8%   DISAGREE 37.2%

- To accept up to 360 calls per hour, per phone line.
- To answer each call automatically. . .not with a tape recording subject to mechanical failure, but with a trouble-free SYNTHESIZED VOICE.
- To instantly register each vote.

AGREE 3140   DISAGREE 1860

- To keep a running total of the votes as they come in.
- To present that total on a digital readout on the equipment (see A), and through your own switcher, instantly project it onto the television screen by means of its own built-in character generator.
- To convert, instantly, the running totals into percentages and present them on screen. (B)

- To present both totals and percentages, by the flick of a switch, in a synthesized voice readout.

- To hold running scores in its memory bank even when the equipment is turned off, or in the event of a power failure. (C)

- To request and record responses to questions phrased in six different ways:

Yes	True	Agree	Like	A.	For
No	False	Disagree	Dislike	B.	Against

(Almost any question can be phrased in such a way that one of these answers will apply.)

- To diagnose its own malfunctions and supervise its own adjustment; e.g. should a phone connection work loose or a switch be incorrectly positioned, TELEPHONE POLL "systems check light" (E) will signal and a digital readout on the equipment (A) will lead you step by step to the appropriate remedy.

With engineering telling me they were four to six weeks away from refining the equipment and printing manuals for stations' usage, I couldn't wait any longer to start selling. Meeting one of the salesmen in Las Vegas, we called on the CBS affiliate, KLAS, and made our first pitch on Telephone Poll. Not having any brochure material, just a presentation tape, I let the tape speak for itself. To my amazement, programming, news and management hit the ceiling with excitement. Without my having even quoted a price, they were contemplating leasing the equipment and placing it directly in the news room so that their anchor people could instantly start a poll and get the results, all while on the air. I didn't have contracts with me, so we took a purchase order after negotiating a very lucrative price.

From there, we proceeded to San Jose, Bakersfield and San Diego, picking up purchase orders from each city. Every station that we called on bought Telephone Poll. Returning to the office, we quickly printed up contracts and sent them out.

Several days later while visiting my mother in Buffalo, I sold both radio and television there. It was thrilling and fun. Stations realized the potential of Telephone Poll, and loved the presentation.

Next I flew down to Charlotte, North Carolina, rented a car and made one call there, to WBTV. I did not get an answer, so I told them I was hitting the other stations in the market that afternoon, and I gave them the name of the hotel I was staying in for the evening. At noon, I received a call at the hotel, and I never made another presentation. WBTV confirmed their purchase on the phone, and I went back for a contract later that afternoon.

I went on to the Greensboro-High Point market, and was successful there as well. It had worked on the west coast, in the east, and the south, so I was certain we had a big winner with Telephone Poll. Although the salesmen would be protected in their territory, regarding commissions, I did not give it to them. I was having too much fun making the sales myself. My salesmen had a lot of product and were doing very well, and I was having the fun of selling—still my first love in this wonderful industry.

I also knew that the equipment could not be delivered for several months, and the company had to generate sales with our present products to help pay for Telephone Poll's production. I had made arrangements with our bank for an additional quarter-million-dollar loan, which I felt, with our cash flow would more than see us through. Those were very exciting times.

Channel 9 Network—Australia

It was early October and I knew full well there was no way we could deliver any equipment until after the first of the year, so I decided, with Max Stuart's assistance, to once again go around the world. It was also a great opportunity to test Telephone Poll and find out what had to be done to meet the local Tel-Com minimums. From my "TV POWWW" experience, I knew we had to find a way of shielding and building the equipment to 50-cycle and 240 volts. Max had promised to set up appointments with the heads of the three major networks in Sydney. He had been apprised of what we were doing and, being a great salesman he was very much "hyped" before my arrival in Sydney. When I showed him the presentation tape we had produced, he became ecstatic with anticipation of making a pitch to the networks.

Max, having been a general manager of Channel 9 in Melbourne, was well-known and liked in his own country, and it was not difficult for him to make appointments with the top brass.

Our first call was to Len Mauger, President of Channel 9 in Sydney. Len was about 5' 8", with thinning hair and a little bit round about the middle, but he was a very astute businessman with a charming personality. After the initial presentation, Len called his chief engineer into the meeting and we proceeded to re-play the tape. I have never seen two people so excited, and Max and I never got further than Channel 9, which, at the time, was the number one network in Australia.

Since they owned Sydney and Melbourne, and had affiliates in the other major markets, covering Adelaide, Brisbane and Perth, the deal was to be exclusively theirs in their network major markets. Naturally, everything was subject to Tel-Com approval, which, from experience with "TV POWWW", would prove fairly easy to accomplish.

Knowing the size of these markets, I had offered Len a fifteen-line unit, rather than a five-line, and felt it would be ample. We then got to pricing, and Max Stuart took over, asking for half a million dollars for a three-year lease, with all equipment being supplied by us including spare parts.

I opened my mouth at the wrong time during this portion of the conversation by telling Len that if they needed more than fifteen lines in each market, we would be glad to oblige at our cost, which I felt would be minimal. When Len accepted the terms, Max had another brilliant idea that, fortunately, wasn't accepted.

In 1981, the Australian dollar was worth 114 cents American. Max suggested to Len that they pay in Australian dollars, at which Len blew his stack, stating, "You will take American dollars!" I never said a word. A few months after this meeting, the Australian dollar dropped to somewhere between sixty and sixty-five cents against the American dollar.

We now had a letter of commitment, and contracts were left subject to Tele-Com approval. I arranged to return with our chief engineer in sixty to ninety days and expected to bring the units with us. Bob would install the units for them in Sydney, and their own engineering staff would install the units in the other markets.

It was a thrill to start off with a contract like that for a new product, but Max Stuart still wasn't finished in Sydney.

While I was talking with Len, Max vanished, and when he returned a half hour later he was red as a beet. I asked him what happened, and he told me he had gone down to Channel 9's radio station, TCN9, to talk with Sam Chisholm, the president. They had never gotten along, and Max let him have it. As it turned out, Sam bought for the Sydney market radio, adding another $60,000 to our sales.

Australia was our first delivery of Telephone Poll, and Bob and I flew back to Sydney to install the equipment. After installation and a test run, I heard whispers by the Channel 9 engineers as to Elder's "genius", and their chief, Bruce Robertson, tried to hire him. Several days later, when the equipment was finally installed in the other markets, their first national use of it proved disastrous. So many people tried to vote that it knocked the entire telephone system out.

Len Mauger called, irate as hell, demanding we supply additional telephone interface units (TIU's) and, although we lost our shirt, we delivered twenty-five additional units per station for $50,000. It was truly a loss for us, but I doubt that Len ever believed us.

Three years later, going in for a renewal, we were turned down emphatically, and Len never talked to me again. When the equipment was returned to us at the end of the contract, we discovered that all the additional TIU's supplied had never been used. In fact, the original shipping boxes hadn't even been opened. I wrote Len Mauger about this, but I never got the courtesy of a reply.

Leaving Sydney, we once again went on to Wellington, New Zealand, to see Des Monaghan, whose staff also flipped. On Bob's return to Australia, he would also spend time getting Telephone Poll through the New Zealand Tele-Com people.

The Japanese can be a very charming people, and they are very well educated. But I have been told there isn't a word for "yes" or "no" in their language, and I know from my own experience that they are anything but honorable in business dealings. Twice now I had been promised deals in Japan, only to find thirty to sixty days later their apologies in a letter stating they had "discovered they were already doing it".

Max and I went to see Masayuki Nakamura, Vice President of Tohokushinsha Film Corporation, one of the top companies in Japan. When we presented Telephone Poll to Masayuki, he brought many people in for a second presentation and appeared very, very excited about our polling equipment.

That evening, Masayuki took Max, myself, and two members of his firm to an incredible steak house. During the dinner conversation, he confided in me that his people had for years had an inferiority complex, and he felt that Telephone Poll would prove a sensation in his country. I would be hearing from him quickly as to a decision.

I mentioned that conversation to Max later that evening, and I felt, at long last, we had found a way to break a product in that country. Two months later, I received a letter from Masayuki apologizing deeply for not going ahead with a contract; they had discovered they were already doing it. At the next MIP convention in April in Cannes, he came to our stand and asked what we were currently involved in. I stated (as the Japanese so often do) that I really didn't want to do business with him since I had "lost face".

From Tokyo, we went on to London, where we also were successful in selling BBC in one of their markets. While there, I met a man through Max who sold our Telephone Poll to Canal Plus in Paris, a cable operation just getting started. That meant we had to go through France's telecommunications system, requiring another trip to Europe with engineers. Surprisingly, Canal Plus and their cable operation in France took care of it for us.

British Telecom was another story. Although they were well behind our telecommunications system in the states, setting up equipment for their acceptance proved aggravating, to say the least. Their engineers marveled at what we had done, and could find nothing wrong with giving us immediate acceptance, with one very big exception. The head of British Telecom, with a smile on his face, stated, "We never give authorization on the first trip. You'll have to come back in six weeks, at which time we will clear your equipment." Sure enough, although we did not send engineers back to England, BBC took care of this for us, and our authorization was finally received.

247

21.
The NATPE Convention

I had been in the broadcasting industry for many years, and each week as I read the trade magazines from cover to cover I always dreamed of some day being in a position to take more than a half-page or full-page ad. With the success of Telephone Poll, having already sold 41 stations including Australia, I decided to make that dream come true.

We designed a four-page ad for the trade magazines, with two and one-page ads following, to coincide with the NATPE Convention. We told the entire story of Telephone Poll, including how we would guarantee the equipment during the life of a station's contract, and how we would update the equipment continually, including remote capability, allowing listeners to call the station and automatically give the final results. We would make the equipment compatable with their character generators, etc.

We explained how initially we would give them six responses, and continue to add to that list as we went along. In other words, we said it all in a four-page spread, explaining that our first delivery had been a complete sellout.

We brought our entire sales staff to the convention, and wondered whether this dream of spending a lot of money in advertising would pay dividends.

In my many years in this wonderful industry, I have had many successful conventions, but nothing compared with what happened in our suite that first day. It was so crowded and we were so busy that it became difficult to quote pricing of the markets since our rate card was based on metro population. Where possible, we made appointments for them to come back during the course of the convention and we wrote dozens of contracts.

We had to add additional engineering staff since we were now building our own equipment, having farmed out the many assemblies, including circuit boards. Our job, basically, was to assemble and test prior to shipping. Although our payroll increased twofold, the company was doing exceptionally well.

Broadcasters, are a strange lot, and their engineering departments can make life somewhat difficult at times. Why is it that no one likes to read instructions? We had spent a small fortune putting into a manual the answer to any and every conceivable question. We had given them a simple way to troubleshoot, with nothing more needed than to let the equipment do it for them, or read the manual.

A few days after a station received its equipment, we would get an irate phone call from the engineers or the manager, telling us our equipment didn't work. We immediately would put one of our engineers on the phone, and it was quite humorous at times to listen to the conversation that ensued. Often, their calls would state that the equipment was inoperable, and our engineer would very seriously ask whether the switch on the right lower side of the equipment had been turned on or not.

I walked into a major market station where the management was very upset because they could not get the equipment to give totals instead of percentages. I walked down to where the equipment had been installed and, in front of the general manager, pushed a button. I saw the expression in his eyes when the realization hit him that no one had bothered to look at the schematics or read the manual.

Our stations had a wonderful time using Telephone Poll. Some of them increased their ratings in shows like *People's Court* by asking the audience during a commercial break to vote on what the decision would be. Others went so far as to ask viewers' opinions on programming. Viewers could note on what programs they would like the station to broadcast on a continuous basis.

Others used it continuously in their newscasts, covering local news, political questions, special current events, etc. A few times, stations called us to tell us that viewers had called the telephone company to have their telephone locations switched to the living room or den, next to the television set, so that they could vote without missing the news.

Opening The World

With "TV-POWWW" and Telephone Poll rousing success stories, we decided to take a stand at the MIP convention in Cannes, and go after the European market. At the time, the rental of a stand that was built to our specifications cost $10,000 with airline, hotel, meals etc. our costs approached $20 to 25,000. We had great hopes that we could quickly recoup the outlay.

The MIP people had made a reservation for us at a hotel they claimed was four-star, and located about five miles from the center of Cannes. Taking our chief engineer and one of the salesmen, I took a cab to what was to be our home for the next ten days.

From a distance, our hotel appeared to be on a high knoll overlooking a village and some farms. When we checked in, the accommodations were a disaster, and we weren't quite sure what we should do about it.

That first evening, we found a restaurant in an old cellar and discovered to our dismay that no one spoke a word of English. While we grappled with the menu, two very attractive young ladies who were sitting nearby discovered our problem and quickly offered to aid us. We invited them to join us, and discovered they had been brought up in France, but were now working for the ABC network in New York. They, too, were at our infamous hotel, and discussions with them gave us a glimmer of hope.

Along the Croisette, in addition to hotels, were many attractive apartment houses. One, in particular, was brought to our attention. We should check with the apartment manager to see if we could rent a furnished apartment for one or two weeks.

Early the next morning, to our delight we were able to rent a two-bedroom unit for $75 a week, with a guarantee of two weeks whether we stayed or not. That, coupled with an additional $35 for soap, toilet paper and towels, and we were set up very comfortably. We even had our own telephone, and we made arrangements with management to pay any costs incurred.

That first evening, I tried calling the office so they would know where we were. I must have spent an hour trying everything humanly possible to get through to the United States. Admittedly, I was doing everything wrong, but I didn't realize it. I finally got an operator who could understand English, and when I started berating her, she connected me with the home office in Paris. After telling the operator in

M.A. KEMPNER
TELEPHONE † POLL
© 1982 M.A. Kempner, Inc.   Pat. 4,451,700

equipment is presently
in operation in AUSTRALIA, COLOMBIA,
FRANCE, GREAT BRITAIN, ITALY and the
UNITED STATES, and has proved to be the
easiest and most effective way for television
stations, radio stations, newspapers and
business organizations to get instant, and
constant, readings of the public pulse!

MICROPROCESSOR

A. Mains Power Switch and its Indicator Light.

B-1 thru B-8. LED Indicators show the status of the machine in operation, indicate any irregularities and assist in corrections.

C. Display Screen through which the machine communicates with the operator.

D. Word Select Control - for selecting one of the following set of responses:

Yes/No	True/False	Agree/Disagree
Like/Dislike	For/Against	
A/B	A/B/C	A/B/C/D

E-1 thru E-6. Push Buttons for communicating with and programming the system.

F. Three Position Key Switch:
1. System Check.   2. Run Position.
3. Count Reset - a safety feature making loss of count impossible even through power failure or by turning the whole system off. Count only returns to zero when key is turned to Count Reset position.

Z. Speaker - for monitoring the phone message going out to voters.

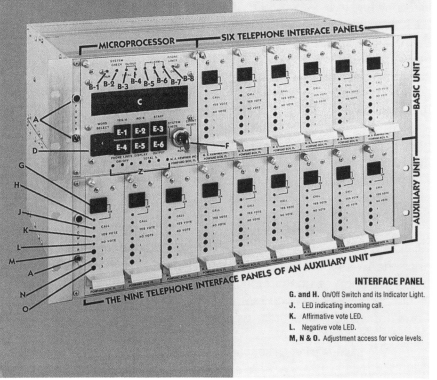

MICROPROCESSOR — SIX TELEPHONE INTERFACE PANELS

BASIC UNIT

AUXILIARY UNIT

THE NINE TELEPHONE INTERFACE PANELS OF AN AUXILIARY UNIT

INTERFACE PANEL

G. and H. On/Off Switch and its Indicator Light.

J. LED indicating incoming call.

K. Affirmative vote LED.

L. Negative vote LED.

M, N & O. Adjustment access for voice levels.

Paris my problem, a minute or two later she came back with, "Zo zorry, zee United States, she is out of order." I don't think I will ever forget that remark. Shortly thereafter, with the help of a man I met in the lobby, I easily reached the country that "was out of order."

This was our first MIP convention being totally on our own. We found it difficult, being a new entity, to be recognized. Max Stuart had his own stand, and he was very helpful in sending people to us, but it was a learning experience. As we found out later it takes two to three years before you are accepted, but we were able to sell enough to pay our expenses.

One major sale was to Achille Mauri who lived in Milan. He could drive one bonkers because he would never pay his bills. For years, he would meet us at the MIP convention with 20,000 to 30,000 dollars in $100 bills. The U.S. government would not allow us to bring back more than $10,000, so we used to split it up, each of us returning with a legal portion.

In many countries, not only in Europe, but South America as well, one had to face the fact that one will never receive one's equipment back. Having sold Telephone Poll to Achille, he got the equipment into the country without paying duty. That meant there was no way we could ever get it out. Achille used our Telephone Poll for years, and, although collecting from him was a trying experience, we always got paid.

The man who handled Mr. Mauro and finally walked away from him, was Maurice Cohen, an Egyptian of Jewish descent who lost his right arm at the shoulder during the Israeli-Egyptian war. He had moved his wife and young children to Monte Carlo, and always worked very diligently to help us with Achille.

MIP aided us in selling Spain, The Netherlands, Sweden, France and England, and we learned to look forward to those conventions in one of the most beautiful areas in the world.

Nice, Cannes, Monte Carlo, and the many beautiful towns and villages in between, are difficult to describe. In the evenings, we would drive the twenty-two miles to Monte Carlo, have drinks and dinner in the coffee shop of Loews Hotel, and listen to one of the finest pianists in Europe. We befriended him and learned he was a fixture at Monte Carlo for years. Of course, we all bought his records each time we visited.

We always tried to stay an extra day or two to sight-see and visit the principality of Monaco. We visited the grave of Grace Kelly, who was the only commoner ever interred in the famous church there.

My favorite stop used to be Le Columne D'or, a restaurant in a small inn that had four or six bedrooms upstairs. Richard Burton and Elizabeth Taylor stayed there on their honeymoon years ago, but what fascinated me most about this restaurant and inn is that it is in a medieval walled city on top of a mountain overlooking miles and miles of terrain.

What made it so unusual was its history. The artists years ago could not pay for their food and, in lieu of cash, gave paintings to the owner. Imagine if you will, having lunch with the likes of Renoir, Monet, Van Gogh and Picasso. It's a lunch one can hardly forget, even though today an appetizer, fish entree, dessert and wine will cost you $100 or more.

Having seen the sights around this centuries-old playground for Europe, one readily understands why it continues to have such a magnetic pull. I still love visiting and finding little cafes a few blocks away from the sea. The food and people off the commercial Croisette are wonderful, not arrogant as those found in the hotels or tourist spots.

The city of Cannes had built a new palais along the waterfront, three or four times larger than the original. But through the years, with the convention growing larger, the aisles became narrower and today, stands go from the basement to the fifth floor.

The second year at MIP, we again rented the apartment but we decided not to continue that practice. We received a phone call from the owner wanting to know who the hell we were! The manager was pocketing the money by renting out apartments without the owners knowledge. After that second year, we were well-known, and we were able to get accommodations at the Martinez, Majestic or Carlton. All were beautiful hotels, and one always looked forward to staying there.

A year or so after we started going to MIP, they added a second convention, called MIP-COM, which was held in October. That doubled our expenses annually, but we continued to hit both meetings for years. The only mistake ever made by the MIP people was in deciding to attempt a convention in the United States, called A-MIP. It lasted two years in Miami, after which they gave up and concentrated on the fall meeting in France.

22.
The Amex Corporation

Having filed for patents on Telephone Poll, we got some great newspaper coverage. To our surprise, one day we received a request to attend a seminar in Washington in which the federal government was involved. The Federal Aviation Administration was upgrading all of the airline weather systems in the major markets, and since we were involved in voice-activated automated equipment, we were invited to a two-day seminar.

I flew up with Bob Elder, and we listened with great interest as we were told that there would be a two or three billion dollar investment made in upgrading weather equipment. Bob felt with what we had accomplished we might have a very good chance of applying for and receiving a subcontract.

We were told that the contract was being awarded to a minority company, one that was classified as a small business. We learned that a small business was classified as one that had fewer than 500 employees and did less than five or six million dollars in business annually.

The company chosen was called the Amex Corporation, headquartered in California. Shortly after the seminar was concluded, we contacted the officials of Amex and Bob flew out to spend a day or two with them in the hope that we could file for a portion of the contract. When Bob came back, he mentioned to me how excited they were with what we had accomplished and what we had to offer, so the decision was made to go ahead.

Uncle Sam doesn't tell you, in most instances, the truth when it comes to government contracts. We knew from experience that, by law, they must get at least three bids from different companies before awarding a contract, but I should have known better. Years earlier, I had been asked to bid on a commercial contract for armed forces radio. In Washington, I was taken through their facilities which, admittedly, were brilliant, but I was told that, although they wanted three bids, they had already picked the company that was going to do the job, one they'd used for years.

Not withstanding, I went to Washington to a top engineering firm. Being told we needed professional expertise in making up our bid, we contracted with a firm and spent several thousand dollars doing a very professional job in bidding for the subcontract to manufacture a segment of the government contract.

We took several months to make sure we were on the right track and had crossed every "t" and dotted every "i", but we were well within the time period given us to make the bid. We sent the finished presentation to the heads of the Amex Corporation. They didn't even have the courtesy of responding. We finally telexed them asking for a response, and shortly thereafter received a reply stating they had contracted with another company.

I was so angry that I sent letters to our two senators from Florida, Paula Hawkins and Laughton Chiles. The response from Senator Hawkins still brings a smile to my face. I received a mimeographed standard response thanking me for apprising her of the situation. No wonder she was a one-term senator.

Senator Chiles sent me a personal letter not only thanking me, but stating he would follow it up, and he did just that.

Having been so shabbily treated, we decided to find out just what kind of company Amex was. I believe the name Amex at one time or another must have stood for "A-Mexican", but it sure didn't any longer. In addition to being a minority company, it also had to be a small business. We discovered that our federal government had done no less than 600 million dollars with them the previous year!

Doing business with Uncle Sam requires large sums of money to the politicians and party of choice. An individual or small company will never have an opportunity to gain a government contract any other way.

This brings to mind a phone call I had received from Armed Forces radio and television asking to buy fifteen one-hour sport specials. They told me at the time that the government only allowed them to pay $300 an hour, and when I laughingly declined selling them fifteen one-hour shows that had cost approximately $100,000 each to produce, they came back with a great suggestion. They wanted approximately 400 two-inch tapes, which ran between $350 and $400 each. They suggested that we lease them at $30 a month, they would still pay the $350 to $400 each, and they would return them to us within a thirty-day period. That meant in addition to the $4500 we would get for our film, we could make a very nice profit by leasing the tapes. We did just that, and it worked out beautifully.

A few years later, when they again called, I was delighted until I asked, "Is this on the same terms, that we supply you with two-inch tapes that will be returned?" Their response was, "No, we just want the film. We have a deal with 3M for the duplicate tapes." Angrily, I told them to go to hell.

23.
The World Traveler

For the past few years, I had made one form of around-the-world trip one way or another each year with Max Stuart and with renewals coming up in several countries, I decided to plan a trip covering the major countries and cities where we had interest in our products. Max was selling documentary, specials from Australia and New Zealand, and felt together we could have a very successful trip. The two of us always got along well together. We never had a problem of where we were going to eat or what we were going to do, and we more or less understood each other's shortcomings.

The final A-MIP was being held in November in Miami, and he was coming in from Melbourne to share my stand. The convention was over on a Monday evening, and he was flying out to Los Angeles where I was to meet him on Friday, the day after Thanksgiving, and we would continue on to our first stop in Tokyo.

I caught Pan Am to Los Angeles from Miami, and was supposed to have a three-hour layover prior to catching Pan Am to Tokyo. My flight was hours late, and came in fifteen minutes prior to departure. We had little time other than to run and catch a fourteen-hour plane ride.

The airport in Tokyo is miles from the city and one cannot afford a cab, so we got on a train to the city and then caught a cab to the Hilton Hotel, a beautiful structure almost directly across the street from the Imperial Palace of the Emperor.

When we arrived at the hotel, we saw a stretch Cadillac in the driveway which, naturally, could not be driven, it being (1) American, with a dozen Japanese reasons why it probably was unsafe, and (2)

257

being a stretch, it might not traverse the streets. I guess it was there just as a curiosity, something the Japanese must find amusing with their many laws forbidding anything other than their own product from being used or sold.

Having had no sleep, and with Max setting up appointments all day, I had a very rough time of it. Our last meeting was at 5:00 p.m., and after I had finished my presentation Max took over with his product. I was sitting down and found myself falling asleep. No matter how hard I pinched myself, I just couldn't stay awake. I decided I had better stand up, and I did just that, falling asleep on my feet. Max got me back to the hotel, I had a bite to eat, and I fell into bed exhausted.

The next morning, having breakfast in the coffee shop, I watched with amazement a Japanese gentleman eating two very soft boiled eggs with chopsticks, never missing or spilling a drop. Although we saw several television companies, including the networks, we again left Japan with nothing to show for it. Grudgingly, however, I have to admit their cities and gardens are beautiful, and Japanese scotch is great.

We had planned to go on from Tokyo to Manila, but with what was going on there politically, it was suggested we bypass the Phillipines and try to do business by phone or mail instead. From Tokyo, we went on to Hong Kong where we renewed our contracts, getting a second station for "TV POWWW." Going back to Sydney, we attempted to re-sell Telephone Poll to one of the other networks, but had little success. While there, however, we renewed most of our "TV POWWW" contracts with the fourteen markets Max had sold a few years earlier. It was wonderful finding out how much they liked the program and how successful it was continuing to be.

On to New Zealand, where we did little but service our products, with Max getting an opportunity to make presentations on some documentaries. Leaving Auckland, we flew into Singapore, one of the most fascinating city-countries I have ever visited. The prime minister had taken this city surrounded by Malaysia and literally erased poverty.

The Singapore government subsidizes high-rise apartments and passed some very stringent laws regarding cleanliness and upkeep. For block after block, high-rises and beautiful homes, little shops, restaurants and stores, are all beautifully manicured. One can be fined for dropping a cigarette butt on the street.

The downtown shops are exquisite, with French and Italian wares, all very expensive. There are two buildings covering an entire city block with 700 to 800 shops in them—the bargain area, where one can buy silk shirts for under $5, and little men run up to you whispering, "You want to buy a watch?", hoping you will follow them behind some shop where Rolex copies go for $25 to $50.

I stayed at the Shangri La Hotel, considered one of the most beautiful in the world. Each room is in a garden setting and, with such high ceilings, one gets the feeling of being outdoors. It is unlike any other hotel I've been in. Appointments had been made with stations in Singapore and Malaysia. They visited us at our hotel, and we did most of our business presentations in the garden bar We had meetings on the following Saturday morning, and spent that afternoon shopping, which was an experience. If one sees something he likes, is quoted a price by the merchant and accepts it, they to have no respect for you. Come back with a ridiculously low price, and the fighting becomes not only heated but fun.

I saw an attache case that would sell for about $200 in the states. I offered $30, and thought the man was going to explode with anger. When I showed no interest and walked down the hall, he followed me, screaming. Finally he said, "$35.00?" It was a beautiful case with combination locks, and I went half way around the world trying to find out what the combination was. Someone had set it, and we had no idea how to open it. Somewhere in Europe, Max hit the right combination and my "$200" bag became a real bargain.

Visiting Taipei in Taiwan was the weirdest adventure I have ever been involved in. We arrived by cab at the Hilton Hotel in downtown Taipei, checked in and headed for our rooms, each of us being followed by three girls. They went right up to the rooms, jabbering and giggling, and we had to physically push them away to keep them from coming in with us. Shortly thereafter, we went down to the bar, and girls were trying to climb on our laps.

Prostitution may be legal in Taiwan, but this was ridiculous. Later that evening, I asked the hotel manager what was going on. He smiled and said, "With people coming from all over the world because of the manufacturing being done here, we're forced to allow it." After dinner, we again were accompanied up to our rooms by delightful young ladies jabbering in Chinese, and we forcibly had to shove them from our doors.

The next morning, while having breakfast, I happened to look across from our table at a blond Eurasian with a beautiful face and figure. She was a spectacular beauty. Then I almost bit my tongue in half when she opened her mouth to smile, and she was toothless.

259

We held meetings and had lunch with one client who promised to buy our "TV POWWW" and Telephone Poll. I telexed the office to send out additional material for them, but nothing actually happened. Max was able to place a few documentaries.

We flew back to Hong Kong to continue the trip. I had several hours to kill before our flight was scheduled. While Max was making several phone calls. I sat in the lobby of the Regent Hotel, where I met an American who was working for the Chinese government as an aviation specialist. He made me promise never to fly a Russian or Chinese airline, claiming their upkeep was anything but safe. He and others were in the process of trying to improve their aircraft servicing and pilot training. It was a very interesting afternoon.

Early that evening, we left for Rome, with a stop for refueling in the Arab Emirates. While there, I was intrigued by the duty-free shop. In the Arab countries it is illegal to buy, sell or drink alcohol, but the duty-free shop sold only one thing—alcohol. In fact, we picked up a couple of quarts of Dewars Scotch for just $5 each.

Max had a very dear friend who represented him in Italy, by the name of Italo Tinaro. Italo was a very handsome, tall, thin, graying individual. He reminded me of Caesar Romero. He was charming, spoke excellent English, and picked us up in his tiny Fiat at 8:00 in the morning. Italo had made all of the appointments for us, beginning at 9:00 a.m., and Max and I shaved in the Fiat with my electric razor, stopping at a gasoline station for a cup of coffee en route to our first meeting.

Don't ever drive in Rome. On the side of the main thoroughfares are streetcars, and people drive on the tracks even with a streetcar coming. If there is half a parking space, they park vertical to the street, and you are dodging automobiles all the time.

My contract with Mr. Mauri in Italy was about to end and, rather than have the aggravation of trying to collect money from him all the time, I decided to re-sell it to one of the networks. Although we came close to an agreement, it never happened, and we decided to continue aggravating ourselves, collecting hundred dollar bills every year at MIP. Of course, it had gotten easier, since with two MIPs a year, we were collecting twice a year.

Having arrived in Rome at 8:00 in the morning, I had made plans to meet Maurice Cohen, Mauri's rep, for lunch. Not knowing many restaurants there, I suggested we meet at Harry's Bar. Anyone who has traveled in Europe knows that there is a Harry's Bar in many major cities, and we proceeded to have a delightful lunch. After collecting some hundred dollar bills from Maurice, we continued onto our meetings that afternoon.

Italo got us to the airport at 5:00 p.m., and we caught a 6:00 p.m. plane to Stockholm for a day or two of rest.

Stockholm is a beautiful city, and the people are just as beautiful. We stayed at an unusual hotel called The Grand, located on the bay. Directly across from it is the queen's castle, although the royal family no longer uses it.

The hotel is not only attractive, but old and stately and well-kept. It being Saturday morning, we kept two appointments and finished about 1:00, deciding it would be fun to take a tour of the city. I was impressed by the young people in Sweden, who were mostly blonde, blue-eyed and very attractive. Those that I met spoke perfect English with a very slight accent, and they seemed truly pleased that an American and Australian were visiting their country.

We decided to take a bus tour, which picked us up in front of the hotel. Our tour guide could have been a movie star. She was about 5′8″ tall, blonde, blue-eyed, incredible from head to toe. I could not even detect an accent in her English. At one of the stops, I teasingly asked her, "Where did you learn your English?" She laughingly replied, "UCLA, and I am going back next year."

We saw the old downtown area with buildings and apartments several hundred years old, all with a distinct slant because the foundations had settled. I got such a kick out of our guide when she took us through Embassy Row. She announced that we would shortly be coming to the ugliest building in Sweden. When we passed this monstrosity of modern architecture with glass, concrete and steel, she told us that it was the American Embassy. It was surrounded by very old mansions and buildings that had been turned into other country's headquarters.

We visited the famous ship, WASA, found in the harbor completely intact from the seventeenth century. It had been buried under mud for three hundred years, and was now housed in its own building still drying out. The ship, full of cannons and troops, was top-heavy and went down in the harbor during its maiden voyage, with heavy loss of life. Its massiveness and beauty was fascinating to me.

When our guide mentioned to us that they never had snow this late in the season, I reminded her that I was there and would guarantee it in the next day or so. Sure enough, the next morning we awoke to three inches of snow on the ground. By 2:00 in the afternoon it was already totally dark because of the short days of the winter months.

Getting back to the Grand Hotel, we were told they were famous for their smorgasbord in the dining room, so we went in to make a reservation only to be told they were booked to capacity. I asked for the maitre d' and introduced Max from Melbourne, Australia, and myself from the United States, and asked if it was possible to find room for us. With a smile, he immediately seated us and said that if we wanted to come back a second time, he would see that we were taken care of.

I have had many smorgasbords in my time, but I have never seen a spread like that. We gorged ourselves on all types of fish, salads and desserts. We planned to just take it easy on Sunday, but even though it was in the thirties, with a sprinkling of snow on the ground, we walked all over the downtown area, stopping in little coffee shops and window-shopping. It felt mighty good not having anything planned for a day. Sure enough, Sunday night we went back for a second helping of smorgasbord at the hotel.

The following morning, we flew on to Frankfurt, the one city in Germany that I found very unattractive. It was destroyed during the war, and it seemed to have nothing but modern skyscrapers and twentieth-century architecture.

We had an opportunity to meet many of the German companies and make presentations of our product. Although we came close in a couple of instances, we were unable to make a sale while there.

The Germans, like the French, are extremely arrogant people, and nothing we Americans produce electronically, such as Telephone Poll, is given a fair chance. In other countries in Europe and the rest of the world we always were able to present our product to their telecommunications people, but the Germans, unfortunately, would not even grant us an audience. One large company, Siemens, wouldn't grant us an audience, And their American division proved not only uncooperative, but downright nasty.

Max had received inquiries from the publisher of the newspaper in Koblenz, Germany, since they were planning to introduce a cable operation in the area. The publisher suggested we come to the city, and he made hotel reservations for us. Since we had already sold product to several cable operations, both of us felt it would be a worthwhile stop, so we rented a car and drove up from Frankfurt. It proved to be one of the more interesting parts of our trip, including some incidents that I fondly remember.

262

We rented a Ford Escort and we were able to stuff all our equipment and luggage into the small trunk and back seat. Koblenz is about 150 Kilometers from Frankfurt, and we proceeded on the famous Autobahn Highway. I got a tremendous kick out of the German words for entrance and exit: einfart and ausfart. I can't help it, but it did strike me funny. There we were driving on the Autobahn, gas pedal to the floor, doing 120 kilometers (72 miles an hour), with cars passing us with a "whoosh" sound. It felt like we were standing still, but that was as fast as our little Ford could go.

Arriving in Koblenz, we spent an hour trying to find the hotel and, unfortunately, when asking directions, we could not find youngsters who spoke English. Having taken every other road imaginable, I suggested to Max, who was driving, that we go up a winding, hilly road and see where it led. Sure enough, on the top was our hotel.

The lobby was large and nicely furnished, but our room was like a jail cell, perhaps eight feet long and six feet wide with a narrow metal cot-like bed. The bathroom was about the size of a small closet. When looking out a window of our room, we discovered a very large swimming pool with dozens of people taking advantage of it. Here we were in December in Germany, having been given a reservation at a spa with a heated outdoor pool. A heavy fog rose above the water. That afternoon, Max and I explored the hotel spa, discovering people had come from all over Europe to take the baths.

An Evening in Koblenz

We had been invited by our host, Werner Thiessen, to his home for the evening, and he would pick us up at the hotel at 6:00 p.m. We had no idea what plans he had made, assuming that we would have dinner with him and his family, and we were looking forward to a home-cooked German meal.

We were picked up as scheduled in Werner's beautiful Mercedes, and a few minutes later arrived at his home. From the outside, it appeared to have a small circular drive, and was situated on a hill, although little could be seen from the entrance. It did not appear to be more than an average size house until we entered the foyer. Our host spoke fairly good English, but his wife, of Russian descent, spoke none, and we were quickly introduced to his young children, but they soon vanished with the governess for the evening.

We were shown part of the house, including a large den, library, and a living room which I estimated to be about thirty-five feet long.

One wall consisted of glass doors from floor to ceiling, all opening individually, leading to a small three-foot wide porch with a railing its entire length. The "hill" the house was situated on must have been a small mountain since the view was spectacular overlooking the winding Rhine river. All of the furniture appeared to have been custom-built of natural wood, and what I had seen so far was truly magnificent.

A few minutes after our arrival, other guests appeared. I feared we were in for a very difficult evening since no one but our host spoke English. The first person we were introduced to was a gaunt 6'7" German. During the introductions, he almost stood at attention, clicking his heels with a look of utter disdain on his face. I immediately thought "Nazi". He spoke no English, and I had no idea what he was saying. I later discovered that he was considered one of Europe's top media experts, but I never did find out which media he was involved in, although I suspect it was newspapers.

I was then introduced to his wife, an attractive blonde, who did speak some English and was quite charming. When introduced to her, she asked me, "Mr. Kempner, are you related to the Kempner of the Nuremberg trials?" What a start for an evening!

Next, the conductor of the Koblenz symphony arrived, accompanied by his wife. They both proved very charming, jabbering away in German, of course, and once again, not knowing what was going on, I smiled and nodded my hello's. Another gentleman arrived alone, and for a while I had no idea who he was or why he was there.

Our host, who proved warm and pleasant, escorted us into a lovely sitting room where he served us Dom Perignon champagne, but Max and I, knowing little, if any, German for conversation, felt a bit out of it. Then something very delightful happened. The conductor of the Koblenz philharmonic orchestra came to me and whispered in my ear, "Mr. Kempner, I was born and raised in London. My wife is from Scotland. Don't worry, we'll keep you informed of everything that is going on."

After champagne cocktails, we were escorted downstairs to a huge room with approximately thirty theater-type seats facing a stage which held a full-size grand piano. Seating himself at the piano, the conductor of the Koblenz symphony smiled and nodded at our host, who, violin in hand, proceeded for an hour to entertain us in concert. The pianist was great; our host, the violinist, reminded me of Jack Benny. Still it was fun.

After the concert, we were shown our host's wine cellar, which must have been 2500 to 3000 square feet. It was thermostat controlled, and had a collection of wine from all over the world. Looking at Max, who had a twinkle in his eyes, I remarked very quietly to him, "What next?" It was 8:30 in the evening, and champagne cocktails for dinner just wouldn't do.

After touring the wine cellar, we were escorted to a wood-paneled room, not large in size, but ample, with a large table in the center and very comfortable easy chairs surrounding it. Again we were introduced to the mysterious single gentleman who had arrived with the other guests. We were told that he was a wine expert, and we were now going to taste many wines and compare them. The area where Koblenz is situated is world-famous for German riesling wine, and our evening was to be spent tasting the many rieslings from the various local vineyards.

On the table were several baskets of bread broken into small pieces so that after tasting a wine, we could cleanse our palate and get ready for the next bottle. After each wine, our wine expert would describe where it came from. Each of us was asked our opinion as to taste, aroma, etc. Our host, realizing that Max was from Australia, purposely had found an Australian wine. I found that the Australian riesling was the most flavorful, and I liked it the best.

It was after 11:00 when we were escorted upstairs to the dining room where the cook, who must have been Russian, served us borscht and sour cream, together with German breads. I looked at Max and whispered, "We're finally going to get something to eat," and he smiled, telling me how hungry he was.

I have always loved caviar. A few years earlier, flying with Singapore Airlines, the stewardess came up and asked if I would like some Iranian caviar with my cocktails. The hostage mess was still going on in Iran at the time, I looked at her with a smile and said, "Don't tell anyone, but you can give me a double portion."

After the borscht, our main course was a plate full of caviar for each of us, and it was quite a disappointment. Some of the caviar was the size of a vitamin capsule, and made castor oil taste almost palatable. I kept watching everybody pushing their caviar from one side of the plate to the other, making certain after tasting everything not to go back for a second mouthful. I even watched our hostess doing the same thing but naturally none of us said a word.

We then retired to the sitting room where we were served coffee in demitasse cups, and our evening was complete. I will always remember that night as an unusual experience, to say the least. We were driven

265

back to our hotel, and met the following day with Werner regarding his cable potential. Although we worked on Telephone Poll and other projects with him, he never did raise the required 20 to 30 million dollars, and finally gave up his proposed cable channel.

Munich - Amsterdam - Paris - London

Driving back to Frankfurt, Max and I caught an early evening plane to Munich, where we had meetings set up for the following two days. Munich is a very beautiful and historic city. That evening, while taking a cab to the hotel, I became intrigued with Munich and did manage to grab an opportunity one afternoon to do some sightseeing.

Max had set up an appointment with the president and owner of a company called Polyband, which produced video cassettes, all types of videos, and phonograph records. Max mentioned that I was about to meet the owner, Wolfgang Winkel. With a smile on his face, he said I would soon learn whether he liked me or not.

Wolfgang was in his mid-seventies, of small and thin build, with graying hair and very serious demeanor. After Max's remark, I didn't know quite how to take him, but he seemed pleasant enough and introduced both of us to his daughter, Daniela. She was not a beautiful girl, but attractive, and had a certain amount of charm. I made my presentation of "TV POWWW" and Telephone Poll to them, and then Max headed out to another office with Daniela to go through the feature films he was representing for possible sale to Polyband to reproduce them on video cassettes.

Suddenly, Wolfgang looked at me and said in a demanding voice, "Mr. Kempner, are you Jewish?" When I replied in the affirmative, he warmed right up to me. He told me he was Jewish and he had spent World War II in the Russian army. Upon finally being released, he came back to Munich to form Polyband. He also told me of his son, who was not on speaking terms with him at the time, and the problems he was having with his daughter, who had been recently divorced. He announced, "You are having dinner with me tonight. I will make all the arrangements."

Wolfgang, with his daughter, picked Max and me up at our hotel and took us to a tiny German restaurant in the heart of Munich. It was not a fancy place, and one we probably never would have discovered. It was more a family restaurant.

Wolfgang was greeted by the owner, a man I took to be in his late sixties or early seventies. He was a real beefy German 300-pounder

266

with red, jowly cheeks and balding, but very jovial. The two men hugged and Wolfgang whispered something in his ear shortly before we were escorted to what I took to be one of the nicer tables in the place.

Wolfgang, looking at me, smiled and said, "I'm ordering dinner and I know you will enjoy it." A few moments later, they served us some form of "white lightning" (maybe it was slivovitz) in a long thin glass, with a large schooner of beer. Doing as Wolfgang did, we quickly drank the alcohol, followed by the beer as a chaser. The alcohol was a delicious, though strong. After several of those and more beer, I had the opportunity to taste a German delicacy unlike any I had ever had before.

I am not a great lover of duck, or most fowl for that matter, and this was my first experience of eating goose. Normally goose is very greasy and fatty, but it had been superbly prepared in such a way that it had a very dark brown crisp skin and a very moist, but not a fatty, interior. It was one of the most delicious dishes I have ever had. My only problem was that Mr. Winkel continually talked and asked questions, so unfortunately, I only finished half my goose before dessert, crepes suzette, which were made at our table.

After several liqueurs with coffee, Daniela, who had been conversing with Max, announced that we were going to a disco that evening. Just what I needed! But Max had made the date, so we had to go.

In the early eighties, discotheques were the "in" thing, and we were taken to the largest one in Munich. There must have been 2,000 people there and the music, three or four decimals above screaming volume, was ear-shattering. The disco itself was beautiful. The stage was a huge airplane with multicolor flashing lights set to go on and off with the rhythm of the tunes being played. Wolfgang (smart guy that he was) had taken leave of us and gone home, but Daniela wanted to dance. Max and I finally dropped her off in a cab at 5:00 a.m. in the morning.

Back at the hotel, Max decided he wanted a nightcap. He came into my room, opened the mini bar and made himself a scotch and soda. I protested that I had an 8:00 a.m. meeting, and finally got rid of him at 6:30, caught an hour's sleep, kept my appointment and got back to the hotel about 11:00. Upon entering, the phone rang. It was Max, asking how my meeting had gone. I told him, then asked what he was doing. He said he was was still in bed, but would shower and shave and meet me in an hour.

The following day, we arrived in Amsterdam, staying in a little hotel directly on a canal. The hotel was called The America, and was at one end of a large square, overlooking a plaza in the downtown area.

From this plaza, one could see three "nostalgic" restaurants, all within a block: McDonalds, Burger King and Kentucky Fried Chicken. The hotel itself was charming and had a wonderful European flare about it. Everyone knew our names, the concierge couldn't do enough for us, and it was just a delight finding a place where pampering was included in the hotel's daily charge.

Our first meeting was with a company that Max had representation with in Europe, called DBS International. It was headed by Herman de Koster and Pieter Gosselaar, both of whom were 6'5" or 6'6" in height and pure Dutch in character. Herman had a strange manner about him and couldn't look me in the eye. There was something distrustful about him, but, although he was only twenty-seven years of age, he had built quite a following in the television industry in The Netherlands. Still, there was something wrong, and I could not put my finger on it.

Pieter was the handsomest, most charming idiot I have ever known. He was the personification of a great salesman and like many others I have known, had no business acumen whatsoever. As sales manager for DBS, he was doing a brilliant job as long as someone else took over the details and followed through.

Herman and Pieter were both single, but Pieter had been married once and had a two-year-old son. Both of them were incredible womanizers. Pieter could mesmerize women and literally have them in bed an hour after he met them. Herman had a more stable personality but, as I mentioned, there was something wrong with him, giving me an uneasy feeling.

Their office was an old five-story-house, the top two stories being bedrooms. I spent the morning with them working out details on Telephone Poll and "TV POWWW" and, through Max, authorizing their non-exclusive sale in Europe for us. That afternoon, finding out from Pieter of the bedrooms upstairs, I excused myself, left Max with the boys, and got a wonderful three or four hours sleep.

The Netherlands had the strangest television setup. It was fully government-controlled, and the government sent out for bids covering time periods. As I recall, there were about seven companies that had anywhere from three to ten hours a week. Once the bid was granted, they could sell anyone they pleased. A great amount of time was kept for political, educational (and some entertainment) programming by the Dutch government.

The first evening we were guests of Herman and Pieter. They took us to a restaurant where I ordered grilled filet of sole, and I have never tasted the likes of it anywhere else. One receives an entire fish, eats the top portion first, removes the bones, and then eats the lower end. It was a type of sole found only in that part of the world, and it was incredible.

We also visited the red light district, which is a two-block area of Amsterdam. It is completely government-controlled, with physicals for all the participants on a scheduled plan. We drove down the street seeing tiny shops, mostly with plate glass front, with semi-clad girls sitting inside on couches or chairs. It was astounding. If the drapes were closed, it meant they were busily engaged. Driving down those streets, one saw unusually beautiful young girls, as well as some six feet two inches tall, or five feet tall and five feet wide.

From there, we were taken to a casino where I took $50 to spend on a game I had never played before—roulette. I really wasn't interested in gambling, being very tired, but I took my chips ten or fifteen at a time and placed them on numbers. Somehow, not even knowing what I was doing, I couldn't lose, while Max, Herman and Pieter were losing their shirts. Borrowing chips from me, they had a great time and, although no one ever paid me back, I still left the casino a couple hours later a winner.

Pieter did a fine sales job for us, not only in the Netherlands, but in Sweden, Spain and a few other countries. My only problem, a couple of years later, was discovering that Herman had absconded with over a million dollars and left Pieter holding the bag. With Pieter's help, however, we were able to get those who had bought our product to pay us directly. Herman, aside from serving a prison term on a drug charge, has not been seen or heard from since.

While in Amsterdam, I had met another producer, Burt Vegter, who had been head of promotion for CBS records prior to setting up his own company. Pieter subsequently went to work for Burt and, although it took several years, fought his way back very successfully.

We went on to Paris, where we called on Canal Plus, the new cable entity that was using our Telephone Poll. We made a few other appointments while there, but on the whole were not too successful. We decided to leave a day early and go on to London.

Calling on the BBC to check on Telephone Poll and "TV POWWW" proved to be an experience. They were very unhappy with "TV POWWW," which was running in a children's program, because

269

they were having so much trouble setting up the equipment. We had given them a simple manual to follow, together with all the instructions, games and equipment. When their head of programming complained to me about the problems, it didn't take too long to discover what was wrong.

The government-controlled broadcasting facility had at least three people doing each man's job. A different engineering staff was being used every time they played our game. No wonder they were having problems! Nobody checked the manual, and it was very apparent that, as with any government organization, nobody knew what the hell was going on. We straightened them out as best we could.

Telephone Poll was doing well, and there was little else I had to do while there. The last two days we spent in London proved to be a complete waste of time. We had been in fifteen countries in twenty-seven days, and we were just too tired to be productive in any way.

Max had a twenty-six-hour trip to get back to Melbourne. I put him in a cab at 6:00 p.m. on the evening of December 23rd to head for the airport. After a handshake and a hug, he looked at me and asked what I was planning to do that evening since my plane didn't leave until 11:00 the following morning. I told him I was going to bed, even forsaking dinner, and the realization suddenly hit both of us—we had had quite a trip. It was very successful, but it was damn tiring.

I had picked up a Russian wedding ring, a cultured pearl necklace from Singapore, a leather handbag from Hong Kong, a scarf from Paris, and two or three other gifts for my wife. Max had done the same for his wife since it was Christmas. On the 27th of December, Max called me from Melbourne to find out how Jeanne liked her presents. I laughed and said, "Dammit, Max, while I was gone she bought herself a mink coat!"

Although that proved to be the last around-the-world trip I made, trips to Southeast Asia and Europe continued for many years. That twenty-seven days with Max, however, will always be a highlight in my life in broadcasting.

24.
Hollywood Dreams—Making Movies

Early in 1984, I was introduced to John Feeny, a very attractive man with an incredible personality. He was a graduate of Miami University's School of Communications, and had been vice president of public relations for the NBC network. He was about 5'10", of slim build, and could charm the hell out of anyone.

According to the story he gave me, he had moved with his wife from southern California to the south Florida area, and was interested in securing employment. Strange how one who thinks he knows people can be so easily taken in! It is also amazing to me how so few people will be honest when discussing the job background or history of a person in this wonderful industry.

I have always disliked knocking anyone, but if I found someone who had one or more bad traits and a history of failure, I would be honest with those who called for references.

In checking on John Feeny, I was told of his brilliance, even by those at NBC in New York where he had worked. The only negative comment I ever received was that he had had a falling out with the network, but deserved a second chance. I liked the way John talked and the manner in which he handled himself, and I decided we might use him in opening up new avenues for the company. Thus began a frustrating and expensive year for the company.

John's wife, a writer, went under the professional name of Jo Montgomery. She was an Oklahoma gal, and had several scripts produced for different television series. She was a very attractive young woman, tall, with a beautiful figure and an unusual background. She was in the process of writing a book, and she seemed, to me anyway, to have a great deal of moxy.

After several discussions with her, I became quite excited about the potential of getting involved in the production of motion pictures. With her contacts, and John's as well, I felt with a good agent we could find the financing and produce feature films. The company was doing exceptionally well, I always liked a challenge, so I decided what the hell—let's go for it. We hired Jo, who was to come up with some ideas for the initial one or two scripts.

Jo had written one motion picture, a comedy about a ne'er-do-well stockbroker on Wall Street who saved the life of a chicken and discovered that the bird could peck out a stock daily in the Wall Street Journal with sensational results. The story line was a tongue-in-cheek comedy with the bird being kidnapped, ransom, and all kinds of other crazy happenings. She had another idea about a crooked preacher who had found a way of taking care of everyone on Social Security. Her ideas seemed to have promise, but Jo's writing just didn't make it.

I soon discovered John Feeny's major problem. I have known many people who were drunks, but he was the first real alcoholic I ever had to deal with. He had been told years before that the next drink would kill him because most of his liver was shot, but he would still go on seven or ten-day drunks, after which he would be committed to a hospital to dry out, come back for a week, and the same thing would start all over again.

Jo, in total frustration, divorced him. I was completely disillusioned and just let him go. While that was going on, Jo and I continued to fly out to the west coast, where I probably met most of the four-flushers, phonies and ne'er-do-well agents in the industry. It was finally decided to hire a Hollywood writer to re-script our story on the preacher. The writer flew down to Florida, where he spent a couple of days discussing the idea, his remuneration, etc.

We gave him a time limit of several weeks to rewrite the entire script, paid all his expenses plus the salary required, and sat back to wait. Looking back, I can only smile at how naive we were. We had little if any experience with the Hollywood crowd and they must have thought, "here comes another sucker". I met enough near-winners and almost-losers in the coming months to last me a lifetime, and I won't go into further detail. I also met some wonderful people, and some fine television and motion picture stars, so I have to admit it wasn't all bad.

After months of excuses as to why our second script, as well as the first, for that matter, were not being picked up, Jo Montgomery set up a luncheon meeting for us with a friend, someone she had written television scripts for in the past. Roy Huggins was probably the most incredible man I met in the motion picture and/or television industry. He was of medium height, a light complexion with rosy cheeks, and a head of snow white-hair. I took him to be in his early sixties, and I liked him immediately. When I discovered he had produced many television programs, including *Bonanza*, *Maverick*, *The Rockford Files*, *Baretta* and *Hunter*, I thought I was finally going to get an honest response as to whether we were wasting our time. You never know when you're going to find the right person with the right contact to get that first big break.

At the time we met, Roy Huggins had been replaced as producer on *Hunter* because he was too old. He was in his early sixties, and they were looking for thirty-year-olds. (Maybe that's why every program or movie on television has to have a torrid bedroom scene, a car chase or bloody gore.)

The entertainment industry is like a big clock—what goes around comes around. The same programming, with a fresh approach, will continuously reappear. Medical shows, courtroom series and situation comedies will be replaced by westerns, prime time soaps, adventure series, etc. There really are very few new ideas. Talk shows are successful in syndication because they can be produced so cheaply. Comedy will always be with us, in some form, because it is escapism, and even musical variety programming will eventually come back in a new format.

After lunch, Roy sat Jo and me down and told us honestly our script, to put it nicely, was "lousy". Swallowing hard, I decided I didn't have the time or the stomach for this type of business. Roy gave us several suggestions about re-writing but told me our chances were still slim.

To this day, I am flabbergasted by what gets on the silver screen and on television. I can only figure that it isn't what you have or how good it is, but what contacts you have and who you know in the top echelon. Unknown writers have a very difficult time getting their first works produced. If you get a book published first, even if it is a flop, it is almost an entree to the motion picture and broadcasting people. Years later, an unusual mini-series was presented to me. I contacted one of the writers for Steven Spielberg, whom I knew, and he said, "By all means, send it to me." A few days later, I received the materials back with a note saying that unless the writer had some background, they weren't interested, and besides, his agent was too busy to do anything anyway. I couldn't help but smile reading his remarks. The writer is not only well known and respected for his talent but many of his scripts have been sold to the industry. I decided to send the mini-series to a close friend and literary agent who, after reading it, sent it on to paramount. Their comments included the word "brilliant" in describing the writer's work. It was turned down because of budget restraints at the time. Although the author received option money twice, the project never went forward.

25.
"Escape 600"

In my many years of broadcast programming experience, I have always been amazed at how some of our ideas and products were developed, sometimes years too early. "TV-POWWW," although running for more than twelve years, could have been that much more successful if companies like Mattel and Fairchild Camera Instrument Corporation had realized what they had in their electronic game shows.

Telephone Poll was another example. We had the only polling equipment that gave the viewer at home an opportunity to vote at no cost. We were licked by AT&T and others primarily because we could not give more than 5,000 responses an hour, while their equipment, using two computers, could do three to four times that—but only a "yes" or "no." We had multiple choice, and it cost the viewer nothing for a local call.

But the public paid fifty cents for the privilege of voting. Broadcasters wanted large numbers, even if it cost their viewers money. Perhaps the telephone company paid the broadcasters a portion of the fifty cents (which today, is now ninty-five cents). We Americans are strange animals; volume, rather than quality, is all-important.

For me, the fun in building a new product was if it was out-of-the-ordinary or something not done before, and we were about to do it again in the coming months. I started having meetings with our engineering people, asking many "what if" questions. Our Telephone Poll had been a resounding success, and is still being used in the mid-nineties. It is not scientific, in any way, but gives stations an instant response as

275

to local affairs and national topics. "What if" we could build a piece of equipment that could be scientifically accurate in taking a poll?

Research companies charge from $5,000 on up for polling and completing as few as 300 calls. National pollsters claim accuracy of plus or minus three percent, with telephone operators often calling fewer than a thousand homes. "What if" we could build a piece of equipment that could do what the pollsters did for a fraction of the cost?

In our discussions, we talked with several research companies, as well as their personnel, and received such a positive response that we decided to go ahead. Electronics in this field had advanced so much that we knew we could take a synthesized chip and copy any human voice. It could be easily programmed in an office by a company official, a favorite on-the-air personality, or a famous guest. The chip would give a faithful reproduction of the voice used, and it was felt there would be little problem in developing our equipment with the use of this chip which was already available on the market.

We then decided to explore voice recognition. "Wouldn't it" be wonderful to install our synthesized chip in a telephone, and those that were called could answer verbally? I flew all over the country visiting companies that claimed they could offer voice recognition. IBM was involved, and had developed a computer that could be trained to accept an individual's voice. The problem, however, was the number of accents in the English language. I met with a company in Atlanta, and after they had gone through their entire pitch to us, they suggested that we try it ourselves. Sadly, it couldn't recognize a southern drawl, Yankee twang, or any voice at all except pure simple English.

Foreign accents would be another problem. We found a company from Japan, a country that only has two or three different accents in their language, but it was worthless for what we had in mind. After several months of fruitless searching, we gave up, with the realization that voice recognition was several years away.

Our next major problem was telephone equipment. We had been making phone calls with our equipment at random. There was no problem with touch tone phones, but pulse or rotary dials were proving to be almost insurmountable problems. Telephone companies have equipment for the rotary dial system, but after five clicks, sometimes three or four, their units would disconnect, reading the clicks as a hang-up. Thus, if we wanted someone to give us his age, and it was twenty-nine, the two was fine but the nine would not register, and the telephone company disconnected. Although, at the time, most of the telephones in the U.S.

had touch tone capability, there were a lot of areas that still relied on the old rotary dial.

After months of work, we devised a way, and developed a piece of equipment that worked with rotary dial phones. Although our country was heavily invested with touch tone phones, the rest of the world, at that time, had less than 10%. Our engineers worked out a system, and we filed for patents, which were granted three years later. While all this was occurring, my chief engineer, Bob Elder, was having an affair with Jo Montgomery. He had filed for divorce from his fourth (or fifth) wife, had moved in with Jo, and had gone back to drinking. He would come into the office for two or three hours, leave for lunch and, in most instances, would not return.

After several days of this, he came into my office one morning demanding a large increase in salary. I turned him down. With his salary, two percent of the gross, and full medical coverage, he was already making one hell of a good living.

A few days later, I received a registered letter with his demands in writing, followed by his resignation if I did not honor them. I tried several times to reason with him, but he was adamant. I let him go, and we started looking for a new chief engineer. Although I was very upset, it wasn't long before the realization hit me that with his background and training it would have been nearly impossible for him to develop the sophisticated piece of equipment we had in mind. When I discovered that Jo Montgomery had written the letter for him, I gave her two weeks notice. Her four-letter-word response on the telephone was something to hear—and I always thought she was a "lady"! Shortly after, Bob Elder drove her out to California, where she dumped him, and he came back to southern Florida. He's been working since as an engineer for a large company, making less than one-third what we were paying him.

After Bob's return from California, I came home one evening to find my automobile stolen from my locked garage, as well as all of my jewelry from the bedroom. Unfortunately, Bob knew my home alarm code, and I can't believe a professional thief would take all of my jewelry, leaving my wife's in a drawer next to it. Naturally, I can't prove it, but I will always feel he was responsible.

After weeks of an intensive search, we finally found a new chief engineer, Dick Walker, whose credentials were excellent. He was in his mid-forties, and he had excellent experience in electronic development. He was a good-looking guy, and I felt he would prove a good investment for us. We worked his butt off, and soon discovered he was short-tempered, extremely cheap, and, at times, a nervous wreck, particularly if he had to buy some one a cup of coffee. I still think he has most of the money he ever made in a "Jack Benny" underground vault somewhere. After getting used to his idiosyncrasies, and he had many, we found a way to continue successfully with few problems in the development of our new product.

Doing the Impossible

Several meetings were held with Paul and Marge Nagle from the University of Miami, as well as Mitch Shapiro, who was a professor in the Communications Department at the University, taught research and had his own consulting firm doing work for national accounts. We gave Paul the opportunity to write up the Escape 600 concept, with Marge designing our brochure. We hired Mitch as a consultant, and planned to use him in our presentation tape, as well as helping train station personnel in the use of the equipment.

We devised the name Escape 600 as an acronym for Electronic Synthesized Computerized Automatic Polling Equipment. The 600 was added only because IBM had a unit called 1200, and we divided it by two. It really meant nothing. When I realized that what we were building was so far ahead of the industry, in some ways it was frightening. Years later, the realization hit me that we could have built a piece of equipment much simpler in design that would have done much less, but still would have been very successful.

The Escape 600 unit was totally automated, could operate unattended for any pre-programmed time period, could be set to go on automatically, and could discontinue calling at certain times of the day or night. The synthesized voice could easily be programmed by anyone, including a favorite on-the-air personality, a famous guest, or, for that matter, a politician. The faithful reproduction of the voice contributed to the percentage of people responding to the questionnaires.

One of the more exciting concepts was its random digit dialing that could be programmed for each survey. The Escape equipment could make a certain number of calls in a certain number of exchanges, since one of the principal determinants of the accuracy of any survey is always the relationship of the size of the sample to the total population—the larger the sample, the lower the margin of error. That meant that in a coverage area you could make 20% of the calls in a 954 area code,

42% in a 305 area code, 38% in a 407 area code, etc., and could pre-set the equipment, which would continue running by itself until it had achieved the exact number of completed calls from each exchange.

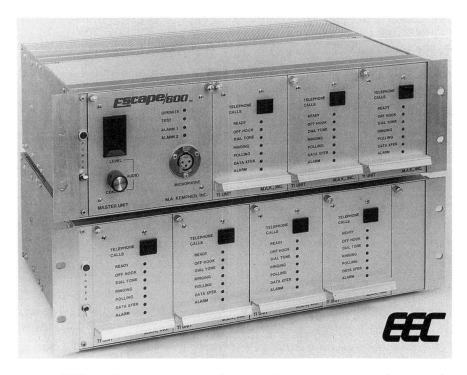

With no live operators and no overtime to pay, it just kept work-ing until the job was done. Escape could recognize a busy signal, an answering machine, even a prankster. For busy signals or answering machines, it would note it and automatically replace the calls at a later date. If it received a ridiculous response, it would branch to a "thank you," disconnect, and take that telephone number out of its memory. With no answer, it would automatically redial later.

We were going to deliver a seven phone line capability and, should one want to, he could add up to 100 telephone lines. All the people at home had to do to respond was to dial or press certain num-bers on their telephones. "One might be for "yes," two for no," or to answer how old you are, you would answer by touch tone or dialing the correct set of numbers. In asking the first question, the equipment in-stantly could determine whether the telephone was touch tone or rotary, and would branch to the necessary changes needed to continue. A rotary phone had its own special retrieval system, which now worked beautifully.

The equipment was incredible because of this "branching" ability. One might start a poll by asking if the interviewee wanted the question asked in English or Spanish. If he dialed "One for English or two for Spanish, the equipment would instantly branch into that language to continue the poll. If the age of someone determined an entirely different set of questions, the equipment would instantly respond.

The results of each poll would be on a computer printout, and the results would be printed out in response to each question, the frequency of that response and the percentage of calls with that response. If a specific question was answered "yes," the equipment could print out every telephone number that responded with a "yes". If one wanted a total of those 18-39 years of age who responded, it could be quickly printed out, with telephone numbers if requested.

Because everyone was polled and questioned by the same synthesized voice, there could be no "interviewer bias" or "staleness". That made Escape 600 a much more scientifically accurate method of gathering information.

At the conclusion of the poll, the equipment thanked the person for responding, broke the connection and programmed the information into its computer, continuing on to more automatic phone calls.

After much discussion, we decided not to sell the Escape 600, but rather, lease it on a three-year contract. In addition, we decided to supply an IBM XT computer and a Princeton printer. I contacted IBM, telling them of our needs and asking whether they would be kind enough to supply computers to us at the dealer's price. In no uncertain terms, we were told to go to hell (we were too small a company). We worked out an agreement ourselves with a local dealer who gave us a reasonable break on the price. At the time, the XT was selling for over $3,000.

We stopped supplying IBM's equipment a year later, not because we were going to another company, but because IBM gave only ninty-day warranties on their equipment. It was costing us a lot of money since we gave our clients three-year warranties and so many computers broke down shortly after their warranty expired. We quickly learned that IBM equipment was costly as hell after three months, and we suggested that our clients use their own computers or purchase one of their choice, the Escape equipment being compatible with other manufacturers. I sat next to a vice president of IBM on a flight to London several months after our units were in use, and he told me how wrong I was as far as

IBM's quality control. He promised to get back to me after checking out what I had told him. I'm still waiting, years later, to hear from him.

The next step in preparing the release of Escape was to produce a presentation tape. We decided to tape from our own offices, and hired a local television production company, using Paul Nagle as our director. With our own secretaries and engineers, we set up an office atmosphere showing how the Escape could work without disturbing anyone. We filmed in my office which was furnished like a living room, having some of my employee's wives answering and taking the poll. It was low key, and it was fun to watch all our amateur actors and actresses on camera.

After a two-day shoot and several days of editing, our presentation was ready, and we were now able to find out whether we had been right or wrong. We still had a lot of bugs to work out in the equipment. Some of the electronic boards which we had farmed out had several mistakes in them, and we had the standard problems one finds in the electronic industry—viruses, plus poor contacts on some of the equipment had to be found and corrected.

We decided to give ourselves an additional six months before start date to be certain our units operated as advertised. We planned to invite every station which leased Escape 600 to choose a member of its staff and fly them down to our office for a two-day training period. Mitch Shapiro and our engineers would be involved in educating members of stations, research companies or universities in operating the equipment.

It was time to find out what we had. After discussions with Mitch and Paul Nagle, we arranged to place a unit at the Univerity of Miami, giving us an opportunity to continuously test our theories and find out what our strengths and weaknesses were. I had lunch with the new dean of the School of Communications, and a whole new world suddenly opened up.

Ed Pfister had recently resigned as president of the Corporation for Public Broadcasting and the University was thrilled to have him. He had a dynamic personality, and his background in the broadcasting industry was brilliant. Over lunch, we discussed Escape 600 and I couldn't help but be pleased with his ideas and suggestions. We discussed many areas where not only the School of Communications could be involved, but all other areas of the university. He was excited and came up with many unusual suggestions for Escape's usage. He made me realize how the equipment could be used on a day-to-day basis.

Ed came up with an idea to find out why students who had been accepted for a coming semester were never heard from again. He would use the Escape 600 equipment to call them all and ask them why they were not coming to the school. Was it money? Had they decided to go to another school? Were there problems or questions that could be readily answered by a follow-up phone call?

Another idea was to have a recognizable name at the university—a football coach, professor, dean of the university—call the alumni asking for donations. With Escape's branching capabilities, the university planned many types of research. After the equipment's installation, so many wanted to use it that Mitch Shapiro, who was in charge, had to set up schedules.

As we had discovered in our conversations with research companies and television stations, an initial seven-line telephone system would be more than adequate. By adding a simple switch to their current telephone lines, there was no need to incur additional expense. Most businesses are open nine to five, and one could readily flick a switch to put the Escape to work after the normal day was over, and use up to seven lines, all working independently of each other.

With our first installation at the university complete, it was time to go out into the field and find out what our sales potential was. Our presentation tape would do most of the selling. I wanted to maintain our sales volume in other products, so I decided not to give the salesmen Escape 600.

In the early 1970's, inflation had reared its ugly head. Eight dollar motel rooms started costing thirty dollars, while gasoline for automobiles began inching up to a dollar a gallon. Maintaining a large staff of salesmen began to cause many problems, particularly for small independent producers, and although we were writing contracts and selling successfully, our costs were skyrocketing. By the mid 1980's, even with several million dollars on our books, our profits continued to dwindle, and it became apparent that we could no longer afford a large sales organization.

In retrospect, I realize I never listened to John Kluge and his success formula for business: "never go into any business with an inventory." Our "inventory" was our engineers and the many people we hired to do assembly work. For a small company, spending $110,000 a month was not only frightening, but worrisome, and there was no possible way for us to increase our pricing or cut down on our staff. Keeping six or seven salesmen on the road had become much too costly.

In order for us to service "TV-POWWW," Telephone Poll, and continue to build the units, as well as developing and assembling the Escape 600 equipment, it was impossible to cut the engineering department.

After much soul-searching, it was decided to cut the sales staff down to two full-time men, and add more traveling on my part to try and take up the slack. In looking back, it was the right decision and, admittedly, I still loved the challenge of working with management and companies all over the world. With some frugality, staying in second-rate hotels and motels, I could do it at a weekly cost of about a thousand dollars, quite a change from the days when we paid $300 a week, and one could travel five days or four nights by automobile for as little as $75 a week.

I hired a nephew of mine, Bob Grossman, as an independent contractor. He was a graduate of Hobart, and received his law degree, at the University of Buffalo. He continued to work with universities and became Assistant Dean of Brooklyn College. His expertise was in marketing, and for several years he had been a professor at Marist College in Poughkeepsie. In his spare time, he did consulting work for large companies in New York. Bob was fascinated by our business, but he didn't want to give up his consulting business or his teaching. However, he felt he could give us at least two full days a week. We would pay all his expenses, and he would work on a straight commission. Just talking to him, I knew he was a salesman.

He was a charming, very well-spoken and handsome young man, even if he had a beard which, to me was very becoming. I decided he might offer a fresh approach, and I certainly needed help in many major markets at that time. First, however, I had to get my own feet wet and see what we had before working with and training him. It meant a few weeks of testing before I'd know where this new product would take us.

We had discussions for months prior to the release of Escape, but nothing is ever a sure thing in the broadcasting industry. Not wanting to go after the "big boys", I decided my first approach would be a small market with a general manager who had always had the reputation of being a leader, and one I could get a decision from quickly.

I called my old friend, Ed Metcalfe, who at the time was managing the ABC affiliate in Ft. Wayne, Indiana. Anytime Ed knew I was coming out, he would suggest meeting me in Chicago for dinner and an evening together. This time, however, in making an appointment with him, I suggested I fly into Ft. Wayne, only mentioning to him that I had a new concept, something I wanted him to take a look at. I flew in the night before, had dinner with him and his wife, and planned to present Escape early the next morning.

After briefly describing the project, I put the fourteen-minute presentation tape on. It was the first pitch I had made, and I had those wonderful butterflies inside wondering what was going to happen. Anyone in sales can look back through the years to his dismay at the products he thought were brilliant, but which fell flat on its face.

When the tape had finished, Ed had a strange smile on his face, a gleam in his eye, and said, "Marv, at the meeting of our station group a few days ago, we discussed the potential of what you have just shown me." He picked up the telephone and called Ken Elkins, President of Pulitzer Broadcasting. Briefly telling Ken what he had seen, he put me on the phone and I immediately was able to make an appointment the following day to meet with Ken in St. Louis. Pulitzer had recently sold their St. Louis station, but still owned Ft. Wayne, Louisville, Kentucky, Albuquerque, New Mexico, Lancaster, Pennsylvania, Winston Salem, North Carolina, and a radio station in Phoenix. My first pitch and I would have an opportunity for a group sale!

Making my presentation to Ken the next morning, figuring he would buy for the entire group with discounts, my hopes were shot down. Ken said, "I'll recommend it, but you are going to have to make the pitch to each of the managers." I quoted prices, with discounts for three or more stations, and said that I would contact the managers and see them within the next couple of weeks.

Before leaving St. Louis, I called Ed Metcalfe and he reiterated to me on the phone that he was buying and I did not have to return to Ft. Wayne. I flew back to the office planning on making a trip covering the Pulitzer markets as quickly as possible. Going home, I was certain we would do well and get most or all of those markets.

On Friday morning, I took a leisurely drive from our offices to Palm Beach, having made a luncheon appointment with Bill Brooks, manager of WPTV, the Scripps Howard station. Bill was one of my favorite people. He was as Irish as "Patty's pig," with that little Irish brogue in his voice and a bit of laughter and deviltry in his eyes. The former manager, Bob Regalbuto, had been promoted to general manager at the flagship station in Cincinnati a year earlier and, unknown to me, would soon be leaving to take over management at KSTP in Minneapolis-St. Paul.

I made my presentation to Bill, who, with his staff present, asked me to contact Bob in Cincinnati with the possibility of a group sale.

Things were really happening and, being in full production, we had that six-month window prior to start dates. Although there were still a few bugs in our software, they were quickly being resolved, and the University of Miami was doing well in the use and operation of the equipment.

The following week, I made plans to fly to Albuquerque and Phoenix, returning by way of Cincinnati. Walking into KOAT in Albuquerque, I found that Ken Elkins had done his job well. I got the royal treatment from management. I was told our Escape equipment was exactly what they were looking for, and had no problems in making a sale. From there I went to Phoenix, and their radio station proved to be our first radio sale. Leaving the market, I had visions of picking up all seven stations.

I flew into Cincinnati and made my presentation to Bob Regalbuto and the whole office staff. I was told to get into Cleveland and Baltimore, and if interest was shown there, a Scripps Howard multiple buy could be made. I returned to the office on cloud nine, making plans to meet Bob Grossman the following week. Since Bob was free on Thursday and Friday, I planned to go into Cleveland, stop in Louisville, and then meet him in Baltimore, going on from there to Lancaster, Pennsylvania.

Baltimore gave us the go-ahead, as did Lancaster, and after two days with Bob, I got the feeling he was just what the doctor had ordered. He had a great head on his shoulders, could think for himself, and was born with a natural talent for our type of work.

I set him up to go into Winston Salem and Omaha, and showed him how to make appointments. Although I wanted to hit New York City, from experience I felt it was not a good place to start, particularly if one wanted one of the owned and operated groups. Rather, it is better to have management at one of their other stations enthusiastically endorse a product to the president of the O&O's, and go on from there. I've always found it much more advantageous, and easier for that matter, to have someone in Detroit or San Francisco or Washington get you to the right people. I suppose it was the lazy way, but one got tired of going from one division to another making several presentations before getting to the people who make the final decision. Getting an O&O station general manager to call his boss for you gets you the meeting with decision makers immediately.

In the release of Escape 600, we had not missed a market. As I had other business on the west coast, I decided to head for Los Angeles. To feel my way, I made several appointments, including Metro Media and John Severino at KABC. John got tied up, and although I made a presentation to members of his staff, I never went back for a follow-up. Metro Media also was excited, but again I didn't follow up.

I made an appointment with John Rohrbeck, Vice President and General Manager of KNBC. After a presentation to him with his news director in the meeting, he immediately asked for an option covering the NBC O&O stations. He called Al Jerome, president in New York, and I was asked to make presentations to management at their New York, Chicago, Washington and Cleveland stations. Since we already had the Scripps Howard station, WEWS in Cleveland, this could become a four market sale, one that in my business was a dream come true.

I called Bob Grossman in New York, gave him the information and told him to contact management at WNBC in New York, WMAQ in Chicago, and WRC in Washington, using not only John Rohrbeck's name, but Al Jerome's as well. Bob did a masterful job, and his commission on those four markets more than helped put his two boys through college several years later. Continuing on the west coast, I was able to make several additional sales, including our first newspaper, *The Oregonian* in Portland. I stayed on the coast for the weekend, and flew back to Cincinnati to sign my contract with Scripps Howard.

While waiting for the plane in Portland, I discovered a crowd around a very handsome young man who moved somewhat in slow motion. It was Mohammed Ali. People came up to him from all directions, and the way he smiled at each of those tugging at him and gave them autographs was very impressive. To my surprise, he sat next to me on the red-eye to Cincinnati that night, and although his movements and speech were somewhat labored due to Parkinson's Syndrome, his mind was clear as a bell. When we landed, he looked at me with a smile and said, "Would you like my autograph?" I smiled back and said, "That's not necessary, champ. Just sitting and talking with you this evening has made my day." One can readily understand why this man is loved worldwide.

26.
AGB—London

The MIP Convention, always held in April, had expanded to include a fall meeting in Cannes early in October. At the same time, someone had started a Multi Media Market Convention in London that ran four days about a week prior to the April MIP, called MIPCOM.

Flying to the London Multi Media Market Convention, I wanted to attempt to see a man I had met with Max Stuart a few years earlier. John Clemens was managing director of a company called AGB Cable and View Data. He was a six-footer with that marvelous British charm and wit, and he headed up the largest research company worldwide. I had written him of what we were doing, and when I arrived in London I called him and received an immediate appointment for later that day. Since our presentation tapes were all made on NTSC, and England was PAL, there was no way I could show him a presentation, but with the brochure material, together with our manual, the meeting proved exciting.

In England at the time, you were not allowed to call people at random and take a poll. The British government had passed laws regarding privacy, so one had to make up lists of those one wanted to call at random and receive prior written permission.

What AGB did was take billboards on trains and buses with pads attached, whereby if you wanted to be called, you would fill out a slip with name, address and telephone number, and state that you would like to be added to the list. Having done this for a very long period of time, AGB always maintained a calling list of at least 50,000 people, and changed those on it continuously.

John was intrigued by Escape 600, and I gave him as much information as I could since the first thing that had to be done was get clearance from British Telcom. John said that he would make whatever arrangements were necessary with them, and I would fly an engineer to London to make a presentation. Bear in mind, once we got British Telcom's approval, it meant spending two to three weeks with two engineers in London changing the software to match their dial tone, there ring, and all the many other facets of that country's telephone system.

About this time, AGB was entering the U.S. market attempting to break the monopoly of the American Research Bureau (ARB) and Nielson. We set up a tentative appointment on his next visit to the States for him to come down and spend a week with us to familiarize himself with our equipment.

I then went on to Paris for a long weekend, meeting my sisters and brother-in-law who were on a tour of Europe. While waiting for their arrival, I walked over to the Eiffel Tower from my hotel and got a kick out of seeing French children trying to play baseball with their hands crossed while holding the bat. Speaking only enough French to not order liver when I sat down to dinner, I tried to show the youngsters how to hold a baseball bat, and when they followed my instruction, their screams of delight were most rewarding. I don't know what their parents were trying to tell me, and I suspect they had no idea what I was talking about either, but I thoroughly enjoyed my afternoon in the park.

Paris in October is pure heaven, with temperatures in the mid-70's. France is at its most beautiful in the early fall months. Glenn Seger, who was running our office at the time, met me in Cannes with one of the engineers, and we proceeded to set up our stand in the Palais.

Although no Escape 600 stations were on the air with our equipment, word of mouth had hit the MIPCOM Convention. People frm the South Africa Broadcasting Corporation, from their director general to their deputy director general and General Manager of Public International Relations, all stopped by and became fascinated with our equipment.

Through the convention organizers, we had leased a VCR that would play not only NTSC, but PAL and SECAM as well. That gave us the means to take our NTSC tape and convert it on the screen to the other systems. Achille Mauri, our old buddy from "TV-POWWW days," arrived with Maurice Cohen. Achille spoke no English, so Maurice, acting as interpreter, went through our Escape and, admittedly, *I* almost wanted to "escape" dealing with Achille. The frustration and aggravation of trying to get paid was never pleasant, but admittedly we always did get paid, so we followed through.

At the time, Maurice and Achille lived in Milan and wanted us to set up the Italian phone system for them immediately. We stalled for time since we did not have the personnel, and suggested they see us in April at the MIP when we would work out the details. The same thing occurred with Des Monaghan from New Zealand, and the Netherlands, all of which we would follow through in April. Our "TV-POWWW" was still going strong in Italy, Sweden, and England, and Telephone Poll was still doing well in several countries in Europe. Even without Escape, the convention was successful financially for us, and we headed back home. Bob Grossman was doing beautifully and had made several sales while I was away. I only wished he would join us full-time.

Training Our Clients

All of our start dates were to begin some time between September 1 and October 1, and we presented the Escape 600 equipment in such a way that training seminars were to be part of the package. It was decided to have three or four stations and/or research companies, newspapers, etc., fly into Ft. Lauderdale to be given their two-day training period together. Upon completion, which included hands-on use of Escape, the equipment would be shipped via UPS and received within two or three days after completion of their training. It was decided to have two sessions a week, Monday and Tuesday, and Thursday and Friday. In that manner, we could complete our training sessions prior to any start dates, giving all our clients an opportunity to return to their offices to get hands-on experience.

Naturally, even if their start dates were two to three weeks ahead, we gave them permission to start using their new-found toys immediately. What a thrill to find everyone so pleased with our training plan and there appeared to be an aura of excitement about everyone involved. We made reservations at a brand new Hilton Hotel within less than five minutes of our offices. Our clients were to pay their airline and hotel expenses, while we took care of their meals and any other expenditures while with us.

Late in the afternoon of our first day of training by our chief engineer, with one or two others helping, we brought in Mitch Shapiro from the University of Miami. We spent several hours going through

289

the equipment, answering questions, and covering in detail the scientific value and accuracy of Escape 600. With the University of Miami using it continuously, and now having had several months experience, we were able to give our trainees the many pluses we had garnered with its usage, but also one or two minuses that they had to be cognizant of.

One major drawback in the polling cycle proved to be that many of the older generation of retirees would not take the poll. We discovered that in order to get the correct percentage of that age demographic twice as many had to be called. It did not skew the final results in any manner.

Prior to our first training sessions, we had paid for a scientific poll, with live poll takers doing a standard survey, against our equipment doing it electronically. The survey was exact in every way, and our results with Escape 600 were comparable to the results of the live poll takers. The major difference was that we did not have to pay $5 per hour for live operators and our only cost was long distance telephone calls. Our first training seminar included television station personnel who after the first day were astounded at what the equipment was capable of. I recall one girl in her mid to late twenties from a Pittsburgh television station stating at the end of the training period how she could have fun herself some evening taking a poll and finding a perfect husband for herself!

In retrospect, not only had our engineers done a brilliant job, they had done much more than all but a handful of our clients would ever use the equipment for. Even I didn't realize how complete the Escape 600 units were, and how it would bring in a new era for us. During the training weeks, we were very pleased with the people sent to us. There were a few exceptions, however, one in particular bothered us a great deal.

We decided to have the NBC O&O station group from New York, Los Angeles, Chicago and Washington trained on the same date. Two representatives were twenty-year-old youngsters who had never so much as seen a computer. I thought it strange, with the amount of money NBC was paying, that this occurred. Although we spent additional time with them, we all felt uneasy about that group. We hoped that when they returned to their stations, they had gleaned enough information to get started.

For days after a training period had been completed, we would get phone calls and talk them through their early surveys. Some stations and research companies picked it up very quickly, and their compliments gave all of us a wonderful feeling of accomplishment. We asked our

290

subscribers to not only send us copies of their surveys and results, but also their success stories.

One in particular still tickles my funny bone. Ft. Wayne, Indiana, had a mayor who had been in office for several years. As the incumbent, he appeared secure in re-election. The Republican party spent substantial dollars with a research firm in Ann Arbor, Michigan, to find out whether or not it was advisable for them to put a strong candidate up against him in November. Our ABC affiliate, WPTA, decided to use the Escape equipment and do their own survey.

Three hundred completions were done by the national research firm, completed at a cost of $5000. WPTA did their survey with 2,000 completions at a cost of $50. When WPTA announced their results, an editorial in the local newspaper decried the poll, claiming it to be totally inaccurate and done in a completely unscientific manner. Ten days prior to the election, the newspaper recanted and apologized. On election day, our poll was accurate to within one percent of the final tally, and a new mayor was elected.

From that success the station formed a separate company and started to sell surveys for clients interested in research. We were thrilled when we heard that the Republican party in the state of Indiana was using our equipment to get necessary data.

Research companies, in addition to using Escape for specific surveys, found it very valuable in cleaning up their lists. Many telephone numbers changed, and large discrepancies were found in their call-out lists. With no one operating the equipment, Escape was capable of taking out those numbers that no longer were current, or should not have been in their directories.

Stations found unusual ways of using the equipment. In one market, an automotive dealer would add telephone numbers to his service department accounts on a daily basis, and the equipment would call customers to see whether or not they were pleased with the service that had just been done on their cars. If they were unhappy, the equipment instantly registered their telephone number, and a personal call could be made to placate them.

A Cadillac dealer that went back ten years on his list of those who had bought automobiles from him, and called each of them to tell them of a party being given at the dealership on a Sunday afternoon where they would be served hot dogs, hamburgers, soft drinks, etc. He also told them, "Bring the kids. We'll have a show all day long"—the new model Cadillac that had just been released.

The same dealer four weeks before Christmas made the same calls suggesting they do their Christmas shopping for their loved ones at his dealership, recommending floor mats, radios and all types of accessories as Christmas presents.

Escape 600 was used on a daily basis, and gave stations and their clients invaluable information. With at least 300 to 500 completed calls, Escape proved accurate to a plus or minus three percent. We were having fun, and though our costs were skyrocketing, we managed to keep our heads above water (although, at times, barely).

Early in September, some people from the Republican party came in to see us, being interested in using our equipment. Unfortunately, the Republican party did not make the decision early enough to give a company like ours an opportunity to have equipment available for them. Early in October, they approached us again, asking us to make 12 million phone calls throughout the United States. When told this had to be completed by the first week in November, we almost laughed, but we came back with a counter proposal.

We would set up a 100-line unit by leasing Wats lines. Using their synthesized voice and the telephone numbers supplied by them on discs, we could complete 800,000 calls within ten days. They then decided that they would ask us to complete 800,000 phone calls in the state of Florida, and would pay us on each completed call. They wanted a thirty-second message. We figured the cost of the lines, plus engineering time, and added a fair profit to those figures.

Having no room in our shop, we used a room supplied us nearby and set up our microprocessor with 100 Wats lines. Each of those lines would work independently, similar to the seven-line units we supplied our clients. We awaited the discs with the numbers and the voice they were going to use. What a surprise when we received a tape from the White House with President Ronald Reagan's voice! An even bigger surprise, however, and one expensive as hell, was that the message ran thirty-one-seconds, meaning our telephone calls would cost us much more.

There was no way we could speed up the tape to get rid of that one second, but we figured this could prove an incredible test for future business with political parties. A few days later the Democratic party came to us, but there was no way we had enough equipment to take on anything more.

We were to set up the equipment and start calling at 9:00 a.m., and stop at 9:00 p.m. Many people would be working, so the equipment would get many no answers or an answering machine, but since those calls would be automatically re-made, we just continued on to the next call.

I loved the message we received from the White House! "Hi, this is President Ronald Reagan calling from the White House. I know you're busy, as am I, so we can't talk to each other, but I need your help." He then proceeded to ask them to vote, thanked them again, and said goodbye.

As planned, we started at nine o'clock in the morning and continued until nine at night. A few days later, I walked into the bank to make a deposit and heard two women excitedly talking about President Reagan calling them last night, and it went on that way for ten days. The public didn't realize exactly what we were doing, and we had a lot of fun turning a speaker on occasionally to listen to people excitedly calling their husbands or wives to the phone, saying, "The President's on the phone!"

Jeb Bush, our president-to-be's son, came in during the first few days. No one could believe that 100 telephones were working individually, and yet you could have heard a pin drop unless you put a speaker on to hear what they were saying. We got fewer than 400 hang-ups, and we completed 800,000 calls in 10 days. In a non-presidential election year, more registered Republicans voted in the state of Florida than ever before.

Now comes the sad part of the story. Since we couldn't handle the Republican partys request for 12 million calls, they supposedly contacted other companies to do it for them, and naturally no one had that type of equipment available to them. Although we had been completely successful for them, the Republican Party never again became involved with that type of promotion.

A company in Marion, Iowa, has built a reputation as one of the top research companies, particularly for broadcasting, in the United States. Frank Magid will research talent to make sure that the anchor people fit the specific markets, and is considered the guru of media. I contacted his office and flew out to make a presentation to him. It was interesting for me to see his operation. In little cubby holes, he would have as many as 100 people doing telephone surveys at a time. I made a presentation to his staff, and got a very affirmative response. I offered to supply a unit to them for testing. Since they were computer-oriented, it was an easy task to ship a unit, together with a complete manual, knowing they would have little trouble in setting it up themselves for testing.

Twenty years ago, if someone called and got an answering machine, he would slam the receiver down in disgust. Today, everyone has them, accepts them and has learned to leave messages. If you want to call an airline, your bank, your credit card company, or any major corporation, you can spend twenty minutes pushing buttons on your telephone before you get a human being at the other end of that line. We call it progress, even if it took years for us to accept it. Escape 600 was something new. It could save thousands of dollars, and was accurate, but, "we've done it this way for years—why change?" Little did we realize in the mid-eighties our design of the escape 600 equipment would become a way of life for corporations and consternation as well as anger for customers trying to reach a human being at a bank, airline, insurance company etc.

After months of trying to get an answer from the Magid Company, we asked for the return of our equipment, and let it go.

While that was going on, a research company in Detroit became involved with us because of a man who wanted to invest in our company. I had flown to Detroit several times to meet with him, and felt we were close to making a deal. Although we were holding our head above water, it was becoming increasingly difficult financially to formulate plans on some very exciting new product, all made available through what we had accomplished with Escape 600. We were asked whether or not we would allow a local research company the opportunity to test our equipment in Chicago, and we jumped at the chance. We made plans to send one of our engineers to Chicago to work with the research company picked by our potential investor, knowing in our hearts it would be difficult not to have a successful test. When our engineer returned to the office, he was terribly upset. When queried, he said, "How could we have a successful test when we were up against a Chicago Bears- New York Giants football game?" The number of hang-ups were incredible, and one couldn't help but get the feeling that another research company, fearful of losing business, gave us the shaft.

Our success stories with Escape were mounting, but so were our costs, and I couldn't help but worry in the coming months. At lunch one day in New York with our attorney, I voiced my worries. We had so many potentially successful products on the drawing board, but it was becoming increasingly difficult to allocate funds for any new product. I asked Mil Fenster what, if any, suggestions he might have, and he asked me very pointedly whether I would be willing to give up control of the company for substantial money.

Ten days later, he called me, telling me of a breakfast meeting he had set up with Lehman Brothers at the Roosevelt Hotel in New York. I jumped at the opportunity, and flew in a day early to sit down with Mil. Where both of us made a horrible mistake was in not discussing how much more we needed to raise, never thinking it of paramount importance. At breakfast the following morning, I told three members of Lehman Brothers what we were doing, what we had accomplished, what patents we had applied for, and what was on the drawing board.

A new concept was just being introduced to the universities whereby one could register college students by telephone. The system, at the time in its infancy, and much more complicated than it had to be, could be incorporated right into our Escape 600 with the changing of a few boards.

We were close to producing a compact electronic device that could upgrade and enhance a standard ultrasound diagnostic machine, making it equal and surpass the capabilities of a much more expensive system. Our engineers felt we could build this so it could be added to existing equipment, saving hundreds of thousands of dollars at each hospital.

I had a wonderful time at that breakfast presentation. Any salesman would have gotten that rare feeling of "got em" when one of the gentlemen looked me square in the eye and said, "How much do you need?" This stupid naive idiot answered, "Three million dollars". All three laughed, and one put his arm around my shoulder and said, "It's too small for us. Too bad you didn't need 30 million dollars." That's as close as I ever got to being a very wealthy man.

27.
Changing Times

In the mid-1980's, broadcasting started changing, basically for two reasons. One, inflation was making it more difficult for small market stations to operate profitably; and two, major market station groups were no longer able to project 10 to 20% increases in income annually. For the first time, they were finding it impossible to maintain such growth.

AM radio, which had proliferated for so many years, was finding it difficult to show profits in standard broadcasting. FM broadcast had become the radio of choice because of its better quality reception, as well as its stereo availability. Only hard rock, country, talk and news formats were holding their own in AM, but news and talk stations found their costs continually rising.

Those stations with multiple ownership were having a particularly tough time. With many of those companies now heavily involved in cable, as well as broadcast groups publicly-traded, it wasn't too long before a cut-back in personnel took place. Major groups gave notices to many of their executives who had been with them for years. Staffs were decimated. People with more than twenty years service lost their jobs and most, or all, of their pensions.

General Electric bought RCA, which included the NBC network. Prior to that sale, NBC would reward its people with up to 15% increases in salary annually. After GE took over, if you proved to be a genius you could get a 3 to 4% increase annually, not even enough to keep up with the cost of inflation.

I knew a vice president who had been with the network for years, forced to take early retirement. He called a meeting of his staff just prior to his leaving and told them that if they wanted to come in two hours early and work late into the evening, that was perfectly fine. He wanted them to understand, however, that under the new ownership they were now only a number. If they were wise, they would work no more than nine to five. Extra time and work would not be acknowledged nor appreciated.

In the 1990's, we have seen a complete collapse of middle management. For the first time in all the years I had been in broadcasting, station managers were calling and begging to be allowed to cancel their contracts with us or, in some cases, buy them out at reduced prices. It was rough for us to have to say "no," We were, in many ways, in the same bind financially that they were. Our operating costs had skyrocketed. Losing even a small percentage of our contracts would have hurt us.

The president of Scripps Howard Broadcasting sent me a letter canceling all Scripps Howard stations. When I replied by letter that we were holding their company to the agreement, the only response I received was that they ignored their monthly billing. It left us no recourse but to sue, knowing full well that the attorneys would have a bonanza. Their arguments in their defense were very weak, and they really had little to go on. I don't think their lawyers knew what was going on, and it was costing Scripps Howard a small fortune.

The arguments given by Scripps Howard for cancellation still bring a smile to my face. Broadcasters are the laziest bunch of people in the world. In the depositions taken by our attorneys, the argument for cancellation was that our equipment didn't work, which was a total fabrication. Escape 600 worked fine but no one at the individual stations would take the time or effort to set up a survey and work with it.

We had given them Colorscope, a very simple way of personalizing all their openings, closings, sport, talk, children's shows, etc. We followed that with Commercialscope, giving them an opportunity to sell directly, or through agencies, tailored animated commercials. Believe it or not, maybe 10% of their stations, after the initial excitement, ever used the product again. The material was not only beautiful, but brilliant for its time, but who was going to make the effort to work with it at the station level?

All that was required to make Escape 600 work, was picking one person at the station part time, putting him in charge, and letting him handle it on a day-to-day basis. It reminded me of the scenario with

BBC and "TV-POWWW," when a different engineering staff had to put it on the air every time they ran it, instead of one or two groups being given the authority and following through.

One man, Bill Brooks at the Scripps Howard station in West Palm Beach, was totally truthful in his deposition. He stated that his station was using the equipment, it worked beautifully, and they were very pleased with it. He also said that one member of his news department had been put in charge of it and they had no problems.

Now I had a dilemma. Bill's boss was president of the group, and Scripps Howard was suddenly becoming very nervous. Their law firm, which was probably charging more than what we were suing for, wasn't very happy, and poor Bill was in the hot seat. I honestly believe had we gone to court we would have won hands down, and quickly. I also think they would have settled just prior to the trial. Had that occurred, I'm sure Bill would have lost his job.

Three days before the allotted day in court, I received, not one, but three phone calls from Bill. The company was meeting in Honolulu. Bill, who would never beg—he's much too fine a gentleman for that—asked me if I would reconsider. Against everyone's wishes, including our attorneys, I settled out of court, something I have had many second thoughts about. Our attorneys did very well, we got some money back, and I kept the friendship of one of the more delightful people I have known in the industry.

To make it all almost worthwhile, Scripps Howard some time later fired that S.O.B. president. (I guess that still stands for Harry Truman's "Son of Brotherhood"?) I Haven't heard of his reappearing in the industry since.

We continued to hit the international conventions, MIP-COM and MIP in October and April. The London multimarket had folded after a few years, since it was foolish to have another convention a week prior to the Cannes Festival.

Burt Vegter, whom I had met in Amsterdam, was very interested in Escape, and enroute to MIP-COM I stopped for several days in the Netherlands. Burt, who had been in charge of promotion for CBS records for years in Europe, had gone to work for an entrepreneur and was fascinated by our Escape concept. When I arrived, he had set up three days of meetings with companies which he felt would be a natural for the equipment.

We had some great presentations, one of which was to a penny stock promoter who was counting the money he could make with it by calling, asking the proper questions, and quickly getting on the telephone with a local salesman to close the deal. Other companies looked just as promising, and Burt's boss decided he would like to buy ten units.

We initially planned to deliver one unit, and fly two engineers over to set up the equipment on a permanent basis for use with the Netherlands' telephone system. Our engineers, when they saw the diagramatics from Holland, were very excited, since many of the problems we foresaw did not exist and they would have a simple task of installation. The Netherlands had a very modern, up-to-date telephone system, and although only 10% of their phones were touchtone, we had few problems re-programming for rotary, on their country's equipment.

Burt's boss, who held controlling interest in the company and financed it, was a most interesting man. I'll not mention his name for fear of reprisal. He invited me to have dinner one evening in a restaurant which he owned. We were the only customers. The place was empty, but the food was great. I didn't think anything of it until the whole story came out at a later date.

Our friend was wanted in Switzerland and the United States for being one of the biggest money launderers in the world. He was very shrewd in that he never personally signed anything, but had his employees sign the papers and deliver the funds. Most of them have been caught and are serving prison terms. He, in turn, has been in prison for short periods of time while awaiting trial in Amsterdam. The last I heard, he had been tried three times and acquitted. No one could find a piece of paper with his name on it.

He owns apartment houses in Florida, and a great deal of other real estate throughout the world. His clients from the States included major gambling casinos, motion picture stars and large developers. He now has twenty-four-hour security guards protecting him from reprisal by his former employees, some of whom have been released from prison.

Our penny stock entrepreneur was also stopped by the government, but I don't recall whether he also went to prison. With all of this happening, we walked away ending up with only one sale of our equipment in the Netherlands.

While at the MIP-COM convention, we were able to sign an agreement with the South African Broadcasting Corporation, and later sent one of our engineers there for several days to set up the equipment to their telephone standards and train their personnel. It proved very valuable to them, and was in use for several years. Our old friend, Achille Mauri, wanted it for Italy, and after getting a renewal for "TV-POWWW" from him, we offered to send two engineers to Milan to re-program the equipment for Italian Tele-Com on the understanding that he pay for it.

A few weeks later, he called, having made airline reservations and taking care of all costs for our people to follow through. Somehow, however, there was a falling out between Achille and Maurice Cohen, our English-speaking go-between. It seems Achille owed Maurice a lot of money, and Maurice resigned and was suing him. Achille never followed through, and our contracts remained unsigned.

John Clemens, while managing director of AGB, had spent a week with us in Florida getting more and more excited about our Escape equipment for use in England. AGB had opened offices in New York and set up their own research to compete with the American Research Bureau and Nielson. Although they spent millions attempting to get a foothold in the States, they finally closed up shop. They were the largest research company in Europe and Asia, but they were unsuccessful in procuring contracts from the networks in the States.

Shortly thereafter, John left AGB and formed a small research company in London. In the interim, we were attempting to get clearance from British Tele-Com and, although dozens of phone calls between us were made, I could never get a response from them. Finally, in a fit of anger, I put a person-to-person call in to the managing director of British Tele-Com and, surprisingly, I reached him. I told him of my problem and received an abject apology with the statement that he would take care of it immediately, and he sure did. Within the next hour, I received phone calls from two different executives of British Tele-Com telling me they would be sending out all the specifications for our engineers. The British are such delightful people—I'm still waiting!

While at MIP-COM, I shook hands with Des Monaghan of TVNZ, New Zealand, on a deal for their television stations. At the time, New Zealand still had two stations owned by the government, while a third, an independent, had just gone on the air with NBC owning 15%. Our agreement was for several hundred thousand dollars, covering the entire country. A few days later, I received a telex confirming the details, sub-ject, naturally, to New Zealand Tele-Com approval, which would be forthcoming.

300

Not too long afterward, Des accepted a job at Channel 7 in Sydney, Australia, and the double-talk from TVNZ began. They must have decided they didn't want to go ahead, and their stalling was intriguing. I suppose we could have sued them, but international lawsuits against government-owned television stations didn't seem encouraging. It was also one of the roughest times in my life because my darling wife, Jeanne, was terminally ill.

I had left MIP-COM early to rush home, only to find the doctors were giving her only a few months to live. I loved my work, but I found it meant little compared with the thought of losing a loved one. Early in May, I was devastated when she died. I sat at my desk for several weeks trying to figure out where this strange new life would be taking me.

Early in the summer, I caught a plane to Auckland, New Zealand, where my son was working for Channel 3. I spent several days with him, my daughter-in-law and my two beautiful grandchildren before heading for Australia, where I met Max Stuart. Max was always a great "picker-upper," and when I left Sydney, I flew to Honolulu for a week by myself.

My first night there, I went to the Royal Hawaiian Hotel. Sitting at the bar overlooking beautiful Diamond Head, my spirits were somewhat buoyed when a gal decided to pick me up. I bought her a drink, and then told her I really wasn't interested, having just lost my wife. She vanished fast, but what it did for my ego cannot be described. That week in Hawaii I kind of got my head screwed on straight and vowed to get back in the thick of things.

The electronic game industry had gone so totally out of style for several years that one could not help but believe it was finished. Then, out of the blue, a Japanese company, Nintendo, arrived with such fascinating and complex games that it took the entire country by storm. Their U.S. headquarters were outside of Seattle. As we still had "TV-POWWW" equipment, I thought it a great idea to make an appointment to fly out to see them. I was very pleasantly received and went through a very simple presentation, giving them the background and history of our game show. I asked whether or not there was a possibility that we might re-release "TV-POWWW" in the States, re-program several of their games, and have the opportunity to initially release new games for them as they appeared.

Knowing their culture, as well as their language, I was surprised to get an immediate negative response. But in looking back, they sure as hell didn't need me or "TV-POWWW," as the months that followed proved. Some time later SEGA arrived, and I got the same answer from them.

One of our engineers, listening to the radio one day, heard a local contest being broadcast where the fifth, or the tenth, or the fifteenth caller would win a prize if he had the right answer. He came into the office stating that we had the equipment and knowledge to build for peanuts a piece of equipment that could be set at any number, answer the telephone, thank each listener for calling, after telling him what number he was, and go on to the next number until the preset number was reached. A sound effect would go off, and a voice would follow, telling him he was the winner and to please hold on.

It sounded like fun, and perhaps an inexpensive product would prove valuable to us. I gave the okay to go into production, and then decided to go to the national radio convention to see what we had. We called the new program "The Count".

How times had changed! Most radio stations had very little talent on hand anymore except for a news reporter. Most music was now supplied by satellite on tape. Very few commercial stations still had disc jockeys, just live announcers for station breaks, commercials or news. Damn few stations were contest-oriented anymore, and most were deficient in promotional know-how. We walked away from that new product very quickly.

Several years earlier, we had formed a second corporation called MAK Electronics, Inc. and, although our Telephone Poll and Escape 600 were all under the M. A. Kempner logo, we had been working on a product called Cine-Disk. It was something we had mentioned when we made our presentation to Lehman Brothers. If properly presented at that time, asking for 30 million dollars would have been definitely in the ballpark. However, I was not aware then of its potential, something I have regretted these past few years.

Cine-Disk was a compact electronic device that could upgrade and enhance standard ultrasound diagnostic equipment. It could equal, even surpass, the capabilities of much more expensive systems. What our engineers had developed was a piece of equipment that adapted to any modality that required film storage, including radiographic, cardiac or vascular studies using any number of imaging techniques, such as ultrasound, nuclear medicine, C-ARM special procedures or cardiology procedures. With the equipment our engineers had designed, we could take the relatively inexpensive ultrasound machines already in use and upgrade them, saving hospitals and doctors from spending $175,000 to $250,000 for a new Cine-Loop ultrasound machine.

We had built a working model, and decided to take it to a medical equipment distributor in Richmond, Virginia, to find out whether there was any interest. After hooking up our equipment in his lab, the distributor turned to me and said he would like to order 100 units, and for the first time in my life I wished I was twenty years younger.

I went back to the office and discussed the offer, and then had engineering give me a breakdown in manufacturing cost. I had learned a great lesson years earlier with engineers. When they give you a time period and amount of money to complete a project, multiply it by at least three, and you might come out with a truer picture of actual time and costs. When the realization hit me that we would need some very heavy bank financing, and couldn't deliver a finished product for at least six months, I made one of the toughest decisions in my years as a businessman. Yes, I decided not to go ahead with Cine-Disk. Although the engineering was pretty well complete, the prints and diagramatics remain today in an engineering folder.

In the early 1990's, I started to cut our staff drastically. With all of our Escape units in the field, we decided not to continue manufacturing. Television stations were on very limited budgets so they could increase their cash flow, that it was silly to continue manufacturing a product that was becoming a luxury. As far as research companies were concerned, although we had sold to several, most did not believe they wanted to do polling except in the old fashioned way.

We are in the electronic world, and researchers love being able to get their percentages and figures electronically but they still want live interviewers, regardless of the bias that takes place. I honestly think the reason for it is a very simple one. They can't, in good conscience, get the amount of money for an electronic poll that they can demand of companies when using live poll takers.

As the saying goes, "You can lead a horse to water but you can't make him drink." The NBC O&O's, after fulfilling their contracts, did not renew, and they returned all units to us in their original boxes unopened. Maybe it's best that television is almost totally automated except for news and sports. You can give them the tools, but if they won't use them, there's nothing you can do.

I was quite upset when the unopened Escape units were returned. I called Al Jerome, President of the NBC O&O's, and got one of the few true apologies I have ever received. I think Al was as angry and discouraged as I was.

Breaking up an organization is a difficult and heart-rending decision. One consolation was that no one, when we let them go, was without a job. It may have cost us some financially, but we made certain that our engineers were placed with other companies, and our assembly people had little trouble finding work as well. We kept one man full time at the office, two engineers and our secretary. One salesman remained on the west coast, and handled everything from Denver west. I planned on servicing the east coast and midwest. Bob Grossman had left us a few months earlier. He had done a fantastic job in sales, but was a big disappointment in servicing the accounts, which added an additional load on my shoulders.

We continued to sell Escape 600 as long as we had equipment, but did little advertising or promotion since it was necessary to maintain materials for servicing. We're pleased that our stations in the late 1990's are still using Escape. A recent sale and success story was Edmonton in Alberta, Canada, where a research company set the Pacific Northwest on its ears using the modern way of polling at a reasonable price.

While downsizing was going on, we continued working with our current contracts, including renewals, and looked for a new challenge. It was time to get out of production, and back into sales and marketing. With our contacts, knowledge and expertise, we knew we could still be very valuable to someone. For years, companies had continued to approach us to represent their products—everything from features to documentaries and cartoons.

I decided to work out an agreement with Max Stuart in Melbourne, Australia, to represent him in the United States and South America. Although documentaries are anathema to commercial television stations in the States, there is a great market for them with cable companies.

A&E, ESPN, National Geographic, Bravo, and the Discovery Channel were always interested, and much of the material from the Southeast Asian area proved salable. I don't know the exact number of great white shark programs that were available, but I do recall that the Discovery Channel would almost buy them over the phone. Max also had an excellent series of cartoons from Europe which had been sold in almost every major country in the world. During the Russian dominance of Eastern Europe, most countries involved were on a barter basis. An animation company in, say, Rumania would produce for the Russian satellites and trade their animated programs for whatever their own needs were.

With new sound tracks added in every language, these cartoons, having been produced similarly to Disney cell animation, were well received. Although we had a rough time selling them in the States, South America was a ready market, and we did well. Many of the cartoons were of an educational variety, so they will continue to do well. We found feature films, off-network series, and many other types of programming, making it available to Max for sales in Europe and Southeast Asia. To this day, we continue to cover conferences such as MIP and MIP-COM in Europe, as well as NATPE here in the states.

A few years ago, the first Asian MIP was held in Hong Kong. It was so successful that it has become an annual conference. I had a great time at the first conference and, upon its completion, returned home by way of Singapore and Australia, having written a substantial amount of business. With the ever-changing world of broadcasting as we approach the year 2000, I find that the international market continues to be a lively market for our many products. In the past six months, however, I can't help but notice the changes taking place in other parts of the world.

The major motion picture companies here in America are starting to make billion dollar deals in France, Germany and Italy. It won't be too many years before much of the world market catches up to what has happened here. China, which for years would pay no more than $300 an hour for anything, has become an incredible bonanza. Already, American companies have found a way to barter their product, taking back commercial time in lieu of dollars for their programming, and selling to major advertisers.

Australia, with a population of 18 to 20 million, has long been commercially competitive with America. A few years ago, they could not pay the prices being asked, and they are just coming out of a very disastrous period when all three networks were in, or close to, bankruptcy. New Zealand, with 3 million people and 33 million sheep, continues in its turn-of-the-century agricultural ways, and broadcasting operations are still mostly government-controlled. Malaysia, Singapore and the Philippines have all been lucrative for us, while Japan, for some, has been spectacular; for others, it is a very tough nut to crack.

In Europe, France and Germany continue to be the powerhouses, while England, no longer overshadowed by BBC, continues to move forward. Italy, with more television stations than any other country except ours, also is growing, and if one knows what he is doing and sells to the proper authorities and stations, one can do well.

Many years ago, over a drink one evening with Chuck Gingold, then Vice President of the ABC O&O stations, and now V.P. at the Discovery Channel, he made a cogent comment. I agreed with him at the time and I still think he will eventually be proven correct.

Chuck's belief is that DBS (Direct Broadcast Satellite) is the wave of the future in broadcasting. In recent years, it has taken off in Europe and become very strong. In smaller countries such as The Netherlands, Belgium, etc., which still have government-controlled television, both cable and DBS are taking hold. In the United States, with billions of dollars invested in cable, it is going to take some time, although I do believe eventually we'll all have that small dish at home, hooked up to a satellite, and be able to bring in programming from all over the world.

The feuds between broadcast cable and the satellite industry are very interesting to follow. The on-going dispute covers whether or not a satellite dish owner has any right to bypass the local network affiliates and pick up their programming elsewhere. Bypassing the cable boys and getting one's programming elsewhere excites me. There's a 1994 satellite home act which is causing a furor. It supposedly does not give home owners the right to bypass the local affiliates. Even the National Association of Broadcasters is threatening lawsuits, because the dish operators are going to supply network feeds to viewers capable of receiving over-the-air signals from their local stations. It's going to be fun in the next few years seeing what happens.

Although it may take a long time, I think the satellite dish will eventually win out. And the pay-per view audience will continue to grow. Having started with prize fighting, today football games and other sports programs are also available on PPV. More and more television programming will be available to us. But we'll be paying for it.

28.
Broadcasting's 21st Century

In retrospect, going back to the early thirties when radio as we know it had its beginning, the changes and growth of all broadcasting have been astounding. So much has happened in our every day life, it's no wonder our children and grandchildren cannot believe the transformation in our life styles. They laugh at us when we tell them of the $2 or $3 hotel rooms, the 10 cent hamburgers, the nickel sundaes, a Ford or Chevrolet selling for $375, a Cadillac at $1400, and you really can't blame them. Today it's difficult to find any motel room under $75, and in major markets, hotels are $200 to $350 a night. That hamburger is now $2.00 to $3.00 and the nickel, 12-ounce Pepsi Cola, in vending machines, 75 cents to a dollar. The minimum wage has gone from 25 cents an hour to over $5, the nickel subway in New York is over a buck, and the nickel telephone call is averaging 35 cents. Broadcasting has grown immensely and our price structure, like everything else, has skyrocketed.

Standards in the industry have changed dramatically for the better, with tape and disk, computer technology, state of the art camera equipment, cable and direct broadcast satellite. What we have available to us is remarkable. We've managed to keep up with the electronic age and we can't help but see continuing improvements with changes still to come. The turn of the century is upon us and we're going to have many additional choices in broadcasting, more miracles no one envisioned years ago.

The present rating structure is intriguing but may have to be reexamined in the not too distant future. Until the 60's, ratings covered all listeners and viewers regardless of age. The Hooper survey covered the entire audience, and time and programming were sold to advertisers using those numbers. It was done randomly by telephone to the home. Pulse, on the other hand, had a "diary" system with several thousand homes, the family filling out forms covering their listening or viewing habits. Then everything changed. ARB (Arbitron-American Research Bureau) and Nielson rating services took hold. The advertiser was educated and started buying specific demographics. Depending on their product and what population group they wanted to reach, they placed time and schedules for viewers or listeners according to age, sex or other specific categories.

What happened to those 50 or older? What is the life style of the 50 plus today? They have been pretty much ignored for years on the premise that their buying habits don't change. They still smoke, drink, buy most products including the new ones, travel extensively and have the dollars for all forms of entertainment.

With advances in medicine, people are living longer and many of the 50 to 60 year olds are acting decades younger. By the year 2000, fifty percent of the population will be 50 or older. Somehow the networks must reach out to them. They have to find some ways to increase their overall audience, since fewer viewers at higher costs cannot continue.

In many ways I miss the days of live programming. It wasn't perfect but it was spontaneous and often funny when the unexpected occurred. Kukla, Fran and Ollie's quarter-hour network program was an example. The show ran at 7 or 7:15 p.m. for years on NBC.

Kukla and Ollie, a little boy and a friendly dragon, were puppets operated behind a small stage by Burr Tillstrom. Fran (Fran Allison) the live attractive lady, stood by the small stage talking with the characters. When the guest, a pet skunk, had an accident, defecating on the little stage, Tillstrom and Allison were unable to do anything but giggle the entire program. Being in on the fun as it happened was talked about at coffee breaks for days.

Playhouse Ninety was another live TV programming example. In a one hour murder mystery, one saw leather-gloved hands of the killer stealthily turning the doorknob, opening a door. Switching to the other side of the door, a camera was supposed to show you the sinister murderer. Instead, one looked directly into a television camera. What fun that was, to see even directors and cameramen not perfect in everything they did.

It was a very special treat to see Jack Parr on the Tonight Show live with Abe Burrows, the writer-producer, director and actor as his guest. After a station break and a commercial for Bufferin, Parr ad-libbed when they came back about how he always took Aspirin for a headache, and realizing what he had just said, apologized and quickly opened a bottle of Bufferin. When he couldn't get the cotton out, he poured water into the bottle and pretended to drink and then recapped it. Ten minutes later, in full view of the television audience, the bottle exploded, leaving Abe Burrows, Jack Parr and the staff white from head to toe.

The next hour was one of the most hilarious ever seen on television, and it wasn't 'til ten minutes before the end of the program that they got some semblance of order back. At that moment, Jack Parr turned to Abe Burrows and said something like, "You have had all kinds of experience in producing, directing and acting, can you give us an idea of some of the interesting things you've been involved with?" At this point, Abe turned to Jack and said something like, "Some idiot poured water into a Bufferin bottle." At that, the program disintegrated into nothing but laughter.

Today one can watch the "Bloopers" shows giving us the fun and laughter found when our TV stars make mistakes or forget their lines. I also get a kick out of seeing some of the outtakes in "Mad About You" and "Home Improvement" while the credits are shown at the end of each program.

I've always loved the challenge of producing the unusual but for years saw how the motion picture industry was making inroads into broadcasting. With television, there was no way to keep them out. They had the studios, sets, everything necessary to do weekly series, comedy, westerns, variety shows, anything, and although every independent producer fought their inroads into the business for a while, nothing could deter them in the long run.

Television, with 8x10 foot screens, two to three inch tubes in depth being available in our homes in the early 21st century, may doom the theatre as we've known it. Look how the large motion picture house has been replaced with multiple screen theaters, each seating no more than 150 to 300 people.

In the twenty-first century, HDTV (high definition television) will have replaced our current system giving us better quality in color and contrast. Our present system using NTSC standards can't compare with Europe's PAL or France's SECAM because of their additional 100-line

TV tube. All these systems, however, have used analog signals and, with authorization from the F.C.C., we in the U.S. will begin shooting digital pictures over the airways some time in late 1999, possibly sooner.

Remember high fidelity popularized in the 50's? All our vinyl records were recorded in monaural. Suddenly, stereo hi-fi came along and monaural recordings sounded very dull. With the change in analog to digital, the new television picture will be somewhat equivalent to what one sees on a movie screen, and the quality will be startling.

The prices of digital television sets initially will cost between two and five thousand dollars when first coming out on the market although eventually they'll come down to about $250 more than what we are currently paying for a set, and one will be able to buy a unit, let's say 25-inch, for around $500.

One of the many questions being raised is whether digital television is just another way to pry billions of dollars out of consumers who have already bought TV sets and weren't planning a new purchase in the near future.

The Federal Communications Commission is activating the digital spectrum starting late in 1998 and some people are estimating it will cost 150 billion dollars to replace the 300 million TV sets nationwide. Some people claim buying a new television set now will guarantee its obsolescence within eight years since analog broadcasting is scheduled to end by the year 2006. Initially, those going to digital broadcast will continue to supply analog programming. No one knows as yet what the demand for this new form of television will be and the commission may have to allow additional years of analog broadcasting.

The computer companies also have their own plans for digital television and several have vowed to flood the market with personal computers equipped to receive digital broadcasts.

There are many pluses involving digital. Your new television picture tube will yield a crisper, sharper picture with a rectangular rather than square picture tube similar to a movie theater screen. Sports fans will find better viewing on this wider screen.

One of the worries about digital concerns the small- and medium-size TV stations, since currently it is estimated to cost them (the station) at least one million dollars for equipment. Every tape machine, camera and piece of electronic equipment will become obsolete in the new HDTV-digital age. It shouldn't be too long however before prices for equipment start falling to reasonable levels.

Digital will be set up in different phases. Those stations in the top ten television markets are required to begin broadcasts with digital use within eighteen months, while stations from 11th through 30th in size will have thirty months.

Several of the networks are leaning toward multi-channel digital broadcast rather than dedicating a station spectrum to a single HDTV channel.

With motion picture features costing untold millions to produce, with large screen digital television sets in the home, I envision the studios will eventually release their pictures on a pay per view basis.

Opening a new movie in a thousand theatres at one time costs millions in print costs. On television, charging five dollars per home would quickly recoup production costs, and a second run, brings in that much more. The movie, "Schindlers List", was seen by 26 million in the theater while 63 million saw it on the NBC television network in one night. Picture using a feature film as WOR-TV New York did in the 50's. They took one film and ran it each night in the same time slot for a week with great viewer results. Charging a fee in this manner would bring in vast amounts of dollars in a very short period of time. No print costs, recoupment of all production costs immediately—wow!

I suspect sports stadiums could become secondary when fifty million people will pay money at home to see a world series game, football playoff or super bowl.

We can't stop progress like this simply because money continues to be our main focus in life, and making more of it seems to be our national pastime. We already pay for cable with much of it having paid commercials. Our politicians will fight for free television for a long while yet, but much of what we're getting now will cost us in coming years.

Recently, our government passed a new telecommunications law, something that has been needed for years. Prior to its passage, the Finsyn laws were overturned, meaning that in the top fifty markets, you could now sell television network affiliates re-runs of off-network programming in the prime access time period (normally 7 to 8 p.m.).

Much of the telecommunications act makes sense. We had to modernize, something all of us realize. What hurts mostly is what we have done to broadcasters. Like Wal-Mart, Home Depot, Office Depot, etc. that have destroyed "mom and pop" stores nationally, we're doing the same thing to individual radio and TV operators, and in many ways could prove troublesome.

311

When the duopoly laws were passed in the early 50's, it was done in order to diversify not only programming but news in each market. No one could own more than one radio AM and FM station or one television station in a market, and supposedly newspapers were not to be television owners. However, grandfathering of all stations and early newspaper ownership initially allowed this. Through the years the FCC continued to give waivers allowing newspaper ownership.

Originally, one was allowed to own a maximum of seven television stations, two of which were to be UHF. (When cable proliferated, these, too, became very valuable.) That changed several years later to a maximum of twelve stations but no more than 25 percent of television homes in the country. Your three basic networks, NBC, CBS and ABC, originally owned approximately 21 to 23 percent of the nation's television homes. Although you supposedly are not allowed to own television and radio stations in one market, this has been waived continuously. The FCC is also considering relaxing all duopoly rules, particularly those which limit a broadcaster to ownership of only one television station in a market. They're now proposing two stations, one VHF and one UHF per market. With cable, UHF's are almost as valuable as VHF's. Much more is required insofar as television ownership and these points and changes from 25 to 35 percent of the American market doesn't really disturb me as much as what they are doing with radio ownership.

The FCC has now eliminated national ownership limits for radio, as well as local ownership caps. The larger the market, the more stations one company may own within it, up to five AM and three FM facilities. What surprises me is that the duopoly law was put into effect many years ago, and now suddenly appears to be unnecessary. Big companies are becoming huge conglomerates or mini-cartels. I wonder if the Sherman Act covering the loss of competition could somehow be used to slow down the large companies in their haste to add multiple stations to their holdings.

One company now owns 30 stations in Florida, 8 in Miami (the maximum) and several in Tampa, Ft. Lauderdale, Jacksonville, etc. Maybe I'm a bit addled but might they not be able to control the state politically through broadcasts? I wonder if or when the FCC or our senators and representatives will stop to realize what's beginning to happen. There's an operator in Hartford, Connecticut, who owns six stations with rankings from 1 to 6 in the ratings. What happens in that market if station ownership takes a stance against a particular politician or politicians? Sounds like it would be fun to find a way to give the opposition party or candidates equal time. I also can't believe the FCC is now considering allowing owners of radio stations to buy daily newspapers in their markets.

We're all used to big companies in the country downsizing insofar as personnel. The same thing is happening in radio where multiple station owners in a given market are doubling one sales staff that now goes out selling, offering any demographic for a spot buy to an advertiser. With six or eight stations owned in one market they now have the ability to sell an advertiser programming in rock, oldies, all news, talk, etc.

I hope this excessive media concentration will not continue to expand. As one who's skeptical, I'm afraid it will shut out minority voices and ultimately undermine our democratic way of life. It's mind-boggling reading the trade papers every week and seeing the number of billion dollar deals so quickly put together. I hope that the Justice Department will look into some of these major mergers, and sales, bringing some sanity back into the media.

With all of its current problems, I feel I'm one of the very lucky ones to still be in an industry so full of fun and excitement, and I've accomplished so many things through the years. To be part of its growth, to go to bed each night looking forward to the next day, to spend a weekend at home waiting for Monday morning, continues to be a lifetime of pleasure.

I have seen it all, from the little guys to the giants. It's not the business we knew forty or fifty years ago, and its growth has always been a plus. I hope, however, that it doesn't become a General Motors or an Exxon, but remain a media for and by those people involved for most years of their lives.

But my dream continues. I want broadcasters to have the opportunity to program their individual tastes and ideas. The thrill of development, doing the untried, the unusual, still makes my heart beat faster. The vast opportunities are still there with so many ways to continue. They're diffent than in the past, but just as exciting and rewarding.

In my lifetime, I've seen little guys grow and become all-powerful multiple-station owners. I've seen radio broadcasters responsible for the development and growth of the huge record, tape and CD industry. Without them, it could never have happened.

I've watched television grow from the early days of the New York Dumont Station in Wanamaker's Department Store—130 degrees under the lights, blue shirt a must for a black & white picture and develop into the wonderful monster it has become. I've been involved in sales of $7.50 for a half hour in radio and a three-station television buy for over $500,000. God, it's been fun!

It's still possible for syndicates to produce programming for commercial television as well as for cable companies and overseas broadcasters. People keep calling for documentaries and all kinds of specialty programming. Got to keep my hand in somehow since it's part of my life, so we have Airlandsea placing some of our features on American and New Zealand Airlines overseas, twenty-six half hours of "All Aboard" railroad shows being run on PBS and all over the world, 200 railroad videos placed in the United States, Canada, Europe and Southeast Asia, and believe it or not, raising a million and a half dollars with sales already consummated for twenty-six half hours of a history of the motorcycle. Remember when I said we still get a kick out of doing the unusual in something new? No one's done anything on the motorcycle before and a major cable company has already committed to it nationally with the rest of the world ours (M. A. Kempner, Inc.) for TV, video and cable. A salesman who I trained 25 years ago came to me recently with a delightful request. As a news network executive today, he wanted to know if we would reproduce a Jane Chastain insert on sports for them, I'm sure as hell going through the original TV scripts and making plans to do a new pilot.

There's a great book written by Alan Jay Lerner of Broadway fame called "The Street Where I Live". He says it best with,

"This is the story of climaxes and endings and the sundown of a decade that blazed with the joy, excitement and triumphs, so much, in fact, that as I look back I'm haunted by the fear that perhaps I drank the wine too fast to taste it. Instead of slowing down to enjoy the scenery, kept my foot on the accelerator and my eyes on the road ahead, gazing only occasionally from side to side and waiting far too long to glance in the rear-view mirror."

It's five o'clock Friday night, time to quit, and I can't wait till Monday morning.